D1544506

THE HUTT ADAPTATION OF THE BENDER-GESTALT TEST

THIRD EDITION

MAX L. HUTT
Professor (retired), University of Detroit
and
Consultant in Clinical Psychology

Grune & Stratton
A Subsidiary of Harcourt Brace Jovanovich, Publishers
New York / San Francisco / London

Library of Congress Cataloging in Publication Data

Hutt, Max L.
   The Hutt adaptation of the Bender-gestalt test.

   First ed. published in 1960 under title: The
clinical use of the revised Bender-gestalt test.
   Bibliography: p.
   Includes index.
   1. Bender gestalt test. I. Title.
BF698.8.B4H8   1977   155.2'84   76-51352
ISBN 0-8089-0990-8

*Acknowledgment is made to Dr. Lauretta Bender
and the American Orthopsychiatric Association, Inc., for permission to adapt and use the
test figures used in the Bender-Gestalt Test. Dr.
Bender and the American Orthopsychiatric Association of course do not assume any responsibility for the contents of this book.*

Grune & Stratton, Inc.
111 Fifth Avenue
New York, New York 10003

Distributed in the United Kingdom by
Academic Press, Inc. (London) Ltd.
24/28 Oval Road, London NW1

Library of Congress Catalog Number 76-51352
International Standard Book Number 0-8089-0990-8
Printed in the United States of America

CONTENTS

Table of Plates   *v*

Preface   *vii*

Part I   HISTORY, THEORY, AND METHODS   *1*

1. The Roles of a Visual-Motor Test in Clinical Evaluation   *3*

2. A History of the Development of the HABGT   *18*

3. General Problems in Psychodiagnosis   *43*

4. Methods of Administration   *62*

5. Specific Test Factors and Their Interpretations   *84*

6. Principles of Inferential and Configurational Analysis   *129*

7. The Measurement of Psychopathology and Adience–Abience   *149*

Part II   CLINICAL STUDIES   *173*

     Introduction to Clinical Studies   *173*

8. Clinical Studies: Children's Records   *175*

9. Clinical Studies: Organic Records   *194*

10. Clinical Studies: Psychotic Records   *210*

11. Clinical Studies: Neurotic Records   *223*

12. Clinical Studies: A Character Problem   *240*

13. Clinical Studies: The Problem of Mental Retardation   *251*

References   *258*

Author Index   *269*

Subject Index   *273*

The Hutt adaptation of the test figures, and packages of the Revised Record Form for the test, as used by the author, are available from the publisher

Grune & Stratton, Inc.
111 Fifth Avenue
New York, N. Y. 10003

Test figures, one set (of 9 figures) $3.00
Record forms and scoring template (package of 25) $9.00

(Prices are subject to change.)

TABLE OF PLATES

Plate 1 The Hutt Adaptation of the Bender-Gestalt Figures 6

Plate 2 A Boy Suspected of Having Organic Brain Damage or Mental Retardation, or Both 52

Plate 3 Clinical-Experimental Trials for the Drawings Reproduced in Plate 2 53

Plate 4 Case Illustration: Tom (page 1) 55

Plate 5 Case Illustration: Tom (page 2) 56

Plate 6 Case A: Donald—Copy Phase 177

Plate 7 Case A: Donald—Elaborations 184

Plate 8 Case B: Catherine 191

Plate 9 Case C: Harold—An Organic Record 198

Plate 10 Case D: Warren 205

Plate 11 Case E: Randolf 207

Plate 12 Case F: Edward 208

Plate 13 Case G: David—An Apparently Benign Record 212

Plate 14 Case H: Bill—An Obviously Psychotic Record 220

Plate 15 Case I: John—Copy Phase 225

Plate 16 Case I: John—Elaborations 228

Plate 17 Case J: Horace—Copy Phase (page 1) 232

Plate 18 Case J: Horace (page 2) 233

Plate 19 Case K: Stephen—Copy Phase 235

Plate 20 Case K: Stephen—Elaborations 238

Plate 21 Case L: Gladys—A Character Problem—Copy Phase (page 1) 241

Plate 22 Case L: Gladys—A Character Problem—Copy Phase (page 2) 242

Plate 23 Case L: Gladys—A Character Problem—Elaborations 246

Plate 24 Case M: Roberta—A Case of Primary Mental Retardation 252

PREFACE

In the third edition of this work I have tried to incorporate the many suggestions that have been offered by kind readers of the previous editions. I have also been greatly assisted by the comments and questions of colleagues during workshops and lectures I have offered on the various uses of the HABGT. In these presentations and discussions in many states of this country as well as in Canada and Puerto Rico, the diverse issues confronted by clinicians working in differing cultural and social settings have been defined more clearly. I have tried to take advantage of the problems and opportunities which these discussions have offered.

Still another source of clinical data has been the consultations I have been privileged to offer in quite differing settings. I have taken advantage of what I have learned from consultations (and court trials) of criminals and felons. Special problems of questionable organic brain damage with children have been particularly revealing. Community health programs have provided still another source of meaningful clinical evaluation of the merits and limitations of the HABGT procedures. And, of course, my own clinical work in psychotherapy with complex personalities has offered a wealth of data on the therapeutic as well as psychodiagnostic possibilities of the experience of the patient in self-examination.

Added to these experiences has been the rich source of research studies—those done by others, and those which I have undertaken. I have tried to review the most pertinent research findings and to utilize them in improving both the projective uses of the HABGT procedures, and the calibration and normative data for the two objective scales presented in this volume. The published research literature is presented in a number of chapters of this book. The revised norms, including norms for children and for special subgroups of psychiatric patients, will be more helpful to users of this method, it is hoped, than those which were previously available.

The book is now clearly divided into two parts: Part I contains a presentation of the history, theory, methods of administration, and methods of interpretation; Part II includes a variety of clinical studies of diverse states of psychopathology and impaired functioning. The methods presented in Part I are illustrated in detail in Part II. There is a new chapter on children's records. Much more attention is given to the experimental–clinical method as an approach to more precise evaluation of dynamics of pathology. The complex problems of evaluating for the psychological effects of organic brain damage and of differentiating primary mental retardation from other conditions are also discussed.

My own clinical orientation has remained basically the same over the years. I believe that it is essential to consider very carefully the specific dynamics and the social–cultural setting of the individual who is being evaluated. Behavioral phenomena are highly important, and their value has certainly been emphasized in recent years, but the meaning of such phenomena cannot be understood without relating them to the *processes* from which they have been derived. Hence, as I phrased this issue in the second edition of this work, ". . . these (behavior and process) are but two sides of the same coin. Both must be fully understood if the individual or psychological principles of human behavior are to be 'known'." Prediction in the individual case, and appropriate therapeutic planning are greatly improved if both are taken into account.

It is impossible to acknowledge properly the many individuals and the many organizations that have been helpful in my work with this test. I have tried to cite all specific sources of assistance wherever this was relevant in the text. I must add a special word of acknowledgment to two groups of individuals: first, the patients whom I have been privileged to work with; second, my graduate students, who have eagerly questioned premise and evidence and have just as eagerly offered suggestions and "sage" advice.

Max L. Hutt

PART I

History, Theory, and Methods

1

The Roles of a Visual–Motor Test in Clinical Evaluation

The Hutt Adaptation of the Bender-Gestalt Test can provide a unique contribution to the assessment process in clinical evaluation: it requires visual–motor functions, and so can offer data for analysis of perceptual and motor maturation; it is essentially nonverbal, and so can provide samples of behavior which do not depend on linguistic development and are not easily influenced by many cultural factors; and it is a "malleable" procedure—it can be adapted to the specific requirements of the individual, clinical case. It can and does have some of the properties of the usual standardized test (see Chapter 7), and it is unusually appropriate for projective analysis (see Chapters 3 and 8–13), but it is particularly useful for intensive clinical adaptation and analysis.

We have come, in this country, to rely excessively on assessment methods that can be objectified and standardized. Such approaches have value, but they are also burdened with serious limitations. We shall delay a more complete discussion of these values and limitations until Chapter 3, for now, but let us point out that they are most pertinent for purposes of group comparisons or comparison of an individual with a group (or group norm). Moreover, objective scores and norms—no matter how sophisticated their derivation and no matter how adequate the population sample—essentially rely on the assumptions of a nomothetic conception of personality. These assumptions include the following. (1) All individuals derive their scores on the standardized test by the accumulation of the same or equivalent elements of the test. (2) Motivational factors in the performance on the test that lead to certain successes or failures are equivalent for all subjects. (3) Previous experience (educational, cultural, and social) is held to be equivalent for all subjects or is held to be insignificant.

None of these assumptions may hold in an individual case and they may be entirely invalid in a great many, if not most, cases that come to the clinician's attention. Perhaps the most relevant is assumption 2. Cases referred for clinical evaluation are likely to be ones in which motivation is abnormal, aspiration level is low, self-concepts are confused or conflicted, and such factors as capacity for attending and for persistent effort have been affected. The nomothetic approach to assessment masks these factors, and many others, and thus obscures from our scrutiny precisely those matters which need to be considered in evaluating the test product and the test score. The core question which the clinician attempts to answer is: "What accounts for this individual's atypical or aberrant performance?" A comparison of the individual's objective score with a group norm only tells us how much difference there may be, but it does not aid us in our inquiry as to how this discrepancy came about and how to effect an improvement, if possible.

In contrast with nomothetic approaches to assessment are two other general diagnostic approaches: *inferential diagnosis* and *process diagnosis*. These two approaches are discussed in detail in Chapter 3, but some brief comments about their nature and their function may be noted here. In inferential diagnosis the psychologist attempts to follow the sequential steps and notes the productions of the subject as he carries out his successive test tasks, noting how he performs, what difficulties he has, and how he copes with these difficulties. At the same time the examiner is attempting to infer what is contributing to the ongoing and successive productions. During this process he raises as many relevant hypotheses (or even speculations) as he can about the test productions, discarding some as they prove fruitless or inadequate, integrating relevant hypotheses, and refining them until he can arrive at the most parsimonious explanation(s) that is pertinent. In this process of attempting to empathize with the subject, the psychologist notes discrepancies in performance level (i.e., whether particular tasks cause difficulty, if there is consistently poorer performance as tasks become more difficult, if there is cumulative effect of failure experience, etc.). The inferential approach involves many hazards and does not, by itself, lead to any firm conclusions. However, it provides rich sources of data and often enables one to explain test phenomena in ways that uniquely fit the subject and that lead to appropriate efforts at rehabilitation and improvement in the subject's functioning. (See Chapters 3 and 6 for more detailed discussion.)

Process diagnosis overlaps with methods of inferential diagnosis but addresses itself more explicitly to the component aspects leading to the final product in performance. It attempts to determine *under what condi-*

tions the subject fails and under what conditions he succeeds. In short, it
is the adoption of an experimental method to test performance. For instance, suppose we ask the subject to copy design A from the Hutt Adaptation of the Bender-Gestalt Test (HABGT). As will be seen in Plate 1,
this design involves a circle and a diamond that are tangential to each
other. Suppose the subject draws this as two separate designs, a circle and
a diamond. After the test has been completed, the examiner may pursue,
for example, the following experimental process procedure to attempt to
determine what led to the failure on this design, i.e., the separation of the
two parts. First he may again show the test card to the subject, placing it
alongside the design the subject made, and he may ask, "Are these two,
the one on the card and the one you made, exactly alike?" If the subject
indicates that they are not, the examiner may ask, "And what's different
about them?" If the answer indicates the subject perceives what is wrong,
he may then be told, "I'd like you to do this one again, making sure to
draw it just like the one on the card." This time the subject may draw two
tangential circles or he may draw the circle accurately but in trying to
make the diamond tangential to the circle, he may distort the shape of the
diamond. The examiner may note that the task appears to be too complex
perceptually for the subject since he could draw the circle and the diamond accurately only when they were separated. He may then test this
hypothesis by asking the subject to copy two tangential diamonds and/or
two tangential circles.

By these and other, similar procedures, the examiner (experimenter,
now) tries to tease out the specific factor or factors which led to the error
in the first place. He questions, he observes, he tries out the same or
similar tasks under differing conditions until he learns precisely what has
caused the difficulty. Suppose the subject said, when asked why he drew
the two parts of this design separately (after he acknowledged that he was
aware of the error), that he did it "the easier way." In the discussion that
follows, the examiner might learn that the subject characteristically did
not attempt to work hard at tasks that he regarded as too difficult for him,
that he had a low aspiration level, that he was hostile to the examiner (or
the examining situation), that he disliked drawing, or that he was fearful in
entering new (test) situations. There might be many other explanations for
the failure. In any event, process diagnosis attempts to elucidate the
cause(s) of the difficulty by experimentally varying the conditions of the
test (experiment) until it becomes clear what the problem is. Such procedures are especially valuable in testing for possible organic brain damage,
as we shall see when we discuss that problem. They are also valuable in
testing for malingering, for cultural deprivation, and for capacity to improve in functioning under certain conditions of encouragement or support. In short, process diagnosis attempts to gain a more complete under-

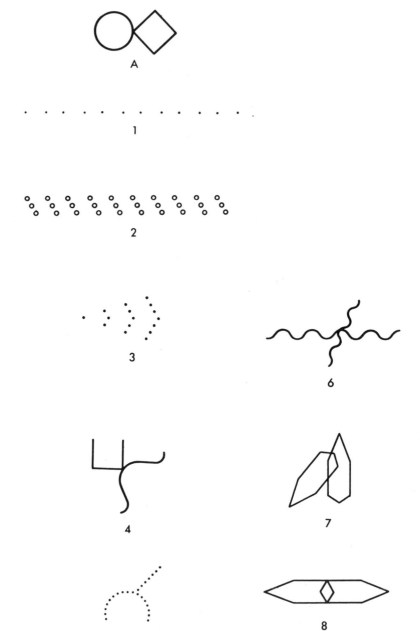

Plate 1. The Hutt Adaptation of the Bender-Gestalt Figures (This and other illustrations in the book have been reduced by about 45% from the original size. The figures are numbered for identification purposes.)

standing of the test performance by testing out the conditions that lead to success or failure.

Now let us consider the nature of the HABGT as we have developed it. It is based on the original work of Wertheimer (1923), who explored Gestalt phenomena by means of many experimental visual designs. His major concern was the confirmation of certain Gestalt principles of behavior as opposed to the then prevalent stimulus–response analysis of behavior. Perception was seen as involving the recognition of *basic Gestalten* rather than as the integration of disparate parts or segments into a total visual interpretation. His focus was on the total complex response and the conditions which explained how and why experiences were responded to in terms of primary configurations rather than in terms of successive steps, which, he believed, could not explain the total, immediate configurational characteristics of the stimulus.

Some years later, Bender became interested in using some of the experimental test designs as a means of studying certain forms of psychopathology (1938). The nine test designs employed by Bender in her clinical study of various pathognomonic groups were designs she had *selected* from the figures developed by Wertheimer and had *adapted* in order "to simplify them or to accentuate some basic Gestalt feature" (Tolor and Schulberg, 1963). Because he believed that these adaptations contained some undesirable features (see Chapter 2), Hutt developed another set of the figures that seemed to him to be more similar to those used by Wertheimer and that did not contain any drafting irregularities which might influence the response (see Plate 1). The usual task given a subject requires that he reproduce these designs freehand without the use of any mechanical aids. This seemingly simple task is far more complex than might at first be suspected. It involves both visual and motor behavior, not only in the reproduction of the designs, but also in the perception of them on the stimulus card. It further requires both visual and motor adaptations in the placement of the reproductions on the page or pages used by the subject as he engages in the "task of the test." In short, the behavior that is elicited is an *integrated whole* and is determined by many factors. As Schilder puts it in his Preface to Bender's monograph (Bender, 1938): "It approaches the fundamental problems of perception and action from a new angle. . . . It shows the continuous interplay between motor and sensory factors." He adds, ". . . gestalt patterns are *experiences* [italics mine] of an individual who has problems and . . . the final configuration of experience is not merely a problem in perception but a problem of personality. This becomes particularly clear when one studies the Gestalt function in neurotics."

The HABGT is an attempt to utilize this procedure as a *projective* device. It goes beyond the classical Gestalt laws of perception (namely, pregnanz, closure, nearness, and the like) and tries to understand both the *process* of responding and the *final product* in such ways as to maximize the understanding of the behaving individual: his idiosyncratic personality style; his needs, conflicts, and defenses; his level of maturation; and his coping methods and ego strengths. Such an approach can make use of both objective scores and complex clinical judgments. It utilizes the large body of evidence which has been acquired concerning the general nature of perceptual and motoric development, the nature of projective phenomena, and the effects of psychological and intracranial damage upon behavioral functions. It attempts to understand the individual's global functioning in the most parsimonious terms that will enable us to describe him and to predict some significant aspects of his behavior under defined circumstances. In subsequent chapters we shall provide a rationale for various methods of analysis of test findings and relate each of these methods to clinical experience, research findings, and experimental evidence whenever possible. However, many aspects of the methods of analysis that are proposed are frankly based on hypotheses which will require considerable research study and further clinical investigation.

First let us consider some propostitions which we hold to be axiomatic, even though there is considerable evidence to support them. All behavior—from the most simple to the complex—is a result of the interplay of conscious and unconscious factors. Of course, it is also much more than this; it involves the physical condition of the organism, its state of maturation, its prior experience, and its immediate state of expectancy at the time of the emergent behavior. In some kinds of behavior, conscious factors may play the decisive, in fact, almost the all-inclusive role. The distinguishing feature of such behavior is deliberate choice, in contrast to automatic functioning in situations of conflict-free spheres of operation. Such behaviors "of choice" most likely lie in the realm of simple, short-term performances, but they may occur in more complicated performances as well. We assume that as civilized human beings we are capable of and usually make such deliberate choices in most of our behavior, but in fact far more frequently factors of unknown origin play a decisive role. Clinical and experimental evidence strongly suggests that unconscious motivational factors play a significant role in our general style of adjustment, in our postural and motoric style of behavior, in our level of aspiration, in our perception and understanding of situations that confront us, and in the specific ways we go about adapting our behaviors to the ongoing problems before us. Not only slips of the tongue, acts of forgetting, distortions of reality, and prejudicial attitudes, but even styles of speaking, facial expression, tempo and movement, and affective tone are, in part, influenced by factors of which we are utterly unaware or only partially aware. Often we can "explain" such behaviors after the fact, but frequently our explanation is of the order "that's the way we are."

Although it is problematic how decisive unconscious factors are in a great many aspects of our everyday behavior, the role of such factors becomes clearer when we examine dream material or when we evaluate neurotic behavior. It is widely accepted that the substance of psychopathologic behavior is largely determined by unconscious motivations which find expression in symptomatic acts or in characterologic traits. Yet, some workers prefer to dismiss the concept of the unconscious, suggesting instead that we view behavior entirely from a phenomenonologic stance. Such an orientation is possible, but I believe that if one takes this stance the very essence of the quality of being human is thereby eliminated and the meaning of motivation in human behavior is entirely neglected. Our problems of analysis of behavior are, in fact, not simplified but only compounded by this outlook, for we are omitting the crucial and meaningful characteristic of the human organism—its striving, actualizing, and self-determining characteristics. Instead, it would seem that although overt phenomena are resultants of the interplay of many factors, unconscious factors often play a central role. Even in so-called normal individuals there is evidence that factors of which the individual is unaware exert a considerable, and often central, influence on the direction and nature of adjustment (Solley & Murphy, 1960).

From a clinical viewpoint, the assumption of unconscious motivation seems highly profitable. Although it is possible to alter overt behavior without understanding the role of conscious and unconscious motivational factors, existing conflicts which gave rise to the behavior may persist or may even become reinforced, and other, ancillary behaviors may develop which may be even more objectionable. An example is the devastating consequences that occur when strong anxiety drives are suppressed or no outlet for them is provided and severely disorganized or psychotic behavior develops. However, when both conscious and unconscious motivations are carefully evaluated and the dynamics of an individual's behavior are understood—even approximately—more effective methods for dealing with pathologic behavior can be devised and outcomes can be more accurately predicted. The methods of dealing with conflicts may themselves be quite diverse, but at least they will tend to be more congruent with the individual's total adjustmental status and more effective in securing some enduring consequences.

Hence, we view it as of great and even crucial importance that the clinician understand the individual's conflicts and their unconscious derivation. A great many methods are available for the evaluation of these problems: structured and unstructured interviews, free associations, dream material, role playing sessions, objective personality tests, verbal projective tests, the use of drawings as projective devices, cartoon-like test devices, and the like. All of these have their place, and sometimes one or another may be most helpful in an individual instance. We suggest, however, that the visual–motor assessment of behavior and underlying dynamics has some unique as well as some common advantages.

As already noted, the use of a visual–motor task in testing personality reactions provides a sample of behavior involving complex functions. Like other projective procedures for assessing personality, such complex examples of behavior offer clues to the general style of adaptation, cognitive methods of behaving, affective types of responses, areas of conflict, specific defensive methods, and maturational characteristics. Unlike many other projective methods, especially those emphasizing verbal comprehension and verbal response, perceptual–motoric functioning has some special characteristics and possible advantages. Perhaps central to such special characteristics is the probability that styles of perceptual, motoric, and perceptual–motoric functioning become established, or tendencies toward such styles are established, very early in life—before language comprehension and usage have developed (Solley & Murphy, 1960; Werner, 1957). Space does not permit a summary of observational and experimental studies of early perception, motoric behavior, and the "integrated" perceptual–motoric behaviors that develop during infancy and very early childhood. Instead we shall note some principles which have emerged and their implications.

The infant has some individual and some general characteristic ways in which, based on constitutional factors, he perceives his immediate world. He is able to make some rudimentary figure–ground differentiation before learning takes place (Hebb, 1949). But his response potential is quite limited because of his immaturity and, more precisely, because he has not yet learned how to mediate incoming stimuli. As Gesell, Ilg, and Bulliss (1949) have shown, the infant soon learns to mediate some of these stimuli by perceptual and tactual responses. Deprivation or frustration experiences tend to disrupt these early integrated response patterns just as they tend to disrupt acts of visual attention (Drever, 1967). The infant's mind grows by the successive laying down of memoric traces which are closely dependent upon immediate experiences (Koffka, 1931). Moreover, probably a great deal of classical conditioning (and imprinting) may occur because of the infant's low level of awareness, and high level of affective need.

When motoric behavior is insufficient to reduce the tension level which internal need and perceptual experience have generated, autistic perception tends to result (Helson, 1953). As Helson puts it, the tendency to autistic perception (or perception that is more determined by inner needs than by outer reality) may result from "memories, residual traces from previously experienced dangers, excessive anticipatory reactions before danger actually threatens, or the result of magnified feed-back mechanisms wherein awareness of one's own bodily process figures prominently." Then, affective needs reinforce autistic perception and only further maturation and differentiation of needs and response patterns can alter this trend; otherwise hallucinatory substitutes for need satisfaction or motoric discharge can provide some partial tension reduction (Rapaport, 1951). With further development, unless traumatic experience is overwhelming, the child learns to utilize improved perceptual–motoric responses to meet his needs and to mediate his experience. Only very gradually does greater "field independence" develop (Witkin, Dyk, Faterson, Goodenough, & Karp, 1967) and does a greater repertoire of coping behaviors emerge.

One implication of these findings is that some important aspects of conflictful experiences are expressed early in life through perceptual–motoric modes or styles of behavior—in fact so early in life that language has played little or no part in them. Even in later years of early childhood, perceptual–motoric modes may be greatly influenced by significant emotional and conflictful experiences. Such experiences and the "memories" of them may, in fact, be "bound" in the motoric style. Sometimes one can infer from the style what the general nature of these experiences might have been. Sometimes *the repetition of the perceptual–motoric act may redintegrate the repressed emotional experience*. As we shall see later, the subject who performs on both the copy phase and the elaboration phase of the HABGT often expresses, knowingly or unknowingly, many facets of his hitherto "covered over" experiences. In any case, his perceptual–motoric behavior may reveal much of his characteristic ways of defending and coping which his verbal behavior may conceal.

Two other special values of a nonverbal, perceptual–motoric projective test of personality reactions should be noted. Since the conventions of what is "good" and what is "bad" behavior are not known to the subject who performs such a task, he is less likely to conceal from the examiner those aspects of himself which he fears to reveal, whereas on a verbal task such conventions are more widely known and can be used to avoid such confrontations. Even when the subject has no conscious intent to conceal, the cultural overlay of language itself may becloud the meaning of the test response. Another way of stating this is that perceptual–motoric behavior is more likely to be idiosyncratic, whereas verbal behavior is more likely to be "culture bound."

In summary, perceptual–motoric test behavior offers a sampling of aspects of behavior not readily available in verbal tests, it may tap earlier levels of meaningful and conflictful experience, and it may be less consciously distorted because its meaning is not so obviously meaningful.

To whom might the HABGT test be profitably administered? The answer depends, in part, upon one's philosophy of testing. In the author's view, psychological testing should be undertaken only when there is a clear, functional use for such testing—first of all, in terms of the patient's or subject's interests; second, in terms of research or administrative interests. (Considering the first of these uses, testing with a particular instrument should involve the probability that the findings will better enable us to serve the patient: enabling him to make more effective use of his capacities; enabling him to understand himself more deeply and fully; or enabling us to understand and assist him toward these objectives.) From such a viewpoint, the following categories or classes of people for whom the HABGT would be most profitable should be considered.

Category I. This category consists of patients whose verbal behavior does not afford an adequate sampling of their personality strengths and deficits *even though they are able to use verbal means of communication quite effectively.* Although it may be true that words "conceal as well as reveal" in all cases, it is especially true for persons in this group, and they are the ones for whom the HABGT is especially useful. Who are these people? First of all, this category includes those whose verbal defenses are so strong or ingrained that their communication acts as a facade—e.g., the obsessive intellectualizer or the verbally facile rationalizer. They may appear on the surface to be far better integrated than is actually the case. Such people may use language consciously to distort the picture of their underlying problems or they may unconsciously present a picture of themselves as different from what is actually the case. In addition to defensive use of intellectualization, such individuals may be detected by their glibness, their inability to express affect spontaneously, or their preoccupation with a fantasy life. In all such instances, samples of behavior derived exclusively from verbal tests can yield distorted findings. They may sometimes show a pseudo ego control in their verbal behavior, as do obsessive people who are able to conceal from themselves and others the disintegration of ego controls which may lie behind such verbal behavior.

A special subgroup of individuals falling within Category I consists of malingerers. Such persons may, for either conscious or unconscious reasons, attempt to convey an impression of greater pathology than actually exists. Or they may attempt to convey an impression of meeting the norms of behavior that they believe are expected of them. In any case, even when the clinician is aware that malingering is occurring, it is difficult to make an accurate assessment and valid differential diagnosis. However, when such people are asked to take a nonverbal test such as the HABGT, they are deprived of their usual verbal–intellectual defenses and are more likely to reveal aspects of themselves—superior or inferior—which might otherwise be obscured. They do not know what various perceptual–motoric kinds of behavior reveal about them and are therefore less competent in concealing or distorting. In later chapters we shall discuss various procedures that may be employed in further clarifying the meaning of test behavior that is engaged in by malingerers.

Category II. This category consists of individuals who are unable or unwilling to produce an adequate sample of verbal behavior for diagnostic purposes. There are several subgroups in this category, with quite different characteristics. There are those whose verbal behavior is significantly impaired. They may have come from culturally deprived backgrounds, or from a culture in which they had little opportunity to master our language. They may show significant inhibition in verbal behavior, which limits the usefulness of their verbal test behavior. For example, they may be severely depressed and unable to verbalize freely. Or they may be markedly withdrawn in all of their interpersonal behavior, including language, as are catatonics or individuals with schizoid inhibition. Sometimes, in cases involving intense, acute, or chronic anxiety, verbal behavior may become markedly disturbed. In these cases not only is the sample of verbal behavior insufficient for evaluative purposes, but even this sample may be nonrepresentative of many aspects of the personality—especially of those healthy aspects which could make for effective growth or recovery. In many instances, the sample of behavior that is obtained with verbal tests is so meager that it is difficult to assess its meaning properly with respect to either the severity of the pathology or areas of conflict. Persons who fall in Category II confront us, then, with two related types of clinical problems: the problem of the representativeness of the sample of behavior which has been elicited, and the problem of identifying the underlying pathology or the areas of most intense conflict.

Category III. This category consists of individuals who suffer from some form of intracranial pathology. Except in certain circumstances, patients who are suspected of having such damage cannot be easily evaluated as having brain damage by means of samples of verbal behavior. Verbal behavior may be least affected by such damage or may reveal such damage only when the condition has deteriorated severely. Moreover, there are many cases of brain damage which are not readily discoverable by routine neurologic diagnostic procedures. In these, tests such as the HABGT can be highly useful in pointing up the possibility of damage which might otherwise be overlooked. In addition, such tests are useful in assessing the type or degree of change which may occur as a result of treatment or surgery, as our later survey of the literature will indicate. Perceptual–motoric tests are routinely useful for both diagnostic and treatment purposes in all instances in which brain damage is present or suspected. Moreover, since the way in which a person reacts to intracranial pathology is a function of both his personality and the type of organic damage, a technique which reflects both of these, such as the HABGT, is useful in the clinical management of such people.

Category IV. We should like to reserve this cateogry for the so-called mentally retarded individuals. The diagnosis of mental retardation presents many special problems. As has now been abundantly demonstrated (Hutt & Gibby, 1976), this group of individuals is frequently characterized by moderate to severe cultural deprivation. The usual verbal intelligence tests, which have a high degree of correlation with verbal skills and with scholastic achievement, are not particularly valid as predictors of intellectual potential or of academic growth in such cases. It is probably true that many children who come from deprived cultural backgrounds obtain scores on such tests that are not necessarily indicative of their mental status or their academic potential if proper and intensive remedial assistance were to be provided, especially in the early stages of their school careers. In order to prevent the inappropriate classification of those in this group who are not truly retarded in the intellectual sphere but are largely or only retarded linguistically and culturally, some measure of intellectual potential which is not so closely bound to cultural experience is needed. Tests of perceptual maturity, in general, and perceptual–motoric tests such as the HABGT are particularly useful in such cases.

Hutt and Gibby (1976) have also shown that many individuals who are classified as mentally retarded may function below average in the intellectual sphere because of severe emotional handicaps which interfere with their intellectual functioning and may produce cognitive inhibition and lower their aspiration and motivation for academic and other achievements. It has been demonstrated that the complex interaction between cultural deprivation and emotional frustration may, temporarily or more enduringly, interfere with intellectual growth and functioning (Hunt, 1961). In order to assess such individuals better, the diagnostic battery should include personality tests which, on the one hand, are not unduly biased by linguistic and cultural factors and, on the other hand, provide some basis for assessing the degree of interference of emotional factors with intellectual functioning. The HABGT and other versions of the Bender-Gestalt Test, as well as other nonverbal tests of intelligence and of personality, are especially useful for such purposes. Tests of perceptual–motoric maturity have been shown to provide useful information in predicting about and in guiding individuals who are handicapped by factors such as those just discussed.

Moreover, many retarded individuals may have some orgainc brain damage, even if slight, or some special personality problems which contribute to mental malfunctioning. The HABGT is a useful device in evaluating the possible contribution of these factors to functional mental retardation and in differentiating those for whom such factors are not particularly relevant.

Category V. The last group contains a miscellaneous population of individuals. Here we would group the illiterates, the uneducated, and the foreign born unskilled in English—all of the individuals who are handicapped in verbal communication. Such persons are likely to give atypical test protocols on instruments designed for individuals with normal linguistic skills and who meet the "normal" conditions of the usual standardization population employed in developing such tests and their norms. Tests such as the HABGT which rely upon more universal background experiences and do not emphasize culture-bound symbol development to so great an extent do not place such persons at an even greater disadvantage in the attempt to assess their intelligence and personality functioning. Moreover, to the extent that perceptual–motoric performance reveals basic aspects of the personality, particularly those aspects dependent upon very early experiences, the HABGT has uncommon advantages for persons who fall in Category V.

The foregoing discussion has attempted to highlight the general categories of individuals for whom tests such as the HABGT are particularly useful. Our emphasis in this discussion was our concern with the individual, and reflects our desire to employ tests in the diagnostic battery that will be most useful in evaluating and providing remedial help when needed. In addition to these considerations, many clinicians have employed the test for other purposes, as Chapter 2 will illustrate. The following listing of the more frequently mentioned uses of the HABGT may help the reader to see the broader vista of the clinical potential of this test.

1. The HABGT has been found useful as a *buffer test*. Every clinicain tries to develop good rapport with his subject. Among the approaches used in developing such a relationship, the use of a seemingly simple, nonthreatening test as the first test in the schedule may be helpful in many cases. Not only is the test not likely to be experienced as threatening, but it is enjoyed by most subjects and lends itself to discussion about the function of the diagnostic battery. In some instances, patients who are covertly hostile to testing find it easy to express their anger by externalizing it upon a test procedure which they see as childish or silly. The skillful clinician will utilize this cathartic expression of feeling to explore the patient's attitudes in order to help him accept the testing situation in his own personal terms.

2. The HABGT is useful as a supplementary devise in rounding out the assessment procedures so that verbal behavior is not overemphasized in the total evaluation.

3. The HABGT is useful when tests involving *minimal examiner–patient interaction* are required. It has been demonstrated that some patients are significantly influenced by such interactions, so that valid assessment is difficult. The HABGT can be administered so as to minimize such "interfering" factors.

4. The HABGT has special value in assessing the illiterate, the uneducated, and the culturally deprived. Such individuals present special

problems in assessment. Although no test can be entirely "fair" in such cases, those relying upon perceptual–motoric performance and involving very little verbal skill are an important part of the test battery in such instances.

5.   The HABGT may be useful in the differential diagnosis of mental retardation. In cases of suspected retardation it is extremely important to evaluate or to de-emphasize the contributing roles of prior cultural experience, emotional interference with intellectual functioning, and possible intracranial damage.

6.   The HABGT is useful for patients whose verbal behavior provides a screen which conceals aspects of personality functioning.

7.   The HABGT is especially useful in cases in which malingering is suspected.

8.   The HABGT is useful in the differential diagnosis of intracranial pathology. Although all psychological manifestations of brain damage are influenced not only by the type and amount of damage, they are also influenced by the subject's personality functioning. The HABGT has been found in both clinical and experimental studies to be quite successful in differentiating some types of brain damage.

9.   The HABGT is often useful in differentiating psychotic process phenomena which are sometimes concealed in verbal projective tests. Perceptual–motoric behavior can reveal evidence of such psychotic processes, especially when they are not otherwise flagrantly apparent.

10.   The HABGT is useful in delineating aspects of conflict areas and defense styles. Among these, problems in identity, sexual identification, general patterns of interpersonal relations, and approach–withdrawal tendencies are prominent.

11.   The HABGT is sometimes useful in determining the degree of psychological regression and intellectual impairment. Among other features of the test, comparisons of performance on the designs which differ in level of maturity can lead to important inferences along these lines.

12.   The HABGT is helpful in predicting some aspects of school achievement. It has been studied extensively in relation to the prediction of the early phases of reading.

13.   The HABGT may be found useful in the study of intercultural differences. Although this device is not entirely free of cultural influences, it taps some important levels of personality functioning which intercultural investigations have been concerned with.

14.   The HABGT may be used in the study of the effects of various forms of chemical and physiological therapy, such as the use of pharmacologic agents and the use of electroconvulsive therapy.

15.   The HABGT may be used in connection with studies investigating the possible effects of psychotherapy.

16. The HABGT may be useful in research studies involving relationships between perceptual–motoric behavior and various personality dimensions.

As we have noted, the above list summarizes some of the more frequent uses of the HABGT. Not all of these uses are equally pertinent for this test and some uses may, finally, be found to be less significant than was at first hoped. And, of course, further research and ingenuity may lead to significant uses for the test which have thus far not been recognized. The listing should be regarded as suggestive. Each user of the test, in this or in other forms, has the final obligation of evaluating for himself the validity and significance of any alleged claims, and each user of the test must decide whether and how to use it in clinical study or in research.

2
A History of the Development of the HABGT

The HABGT constitutes one general method for the clinical use of selected designs from the original Wertheimer experimental designs. Its chief characteristic is the projective features of the test protocol which result from the interplay of the method of administration, the methods of work by the subject, and the test product which is analyzed and scored for evidences projection. Even our objective scales (Psychopathology Scale and Adience–Abience Scale), described in detail in Chapter 7, are based on assumptions germane to the projective approach. It is desirable to keep these considerations clearly in mind when evaluating this approach and when comparing it with other approaches using this or similar test material.

It is inaccurate to speak of the "Bender-Gestalt Test" as if this were a single test instrument. Not only do test cards differ from one version to another, but methods of administration, scoring, analysis, and evaluation also differ significantly. Each of these approaches may have its own particular values and limitations. Thus, we do not have one Bender-Gestalt Test, but rather many procedures for eliciting test behavior and for analyzing test products. This proliferation of test materials and test analyses is welcomed by this writer since it leads to exploration and evaluation which, in the long run, can help us to establish the precise value which each has. Our own interest in the Wertheimer figures is in the special clinical usefulness they have, under certain conditions, in delineating personality problems, in more accurately assessing evidence of mental impoverishment, and in analyzing possible consequences of neurological impairment or deficit. Our attempt has been *to mazimize projective fea-*

tures of the test performance and to provide both clinical and objective methods for its analysis.

Taken together, the various forms of the Bender-Gestalt Test now constitute one of the most widely utilized methods in clinical assessment in this country. They are also widely used throughout the world. The clinical and research literature has burgeoned over the past few decades and several summaries of the findings from these studies are available (e.g., Billingslea, 1963; Koppitz, 1965, 1975a; Landmark & Grinde, 1964; Lubin, Wallis, & Paine, 1971; Koppitz, 1975; Sonoda, 1968; Tolor, 1968; Tolor & Schulberg, 1963). We shall not attempt to describe each of the studies which has been published; that would deserve another volume in its own right. Rather, we shall refer to those studies which are most pertinent to the development of our own approach and which offer evidence concerning the validity of certain test indicators and scores.

As noted in the preceding chapter, the nine figures comprising the usual set of stimuli which are in both the HABGT and the Bender-Gestalt Test were selected from those used by Wertheimer in his studies of Gestalt functions (Wertheimer, 1923). Using a much larger sample of designs, Wertheimer investigated the patterns of visual perception by asking his "apparently" normal subjects to describe what they saw. Bender became interested in the use of some of these designs as a means of exploring deviations in the maturational process in perceptual–motoric functions that were associated with certain pathologic conditions, among which were mental retardation, schizophrenia, organic brain damage, aphasia, manic–depressive psychosis, and certain toxic conditions. For these purposes, she used nine designs, labeling the first one "A," since she conceived of this one essentially as an introductory or practice design (at least in the beginning), and the others from "1" to "8." As she stated: "Only test figures A, 3, 7, and 8 closely resemble the designs used by Wertheimer. The others have been modified usually to simplify them or to accentuate some basic Gestalt feature" (Tolor & Schulberg, 1963).

During the 1930's almost all of the work done with these figures consisted of clinical investigation by Bender, herself, of the clinical groups in which she was interested. A major innovation in using these figures was that subjects were asked to *copy* them, and *not* to describe them. Her position with regard to this test procedure's possible value in assessing personality disturbances was, at first, ambiguous. In her first general summary of her clinical work, speaking of the characteristics of the drawings of her subjects, she maintained, "The final product is a visual motor pattern which reveals modifications in the original pattern by the integrating mechanism of the individual who has experienced it" (Bender, 1938). She also offered little hope that the procedure would be useful in studying personality disturbances in psychoneurotics, stating: "We do not expect to find disturbances in perception or in the visual motor Gestalt function in the psychoneuroses.'' Yet, in the same paragraph she notes, ''. . . it would not be surprising to find that some such Gestalten might become the symbol of the individual's unsatisfied infantile drives.'' Her general position, nevertheless, seemed to indicate little faith that the test could be used effectively in studying personality disturbances. This is all the more surprising in that her husband, Paul Schilder, who interested her in this work and who wrote the preface to this monograph, states: ''Dr. Bender does not forget that Gestalt patterns are experiences of an individual who has problems and that the final configuration of experience is *not merely a problem of perception but a problem of personality* [italics mine]. This becomes particularly clear when one studies the Gestalt function in neurotics.''

As Bender's work continued she shared her drawings with a number of co-workers. Sometimes the drawings were reproduced freehand; sometimes mimeographed copies were available. As already noted, the figures were different from those used by Wertheimer. Moreover, they were inconsistent, varying both in size and in Gestalt characteristics. In these early days, some of the workers utilizing this procedure made their own copies, utilizing the designs available in the 1938 monograph.

I was one of those who found this procedure intriguing, and a valuable supplement to other clinical methods of assessment. Like others, I had utilized the relatively makeshift designs that were currently available. I tried them out with a wide variety of patients, gaining subjective impressions from the characteristics which they displayed both in their methods of work on this task and in the varying products which they produced. In 1944, while a member of the U. S. Army and attached to the Mental Hygiene Unit at Ft. Monmouth, New Jersey, and to the England General Hospital in Atlantic City, New Jersey, I continued the ''experimental'' use of these designs with a wide variety of military patients, and became increasingly impressed with the unique clinical utility of this ''test'' and with its possibilities for the projective assessment of personality.

In 1945, I was assigned as senior instructor in the Officer's Clinical Psychology Program at the Adjutant General's School in Ft. Sam Houston, Texas, and in this capacity was responsible for instruction in projective theory and technique. I considered it wise to include the Bender-Gestalt Test among the projective methods which might be employed. The technique possessed unique characteristics which promised to be of value for such purposes. It was simple and rapid to administer, it was useful for the wide variety of military personnel who differed so much in education and cultural experience as well as in personality characteristics, it was especially useful in assessing the possible effects of organic brain damage, and it relied very little upon verbal communication. In addition to the clinical data which I had amassed, I made use in my tentative interpretations (hypotheses) of the general but limited research evidence on the relations between personality and perception that was already available. I had also been greatly impressed by the provocative findings of Mira's (1939–1940, 1943) work on the relationships of motoric behavior to personality attributes.

However, test cards were unavailable and the designs then currently in use differed in the characteristics already noted. Consequently, I decided to secure "standard" designs, attempting at the same time to adhere as closely as possible to stimuli that met Wertheimer's Gestalt criteria, to develop figures that did not contain irregularities (such as uneven line quality, inopportune angles, varying figure sizes), and to have available easily reproducible figures. In cooperation with F. L. Wells of Harvard University, such a set of cards was produced and distributed to clinical psychologists throughout the U. S. Army.* At the same time, I developed a tentative guide for administration and interpretation (Hutt, 1945a).

Clinical psychologists in the Army and elsewhere became increasingly interested in the projective possibilities, as well as of other potentialities, of this procedure. In the Army it seemed especially useful in the differential diagnosis of organicity, in assessing the severity of psychopathology and its acute or transient character, in differentiating illiteracy from retardation, and in detecting malingering. Some psychologists used the "Tentative Guide" as if it were a well-validated manual of findings, although it was clearly not intended as such, while others were more cautious and experimental in their approach. When I later became Chief, Clinical Psychology Branch, U. S. Army (in the Surgeon General's Office), I urged caution in the use of the procedure and suggested the need for much more clinical work and research study (Military Bulletin, Surgeon General's Office, U. S. Army, 1946).

There followed a very rapid rise in the use of this, and modified, procedures. Before 1945 this test was not even included in the rankings in popularity or frequency of usage of psychological tests employed by clinical psychologists (Sundberg, 1961). The same survey reported that by 1946 it ranked 54th in popularity, and by 1960 it ranked 3rd. In 1961 Schulberg and Tolor reported that 95% of experienced clinicians utilized the "test" and that four of five of these clinicians believed it had value in clinical practice.

It is also of interest that prior to 1945 there were only a handful of papers dealing with this procedure, chiefly by Bender, and no systematic

* These test cards for the HABGT are available from the publisher, Grune and Stratton, Inc., New York City.

research studies. By 1960 almost 300 additional publications had appeared, including clinical papers, research reports on the findings of different methods of administration and scoring as well as on specific validation studies, and reviews of the literature. Two surveys which studied the research use of projective tests have indicated the increasingly greater use of the Bender-Gestalt and its various modifications over the years from 1947 through 1965. In the survey by Mills, (1965), based only on studies published in the *Journal of Projective Techniques and Personality Assessment*, and covering the period from 1947 through 1964, the Bender-Gestalt ranked fourth among the leading 21 projective tests in terms of research use. In the other study, which analyzed the publications in ten other research journals from 1947 through 1965, this test ranked fifth, and was cited in 153 studies during this period (Crenshaw, Bohn, Hoffman, Matheus, & Offenbach, 1968). The latter study indicated that the use of the Bender-Gestalt in research investigations gradually increased over the years. As already indicated, the use of this procedure as a clinical instrument has maintained or even increased its popularity in recent years (Lubin et al., 1971).

In 1946 Bender published her own manual for the clinical use of the "test." At the same time, she made her forms of the test figures commercially available (Bender, 1946). The Hutt form of these figures became unavailable with the conclusion of the Second World War, but were again made commercially available in 1960 with the publication of the Hutt and Briskin volume (1960). The first attempt at objective scoring of the Bender-Gestalt was reported by Billingslea (1948), a former student in the Officer's Clinical Psychology program, and he reported essentially negative findings. However, his scoring method involved the atomistic analysis of what he called "factors" and "indices," yielding 137 indices in all. Thus, although his method was presumably in part based on more global hypotheses advanced by Hutt (and to lesser extent by Bender), it was opposed in basic conceptualization to hypotheses of a projective nature. Moreover, there is considerable question concerning the validity of his criterion groups. Other objective scoring methods developed in this early period were seemingly much more successful. Kitay (1950) presented a scoring approach based essentially on size deviations and found some significant correlations of his scores with Rorschach indices in a population of college students. Pascal (1950), and later Pascal and Suttell (1951), developed an objective scoring system, based on a global score representing amount of psychopathology, which yielded very promising results and stimulated a considerable amount of research activity by others. Pascal's scoring method was, like Billingslea's, influenced to a considerable degree by the thinking and teaching of Hutt in the Army program, and it was developed by him and others (notably Irion and Suttell) on the basis of extensive clinical experience with the "test." Still other scoring approaches were developed by Peek and Quast (1951) and by Gobetz (1953), utilizing operational definitions of test phenomena, and these methods have also stimulated further research exploration by others.

The intense interest that these early efforts generated led to several reviews of the literature and to some rather hastily expressed evaluations of the "test." The reviews included those by Bell (1951), Halpern (1951), and Hutt (1945b). A review and negative evaluation was furnished by Benton (1953). On the other hand, I rested my case for the projective possibilities of this procedure in these early days mainly on "blind" interpretation of clinical cases and the correlation of these findings with the findings from other clinical tests, intensive psychotherapeutic work and reports, and research studies (Hutt 1949, 1951, 1960, 1963). My statistical findings were not presented in detail in the "Tentative Guide," but are summarized for more careful inspection in Chapters 5 and 7 of this book.

Bender's ambiguous evaluation of the possibilities of the projective approach to the interpretation of Gestalt drawings became clearly negative in about 1949. At this time she voiced her grave apprehensions in this regard and noted that researchers and clinicians were misusing the Gestalt principles which she advocated (Bender, 1949). Her opposition to such projective uses was stated even more emphatically in 1963: "Neither can ego strength be defined so as to correlate it with Gestalt function or other performances on the Visual Motor Gestalt Test. Since personality dynamics vary with different schools and sub-schools of psychology, the application of such dynamics to a perceptual motor test is spurious . . ." (Tolor & Schulber, 1963, Foreword). It will remain for further clinical and research study to determine to what extent such judgments are justified.

It should also be noted that in my "blind" analyses referred to above, the predictions which were generated on the bases of the projective approach could be and were checked against criteria based on long-term clinical diagnostic studies and on the therapist's evaluations of the patient's progress. In each case, highly meaningful and precise predictions received striking confirmation. As Cronback indicated (1960, p. 581) in his evaluation of one of these studies, "Such test interpretation is often severely criticized as unscientific. In defense of the method, we may note that Hutt is able to give *a detailed rationale for each of his inferences* [italics mine]. A much stronger defense is that his description of the patient agrees with the clinical picture given both from the MMPI self-report and in the therapist's notes. *Word for word, we find confirmation there of ineffectual defense through obsession, hostile impulses the subject fears to express, and so on."*

In recent years the use of Bender-Gestalt procedures with children, in both individual and group administration, has expanded greatly. The chief interest in these approaches has been in using the test findings to evaluate visual–motor maturity. The work of Koppitz (1963, 1975a) has provided a simple method of scoring and appropriate normative data for ages 5 to 12, although discrimination above 9 years of age appears to be quite unreliable. Haworth (1970) has provided us with a valuable supplement for preschool and primary grade children, between ages 4 to 9, with simpler designs for younger children and with a more refined scoring method. We shall have more to say about the values of such methods in later chapters, but wish to note that even with emphasis upon objective scores for development, these test materials do not exclude projective and other clinical uses of test protocols.

PROJECTIVE USE OF PERCEPTUAL–MOTORIC BEHAVIOR

Research studies dealing with the projective potential of this "test" have been appearing in the literature since 1950. In 1952, Suczek and Klopfer (1952) investigated the symbolic value of the Wertheimer figures that comprise the Bender-Gestalt Test. These figures were presented to a group of college students for their associations. The assumption was that people tend to perceive these designs in characteristic ways. Their findings suggested that their assumption was correct and led them to advance tentative hypotheses regarding the symbolic value of each test figure. Hammer (1955) made specific tests of these prior findings as they dealt with the psychosexual values of certain designs and attempted to isolate indices of phallic sensitization, castration feelings, and reactions to castration feelings. The experimental group was composed of men who were to undergo sterilization under the eugenic laws of the state of Virginia. Men who were to undergo surgery other than sterilization were used as a control group. The testing was carried out on the day of surgery. Hammer found support in his data for Suczek and Klopfer's hypotheses. He was also able to isolate test factors that were significant in distinguishing the experimental from the control group. The majority of these factors involved distortions of the elongated or phallic elements in the test figures.

Another study investigated the possible utility of those determinants proposed by Hutt (in the "Tentative Guide") as indicative of psychopathology (Byrd, 1956). It is significant that, unlike Billingslea, this investigator tested the determinants as defined and scored by Hutt. In all, 15 determinants were evaluted. The experimental and control groups consisted of 200 children each, ranging in age from 8 to 15 years. Each group was further subdivided into 4 subgroups on the basis of age. The contrasting subgroups consisted of 50 "well-adjusted" and 50 "maladjusted" children each. The "maladjusted" children were selected on the basis of clinical study and diagnosis as in need of psychotherapy. One difference in method of administration of the figures from that proposed by Hutt (but favored by Bender) was that the children were required to make all of their drawings on a single sheet of paper (see Chapter 4 on Administration). Byrd found that his data ". . . support the validity that the majority of test factors selected from Hutt are signs of personality adjustment." Further, he found that these factors operated in the *direction* predicted by Hutt. Bryd acknowledged that his study was essentially a test of the "sign" approach, and not an adequate test of the full projective potential when combinations of factors and their interactions were considered. He stated: "Evaluation of a record involves far more than a listing of signs. The total test performance must be considered." It might be added that the methods of defining and scoring the determinants used in this study were arrived at from a study of adult records and their direct applicability to children, especially in the younger age range, had not been proposed.

Clawson (1959) also investigated the utility of some of the factors proposed by Hutt in differentiating emotional disturbance. Again, her study was confined to children, ranging in age from 7 to 12 years. The experimental group consisted of 40 boys and 40 girls who were clients of the Wichita Guidance Center and whose problems could be described clinically "as maladjustive behavior associated with emotional disturbances." The control group, matched individually on the basis of age, sex, and I.Q., and matched on a group basis on socioeconomic status, consisted of a like number of children judged by their teachers to be "normally developing children typical of the age group." Because Clawson's study was sophisticated both with respect to conceptualization and with respect to design, it will be dealt with at some length.

She utilized three kinds of statistical tests to validate test factors: comparisons of clinic and school populations in terms of frequency of occurrence of the pathologic factor; chi square tests between test factors and behavioral symptoms for clinic cases; and chi square comparisons between test factors and Rorschach indicators. Of 48 chi squares which were tested, 19 were significant at the .01 level. The probability of obtaining this number of significant statistics is less than .001. Specific test factors which differentiated clinic from school children (3 at the .001 level, and 1 at the .01 level) were regression, closure, joining difficulty, and erasures. Gestalt factors that were significantly related to behavior indicators (all but one at the .01 level or better, and 1 at the .05 level) were expansive organization (on the Bender) with acting out (in behavior), compressed organization with withdrawn behavior, decreased figure size with withdrawn behavior, incorrect number of units with reading problems, and horizontal page placement with acting out. Similarly, Gestalt factors that

were significantly related to Rorschach indicators (at the .01 level or better) were constricted size with constriction (on the Rorschach), figure
joinings with interpersonal aggression, and uneven figure size with aggressive responses. In addition, it was demonstrated that "use of white
space" was significantly related to aggression and that orderly sequence
was associated with good adjustment while poor sequence was associated
with maladjustment. She concluded: "The results of this study reveal the
presence of meaningful diagnostic signs in children's BVMGT records
beyond a simple ability to reproduce designs of differing complexity. Of
the 13 variables which differentiated the two groups significantly, the data
supported five hypotheses of interpretive significance and demonstrated
three significant relationships between the BVMGT and the Rorschach. It
is believed that Hutt's hypotheses about the *significance of deviations
with adults* [italics mine] have been established, in part, with children."

A number of studies have been concerned with the projective properties of specific types of distortions or work methods on the Gestalt reproductions or with the associations to specific test figures. In examining some of
the more relevant studies, it should be remembered that *no single indicator is likely to have high validity in assessing personality characteristics.*
Any sign may be produced by quite a variety of conditions—such as the
age or sex of the subject, recent traumatic experiences, prior cultural
conditioning, learned methods of drawing, and various psychological conditions. Any proposed "sign" should therefore be interpreted as a *likely
hypothesis* whose probable meaning needs to be checked against other
concurrent evidence as well as against *the accumulation of other signs
having similar probable import.* Even the most valid of "signs" would be
likely to have relatively low reliability (as well as validity) if taken entirely
by itself and should not be used by itself to make predictions in individual
cases. In an individual case, only the concurrent contribution of a number
of signs, *without the occurrence of contraindicative evidence,* would be
highly meaningful.

One of these earlier studies investigated the types of differences found
among aggressive, passive, and a control group of preadolescent and adolescent children (Taylor & Schenke, 1955). Aggression and passivity were
judged on the basis of a questionnaire checked by two raters. The control
group was selected on the basis of intermediate scores on the ratings. A
study such as this raises a number of basic questions: how valid are the
ratings of aggression and passivity; was either the "aggressive" or the
"passive" group homogeneous in other personality characteristics or degree of maladjustment; what type of aggression and what type of passivity
were being rated; and what types of related personality characteristics
(and Bender-Gestalt factors) were expected to be related? None of these
questions is dealt with in this research. It was found that aggressive chil-

dren distorted the size of the drawings more often than did the passive children. Other Bender-Gestalt factors that were studied (such as the sequence of placement of the drawings on the page, and direction in drawing the secant on figure 5) did not significantly differentiate the groups. However, in terms of considerations of basic research design and appropriate rationale for specified hypotheses, a study such as this must be considered inconclusive.

Other studies have dealt with specific types of distortions as indicators of emotional disturbance or of specific personality conflicts. We shall discuss such studies at subsequent relevant points in this book. Distortions involving an increase in the size of the figures have been investigated by a number of workers. For instance, Elliot (1968) found that this factor significantly distinguished between psychiatric patients and normal school pupils of comparable age. Naches found (1967) that large size of the reproductions was correlated with acting out behavior in youngsters. Kai (1972) was able to show that kindergarten children with emotional problems revealed significant differences on this characteristic from those without such problems. A related study by Brannigan and Benowitz (1975) found that the best "Bender-Gestalt" indicators of antisocial acting out tendencies in adolescents were uneven figure size and exaggerated curvature. It should be noted that even when individual test factors are shown to differentiate significantly between different psychiatric conditions or between psychiatric and nonpsychiatric conditions in groups of subjects, the presence of such a factor in an individual case *does not necessarily signify that this is an adequate or sufficient explanation in that case.* The same test factor may occur due to other causes. *It is always necessary to test and evaluate the relevance of other possible explanations of that test factor in a given instance.* We shall have much more to say about the use and abuse of single test indicators and of combinations of test indicators.

In contrast to the above studies, consider one done on the basis of sophisticated theory and rationale (Story, 1960). This investigator was interested in the possible *projective differences* on the HABGT between a group of 30 alcoholics and a control group of 30 nonalcoholic, nonpsychiatric individuals, similar with respect to age and socioeconomic status. The groups were also controlled for educational background. Story begins his report by asserting: "Psychological research in the area of alcohol addictions has been very deficient with respect to the most rudimentary projective aspects of the Bender-Gestalt test." He is also careful to specify, when contrasting his research procedure with that of others he reviewed, ". . . it is first necessary to grasp the *method of test administration employed,* for it differs considerably from the procedure used in the studies reviewed above." Story used the cards and the specific methods of administration proposed by Hutt, including the method of "elaborations" and "associations" (see Chapter 4). He then derived several hypotheses from personality theory and theory of psychopathology *concerning expected dynamics* common to the alcoholic syndrome. He finally selected determinants from the HABGT which Hutt had proposed *as related to these dynamics*.

As an example of the manner in which Story developed these hypotheses, the following may be indicative:

"A low tolerance for frustration and corresponding avoidance of stress are among the most frequently observed behavior patterns of alcoholics. Characteristically, this behavior is to be seen in withdrawal or escape from the demands of interpersonal activities rooted in a deep-seated and pervasive anxiety about interpersonal relations in general. Briefly, rather than endure the satisfactions of unsatisfactory cathexes, the alcoholic chooses to flee from them. We hypothesize that this psychological blocking in the face of interpersonal demands should be evident in the response behavior to certain designs having intersecting, overlapping, or joined lines; e.g., designs A, 4, 6, and 7. On the revised design 6, for example, where the stimulus may be perceived as either two intersecting sinusoidal lines or two separate, nonintersecting, yet still touching sinusoidal lines, we hypothesize that alcoholics will perceive and reproduce these lines in the latter fashion; i.e., as nonintersecting, significantly more often than the control subjects."

As an aside, Story's use of the "revised designs," by which he means the Hutt adaptation of the designs (rather than the Bender designs), makes possible the testing of this particular hypothesis—the Bender designs might not lend themselves to a test of this hypothesis because of their possibly quite different stimulus value. It is also important to note that the expected "response behavior" is predicated on clinical observations already summarized in Hutt and Briskin's published volume on the test, and is not based on armchair or abstract symbolic theorizing.

Story also formulated other hypotheses in a similar fashion. In essence, these were as follows.

1. In their elaboration of design 7, alcoholics will tend to reproduce it as nonoverlapping hexagons.

2. In elaborating design 2, alcoholics will either change the columns of circles to the vertical plane, use solid straight lines, or reverse the direction in angulation of the circles.

3. Alcoholics will count the dots on design 5, aloud or with a finger or pencil.

4. Alcoholics will rotate the upright hexagon in design 7 more than 5 but less than 20 degrees to the left.

The reader will note, especially after he has had an opportunity to read the material in Chapter 5 on specific test factors and their interpretation, how Story wisely selected and adapted test factors *and* test behavior in order to test the relevant hypotheses.

The findings in this particular research study support each of the proffered hypotheses at significant statistical levels. An additional unpredicted finding was that the alcoholics tended to elaborate figure 6 (the sinusoidal curves) as waves, ripples, rivers, torrents, lakes, etc., significantly more ($p < .005$) than the control group, a rather striking and suggestive finding in the case of alcoholics.

Another line of investigation has been concerned with the projective interpretation of *directionality of lines*. I have been impressed with findings from Mira's work, as well as that of Werner (1957), that the characteristic direction in which adults tended to draw lines (as, for example, from the outside inward, or from the top to the bottom) is indicative of some rather basic and generalized attitudinal orientation toward the world (see Chapter 5). In general, the hypothesis was advanced that movement toward the self reflected an egocentric orientation, and that movement away from the self represented both an attitude of greater involvement with the "world" and a more assertive orientation. Similar hypotheses have been proposed and explored in research in connection with drawings, particularly the drawings of children (Alschuler & Hattwick, 1947). Two studies were specifically related to the question of directionality of movement as a possible indicator of egocentric personality orientation. Both used a single phenomenal indicator of direction of movement, i.e., the direction of movement in drawing the diagonal line of dots which forms part of figure 5. Naturally, any test based on this single phenomenon furnishes an attenuated measure of the possible general directionality which an individual may employ in his drawings, and thus may be expected to yield meager results at best. Nevertheless, surprisingly "good" results have been obtained.

Peek (1953) investigated the relationship between direction of movement on the diagonal of figure 5 and specific aspects of the clinical condition of 75 adults. A control consisted of randomly selected hospitalized, neuropsychiatric patients, similar in diagnosis, treatment at the hospital, and measure of improvement, but not selected with respect to directionality of drawing of the diagonal or "spike" on figure 5. The patient's clinical condition was rated on a check list of 40 items—again, not the most valid of indicators of these conditions. Nineteen significant differences (significant at the .05 level or better) were obtained. The results confirmed Hutt's hypothesis that direction of movement from the outside inward was indicative of egocentric personality makeup. Other related findings showed the experimental group to be more dependent, to be more reactive to frustration, and to have more bodily complaints—again, tending to confirm the general traits of egocentricity. Although Peek indicates that the practical utility of this finding is limited by the considerable variability found within the two groups, I am more impressed with the theoretical significance of his findings, especially in view of the limitations of the design noted above.

Clawson, in the study already referred to (1959), tested the power of the same phenomenon, direction in drawing the "spike" on figure 5, with her school children. She found that this single factor discriminated the "maladjusted" from the "adjusted" group at the .05 level.

Findings such as these suggest the potential value of appropriately designed scores, based on a *number* of indicators of a presumably significant characteristic, both for research and for clinical purposes.

Another study, essentially based on the possible symbolic meaning of certain aspects of Gestalt test behavior, investigated the sign "penetration of design 6 into design 5" (Sternberg, 1965). We need not go into the specific method of measuring or detecting this phenomenon nor even its adequacy in terms of rationale. Suffice it to say that this phenomenon was thought to be indicative of suicidal ideation. A group of 25 psychiatric patients showing this sign was matched with 25 other psychiatric patients who did not show it for age, sex, and psychiatric diagnosis. Suicidal ideation was found in 88% of the experimental group, 44% of the control group, and in 48% of a random sampling of the population of hospital patients. The difference in percentages of the experimental and control group was significant at the .005 level.

Other studies, which we shall not attempt to review in this brief historical summary, have dealt with the relationship between anxiety and Bender-Gestalt performance, with attempts to derive a measure of ego strength, with relations to psychosomatic conditions, and the like. The interested reader may consult some of the reviews of the literature referred to earlier. We will however, take this opportunity to make one comment on most of these studies. Whether they produced significant statistical findings or not, most of them were based on only dimly outlined rationales or no rationale at all, and were not, therefore, likely to achieve much significance either in terms of a contribution to theory or to clinical practice. We believe that in the early stages of the development of a projective technique one should either attack the problem with broadly conceived empirical methods, hoping thereby to gain some harvest of findings which can be put to more refined and meaningful subsequent tests, or propose some theoretical model and test it both in clinical and research study, hoping thereby to gain a more sophisticated understanding of underlying, basic processes.

One study of the latter type, which we shall review in detail in Chapter 7, is an attempt to develop a meaningful measure of approach–

avoidance in perceptual–motoric behavior (Hutt & Feuerefile, 1963). The measure, called *adience–abience,* rests on clinical observations that certain kinds of distortions and size changes in the Gestalten as produced by the subject are correlated with some basic qualities of the personality, viz., a general tendency to resist the input of information from the external world, or the reverse, a general tendency to seek out and utilize information from the external world. It was then hypothesized that there existed in each person a general tendency to relate to the world in terms of approach–avoidance and that the basis of this tendency lay in the perceptual–motoric mechanism defined as adience–abience. On the basis of this theoretical position, on the one hand, and perceptual–motoric manifestations on the other, a tentative scale was devised for measuring these manifestations on the HABGT. A series of studies was then conducted to test the plausibility of this formulation and to refine the measure of abience–abience (Hutt & Feuerefile, 1963). These tests, with a population of deaf–retarded patients, involved predictions that individuals who were high on the adience end of the scale would tend to gain more from their educational–cultural–therapeutic experience than those who were high on the abience end of the scale. It was also predicted that there would be significant differences in cognitive functioning and in degree of psychopathology. These predictions were confirmed.

On the basis of these findings, the adience–abience scale, consisting of a number of correlated perceptual–motoric phenomena, was further revised, and additional tests to determine the meaning of the scale were carried out with schizophrenic patients as well as with psychoneurotic patients who were in psychotherapy. Positive findings led to further elaboration of the theory and to suggestions for further clinical and research study as well as to practical applications (see Chapter 7).

There are at least two different types of issues related to the use of visual–motor test materials for projective purposes. One is whether or not such material is valid. This is an empirical question and can only be resolved by empirical data. We have offered some evidence from research studies that valid findings can be obtained from the projective use of the HABGT and other versions of the Bender-Gestalt Test. A subissue concerns whether visual–motor difficulties contribute to emotional problems, whether the reverse is true, or whether the two are interrelated in some other way. Koppitz (1963) takes the position that "emotional problems develop secondary to perceptual problems." She has reaffirmed this position in a later evaluation of the research literature (Koppitz, 1975a). I believe, on the contrary, that emotional disturbance can be causative of disturbances in the perceptual–motoric area (especially of idiosyncratic and symbolic disturbances), as is indicated not only in some of the research already discussed but also in intensive clinical studies. In addition, factors other than either maldevelopment in perceptual–motoric skills or emotional conflicts can contribute to poor or distorted perceptual–motoric performance.

Another issue concerns how projective phenomena on the HABGT (and other versions of the Bender-Gestalt) are to be evaluated. Are single indicators, such as expansion in size, appropriate and sufficient for diagnostic purposes? Are scores for the total number of "emotional indicators" better? Or are analyses (specially derived scores) based on both appropriate rationales and empirical verification more effective? We shall see that all of these approaches have value and that each can lead to different and quite sophisticated use of the HABGT in more precise clinical assessment and therapeutic management.

It should also be noted that research on the projective characteristics of the HABGT has been limited. This is not too surprising since such research is often complicated by difficult problems of measurement, criterion variables, and control. The studies which have been done, some of which will be reported in subsequent chapters of this book, have been productive and offer promise that further research will produce rich yields.

There has been limited discussion, too, of the clinical application of the projective aspect of the HABGT, but increasingly more clinicians are utilizing it, and there has been an emphasis on "emotional indicators" or "psychiatric phenomena" in numerous research and clinical articles. A useful book on the projective use of the test has been published by Lerner (1972).

NONPROJECTIVE USE OF PERCEPTUAL–MOTORIC BEHAVIOR

Psychologists are understandably motivated toward the development of objectively scorable methods of evaluation of behavior, whether on a test or in other circumstances. Such methods reduce the subjective element in evaluations and seem to offer a "scientific" basis for judgments or predictions. However, objectivity that is achieved at the sacrifice of theoretical clarity is often not only premature, but may also inhibit effective exploration, or even definition, of meaningful problems. Sometimes the most significant phenomena are the most difficult to define; if precise definition and objective measurement are required before such phenomena are adequately understood, it may be easier for the tester to discard and lose sight of them rather than be dogged by "insufficient reliability."

One of the recurrent trends in the development of objective scores for perceptual–motoric behavior has been the attempt to develop a global measure of some kind. The scoring scheme developed by Pascal and Suttell (1951), noted earlier, resulted from such an orientation. It can be regarded as a measure of the degree of general psychopathology, or, alternatively, as Pascal and Suttell themselves regard it, as a measure of ego strength. As they state: "If, for the purposes of this discussion, we limit our definition of ego functioning to the ability to reproduce faithfully the B-G drawings as presented, then we may say that ego strength lies on a continuum from very low to very high B-G scores." Clearly, such a definition of ego strength leaves undefined what ego strength really involves. In most of the research work which the Pascal-Suttell measure has stimulated, the objective was to investigate the scale's ability to differentiate different types of psychopathology. It is clear that interjudge reliability in scoring this scale is quite good, the reliability correlations generally ranging from .90 (Pascal & Suttell, 1951) to .99 (Story, 1960). In support of their contention that the score may be used as a measure of degree of psychopathology, Pascall and Suttell present data to show that there are progressive and significant differences in mean score between the normal group and the neurotic and the psychotic. Although some contradictory findings have been published, these conclusions by Pascal and Suttell have stood the test of research quite well: as a rough measure of severity of general psychopathology the scale has demonstrated validity. It is far more questionable whether the scale can be used to differentiate brain-damaged cases from either neurotics or psychotics, and probably other measures should be used for such purposes. Organics may vary considerably in degree of psychopathology and need to be assessed specifically in terms of organic pathology, although the Pascal-Suttell score probably reflects some aspects of each type of phenomenon.

A recent study using very carefully matched groups of patients clearly showed that the Pascal-Suttell scale was very poor in discriminating organics from functionally disturbed individuals (Stoer, Corotto, & Curnutt, 1965). Two reservations concerning the value of the Pascal-Suttell scale in measuring the degree of psychopathology should be indicated. (1) Although it can reliably discriminate between *groups* of normals, neurotics, and psychotics, it does not predict very effectively in *individual* cases. Hence, its clinical utility is somewhat limited. (2) It does not, nor does it pretend to, make available specific predictive discriminations with respect to individual personality characteristics, such as areas of conflict or types of defense mechanisms, and is therefore of no value *in this sense* as a clinical instrument. Pascal and Suttell present norms for adults as well as tentative norms for children.

A sophisticated and well-designed attempt to standardize and validate a scoring system was reported by Gobetz (1953). He developed a set of 82 scoring categories, presumably based on previous work by Pascal and Suttell, Billingslea, and Hutt, but defined essentially in his own way. The objective of his study was to determine whether neurotics and normals could be differentiated on the basis of these scoring categories. He concluded: "The Bender-Gestalt Test, *as scored in the present study* [italics mine], is recommended as a screening device to be used as a supplement to other diagnostic tests rather than as an instrument for the elaborate interpretation of individual personality dynamics." Nevertheless, he did find five global signs that were able to discriminate between normals and neurotics at the .05 level. Major limitations in Gobetz' work, in terms of his own goal of developing an *objective* scoring scheme, were his failure to report any evidence on the reliability of his scoring methods, and the questionable validity of his "normal" population used in contrast with his neurotic population.

In 1960 Hutt proposed a tentative scale for general psychopathology, the "19-factor scale," on which the reported interjudge reliability was .91 (Hutt & Briskin, 1960). This scale was an attempt to provide a cumulative score based on observed clinical indicators of psychopathology and reported research findings on test factors. The scale has been utilized in a number or other research studies with promising results. It is described and reviewed in Chapter 7 of the present work.

A number of scoring scales have been developed for work with children. As in the case of the scales developed for adults, the objective usually has been to develop a global measure of some kind. In most instances the predictive criterion considered was that of achievement in school work. Keller (1955) was one of the first to report on such efforts. Working with high-level mentally retarded children, and utilizing three categories of factors presumably related to maturity of visual–motor functions, Keller was able to demonstrate significant relationships between test scores and teachers' and psychologists' ratings. This study showed promise in the use of this type of score for predicting school achievement, but was limited in terms of its generalizability (only 36 mentally retarded boys were used as subjects) and in terms of an underlying rationale.

A simply rated score, based on "discriminated degrees of quality of production," was developed by a group of workers for application to the kindergarten population (Keogh & Smith, 1961). They found that their method yielded scores which offered considerable promise in predicting school functioning. It was simpler than the Pascal-Suttell scoring scheme, with which it correlated .80, and had fairly good interjudge and rerating reliabilities.

Koppitz has done extensive research with the Bender-Gestalt Test in developing a measure of developmental visual–motor maturity for children between the ages of 5 and 10 years, and has published two books dealing specifically with her method (1958, 1960, 1963, 1965, 1975a). As noted previously, she has also developed a score based on "emotional indicators" in which ten factors are involved. Although in her 1975 volume she suggests the value of specific emotional indicators as predictive of specific personality traits or problems, she does not believe that it is "possible to make a differential diagnosis between neurotic, psychotic, and brain-damaged patients on the basis of EI's [emotional indicators] on a Bender Test record" (Koppitz, 1975a). We might say that this finding is not at all surprising since the EI was not developed for this purpose; but her conclusion should not be taken to mean that other methods of scoring and analyzing Bender test protocols cannot yield such information! Her developmental score is of some value in predicting school achievement in the primary grades, although many other factors need to be taken into consideration. In a recent research report she finds that her developmental score differentiates, in an 8- to 9-year old group, between those with learning disability and a control group, but it did not differentiate between readers and nonreaders (Koppitz, 1975b). She has found that her developmental score is a better predictor of achievement in arithmetic in the primary grades than it is of reading achievement.

Norms for school children in the age range of 6 to 12 years have been provided by other workers (Armstrong & Hauch, 1960).

It should be added that the strong possibility exists that different factors operate in the performance of very young children, say, below 8 years of age, than in that of older children and adults. There is considerable evidence that perceptual and motoric maturity have different developmental curves and enter in differential manner into the performance of individuals at these differing age levels.

Another area of investigation explored the possible presence of primary factors in the Gestalt reproductions of subjects. In a series of studies conducted by Guertin with hospitalized patients, including organics and schizophrenics, an attempt was made to isolate statistically independent factors by means of a factor analytic method (Guertin, 1952, 1954a, 1954b, 1954c, 1955). His first analysis resulted in five general factors: poor reality contact, propensity toward curvilinear movements, constriction, careless execution, and poor spatial contiguity. It was found that paranoids had the highest "loading" on "poor reality contact," for example, and that nonparanoid schizophrenics had the highest "loading" on "propensity toward curvilinear movements." Various meanings were assigned to each of these factors. In one of the later studies, further analysis was conducted on the phenomenon of curvilinear distortions, and this phenomenon was broken down to five subfactors. These studies were limited to specific types of patient subgroups, and therefore the generalizability to other psychiatric subgroups of patients and to nonhospitalized patients may be questioned; however, they mark a highly significant step toward classification and analysis of underlying processes, on the basis of which further progress in understanding the phenomena may be obtained eventually.

A more recent factor analytic study, which employed a number of tests (Bender-Gestalt, Frostig, and Benton Visual Retention Test) with 34 boys between the ages of 8 and 12 years, found 97% of the variance on these tests to be accounted for by the following, extracted factors: global figure–ground discrimination; perceptual differentiation; ability to discriminate positions and size relationships; perseveration; and visuomotor components (Wurst, 1974). Studies such as this one help to delineate primary factors in the total visual–motor performance, but of course they tell us nothing about personality and other correlates.

In contrast, methodologically, is the study by Hain (1964). This investigator selected 31 "signs" on the Bender-Gestalt, and 15 of these were given differential weightings on the basis of their effectiveness in discriminating among brain-damaged, psychiatric, and control groups. Using the 15 "signs" and their weights, a score was derived for each individual. The score differed significantly (at the .01 level) for the organic group and each of the other groups. It identified 80% of the organic group. It was felt that the index was most effective for cases of *diffuse* brain damage and was likely to miss cases of *localized lesions and tumors*. In a more rigorous test of this index and of other scores and configurations, a later study compared the performance of 142 brain-damaged patients (76 cases of traumatic encephalopathy, 66 cases of miscellaneous neurologic disorder) with the performance of 120 control patients (28 cases of neurologic disturbance without brain lesions, 92 cases of acute schizophrenics) Mosher & Smith, 1965). These workers found that both the Hain score and the Peek-Quast score differentiated the brain damage cases from the controls at the .001 level, but they also found that the cutting scores on both scales identified correctly only a relatively small percentage of the cases. In general, they conclude pessimistically that their study ". . . does not provide evidence that the BGT is at all useful in diagnosing these truly questionable cases." They felt that it was best in identifying the severely injured cases requiring surgery or involving skull fractures. Not only is this kind of generalization unwarranted on the basis of the evidence presented—since the composition of the groups, particularly of the control group, poses more problems than it solves—it is also in direct conflict with many other studies that will be referred to in discussing brain damage diagnosis (see especially Chapter 5). However, the study did highlight the relative efficacy of several perceptual–motoric factors: distortion, angulation difficulty, and poor, coarse coordination. In passing it should be noted that they tested five of the Hutt-Briskin signs and found three of these significant (two signs at the .01 level and one sign at the .05 level).

The significant signs, *for this type of discrimination,* were: poor, coarse coordination; perseveration; and, collision. As an example of a study which reported results that indicated that the Bender-Gestalt was significant in predicting minimal neurologic damage (in children), there is the report by Wiener (1966), who found the following significant signs: curvature difficulty, angulation difficulty, and a tendency to gross perceptual–motoric distortion.

Hain's scoring method for detecting possible cerebral dysfunction has been tested in a number of additional studies, and has usually been found to be valuable. A recent study by Pardue (1975) is typical. She compared three groups of patients—brain damaged, schizophrenics, and nonorganic and non-brain damaged—with 20 in each group. She found, using Background Interference Procedures (discussed later), that the Hain scoring method differentiated these groups. Utilization of the Pascal-Suttell scoring led to individually reliable discrimination.

Still another line of study has been undertaken in investigating the possible meaning of basic perceptual–motoric processes. In some ingenious experiments, Fabian (1945, 1951) attempted to explore the meaning of ''rotations'' in the performance of school children and the relationship to reading difficulties. First, the frequency of the phenomenon of rotation was checked. It was found that rotation of the figures was very common in kindergarten children, but as children advanced in age the frequency of rotations diminished sharply. More than half of the very young children rotated the designs, but only 7% of those who were between 7½ and 9 years of age continued to do so. Then, using modified horizontal lines, it was found that 51% of 6-years-olds but only 22% of 6½-year-olds rotated either one or two of the figures. Children were also asked to draw straight lines, without any instruction relating to direction, and almost 70% drew vertical lines. These findings led Fabian to conclude that ''verticalization'' (or rotation toward the upright from the horizontal orientation) was a maturational or developmental process in young children and that the persistence of this tendency indicated a lag in such development or a regression. This lag was found to be related to poor learning in reading. It is interesting that the possible contributions to this lag of emotional factors were not considered, and that the lag was thought to be due to genetic factors, much as Bender had proposed earlier.

Lachman (1960) decided that it was important to explore the possible contribution of emotional factors to the developmental lag in both perceptual–motoric and reading ability. The research design permitted an evaluation of the contribution of each of these factors. A comparison of emotionally disturbed but normal readers showed that such readers also showed visual–motor distortions. It was concluded that the hypothesis of the developmental lag in percepual–motoric behavior could not account, by itself, for the reading difficulty. We might add that it is also quite possible that emotional factors can produce "rotations" and other distortions and that regressive signs of visual–motoric behavior can result from either anomalies in development or from psychological disturbances. In a later chapter of this book we shall comment on the finding, in Fabian's and in others' studies, that certain figures are more likely to be rotated than are others (see Chapter 5).

One intriguing problem concerns the relative contribution of perceptual and motoric processes to perceptual–motoric tasks such as the HABGT. We shall summarize the findings of three studies bearing directly on this problem. In the first (McPherson & Pepin, 1955), subjects were asked to reproduce the designs in the usual way (by drawing them) as well as by placing pieces of felt in the appropriate position to construct the designs. Their evidence seemed to indicate that motor ability is not, by itself, primarily responsible for correct reproduction, and that covert perceptual processes are primarily responsible for accurate performance. In another study (Niebuhr & Cohen, 1956), 40 subjects were administered the Bender-Gestalt under four different experimental conditions. The subjects were divided into four subgroups of 10 persons each: nurses, acute schizophrenics, chronic schizophrenics, and neurologic cases. The results indicated that both perceptual and motoric factors *were* correlated with the severity of the group's psychopathology so that the group with the most severe pathology scored poorest on *both* factors. However, this study does not answer a number of relevant issues: (1) Aside from the nurses, how sure can one be that the other groups differed significantly in degree of psychopathology? (2) Since these workers reported that age and severity of psychopathology, as it was evaluated, were highly correlated, could not the results have been attributed, at least in part, to the age factor? Nevertheless, the findings are suggestive that both perceptual and motoric factors do contribute to performance on the Bender, *as scored*.

A more sophisticated research design sheds some additional light on this problem (Stoer et al., 1965). In this study, discussed above in another connection, four groups of subjects (controls, organics, acute schizophrenics) were matched for age, sex, and intelligence. These adults were then asked to reproduce each of the Gestalt designs on a card exactly the same size as the test card. They were also asked to compare the stimulus with eight other designs (one of which was their own reproduction of that design), and to rank these in terms of a continuum from least like to most like the stimulus. Both the subjects' reproductions of the designs and the designs used in the comparison series were scored by the Pascal-Suttell method. No significant differences were found in the matching task. For the reproductions, variance in the four groups was significant at the .05 level. Stoer et al. concluded that deviant performance reflects "defects in

motor and/or integrative functions.'' They believe that such a position
''. . . is in good agreement with clinical experience concerning the usefulness of the test for the detection of both neurological and functional
pathology.'' Once again the reader is cautioned not to generalize these
findings and conclusions to other methods of scoring, to other nosologic
groups, or to other methods of administration.

It should also be noted that, when there is severe motoric impairment,
performance on the Bender-Gestalt procedures can be grossly affected. A
study of motor-impaired children by Newcomer and Hammill (1973)
clearly indicates this effect. Utilizing the Motor Free Test of Visual Perception and the Bender-Gestalt Test, they examined 90 children ranging in
age from 5 to 12 years. They found that there was progressive deteriora-
tion on the Bender-Gestalt performance with increasing motoric impairment. Nevertheless, all of the findings to date, taken together, do suggest
the essential nature of the integrative function tapped by perceptual–
motoric tasks and indicate one possible reason why such a task, rather
than a ''purely perceptual'' or a ''purely motoric'' task, is likely to prove
more useful in many aspects of clinical work.

One of the most active areas of research has been in the differential
diagnosis of organic brain damage. Such damage can of course take many
different forms, involve ''critical'' or ''noncritical'' regions of the brain, be
of moderate to great severity, be in the dominant or nondominant side of
the brain, or involve small or localized portions of the brain or large or
diffuse sections of the brain. Not only are these different conditions likely
to influence performance on a perceptual–motoric task in quite different
ways and to quite different degrees, but even the same condition may
produce diverse psychological effects in different individuals, depending
on such other factors as their prior physical and personality histories and
the nature of the recovery or compensatory process that may be involved.
It would be inconceivable, therefore, to expect *any single scoring system
or any single method of analysis with any psychological test to be able to
produce anything like near-perfect prediction of the whole gamut of organic deficits*. The aim should, of course, be much more modest: to predict
with *reasonable accuracy* some types of organic defect under some types
of conditions.

In their review of the literature on this subject prior to 1961, Tolor and
Schulberg (1963) stated: ''There is overwhelming evidence in these studies
for the concurrent validity of the Bender-Gestalt Test. Consistently one
notes that the Bender performance of cerebrally impaired groups can be
distinguished from diverse psychiatric groups, either by means of objective scoring criteria or by more global evaluations.'' Yet in a subsequent
review of the literature, Garron and Cheifetz (1965) stated that this test is
relatively inefficient in differentiating *individuals* with severe psychologi-

cal disturbance from those with organic brain disease. Nevertheless, they agreed that the various scoring methods did significantly differentiate the *means* of *groups* of various types of disorders. A sampling of the findings of relatively recent research on this problem may shed some light.

Hain's study, referred to earlier, using a score derived for the weighting of 15 selected factors, found that this index differentiated significantly (at the .01 level) between the brain-damaged group ($N = 20$) and each of the other groups—psychiatric ($N = 38$) and controls ($N = 25$) (Hain, 1964). It was concluded that the index was effective for *diffuse brain damage* (like arteriosclerosis and cerebrovascular insufficiency), but was apt to miss cases with localized lesions. Another worker (Armstrong, 1965) compared the relative efficacy of scores based on the copy phase and the recall phase of the test (see Chapter 4) in differentiation five diagnostic groups: organics, schizophrenics, depressives, neurotics, and character disorders. The total N was relatively small ($N = 72$), and adults over 60 years of age were eliminated from the study in order to match the groups in age. Using objective scoring methods she found that the copy phase differentiated the organics from both the schizophrenics and neurotics at the .001 level, and that the recall phase did an even better job in differentiating the organics from the nonorganics. With the latter score, there was almost no overlap between the two major groups and only 21% of the nonorganic patients achieved as high a score, or higher, than the organic patients.

A later study, whose objective was the testing of the Hain and the Pascal-Suttell scores in differentiating organics from nonorganics, also achieved highly positive results (Kramer & Fenwick, 1966). Both scores differentiated the means of the two groups of adult patients at the .001 level, but the Hain score, *designed specifically for this purpose*, achieved the better results. Moreover, *it gave no false positives* while accurately classifying 76% of the patients. Interestingly, an "expert" with the Bender-Gestalt, using clinical judgment, obtained 81% correct classification—a finding in keeping with similar results achieved by a number of Bender "experts" in other studies.

It should be noted that of the two studies referred to earlier [Mosher and Smith (1965) and Wiener (1966), which seemingly gave contradictory results], with patients showing minimal neurologic damage, the one which utilized *a scale of degree of neurologic deficit* based on perinatal data and early neurologic facts, and which also *controlled carefully* for race, sex, social, and maternal variables in a large group of subjects (822), did obtain results with the Bender-Gestalt that significantly predicted neurologic impairment in children. Although Wiener's positive findings need to be replicated, they are highly suggestive of the value of the "test" when appropriate factors are carefully taken into consideration. A related study (McConnell, 1967), conducted with children, also found that the "test," this time scored in terms of Koppitz' developmental norms, significantly differentiated 120 children who were divided into three levels *in terms of severity of organicity.*

An intriguing study, in this respect, is that reported by Landis, Baxter, Patterson, and Tauber (1974). They evaluated the use of the Bender-Gestalt Test, employing the Pascal-Suttell scoring method, in the detection of neurological damage following open heart surgery. In the usual surgical procedures extracorporeal blood circulation can create microemboli in the blood and thus lead to neurological damage. A new filter, designed to remove such emboli, was assessed by preoperative and postoperative Bender-Gestalt records. The patients, 28 in all, were between 38 and 66 years of age. It was found that (1) postoperative impairment in the Bender-Gestalt performance was consistent with ultrasonic counts of microemboli, and that (2) under conditions of the use of the new filter, there was less visual–motor damage that is associated with neurological defects. Corroborative evidence of the sensitivity of the Bender-Gestalt to the effects of brain damage was obtained in a study by Bravo (1973). The data on the test differentiated between patients with infantile minimal cerbral dysfunction and a control group.

It seems appropriate to conclude that certain kinds of scores derived from perceptual–motoric tasks, and certain kinds of global judgments, are highly useful for some purposes in the differential diagnosis of organicity. There is also considerable evidence that some kinds of organic defects yield test and behavioral data which tend to distinguish between organics on the one hand, and various other clinical and nonclinical groups on the other.

Special adaptations of the Bender-Gestalt Test have been developed in attempts to increase the capacity of the "test" to discriminate between patients with neurological damage and those without such damage. One of the promising procedures, which we shall discuss in greater detail in Chapter 4, is called the Background Interference Procedure. As developed by Canter, it involves administering the test on paper with background, wavy lines which tend to increase figure–ground difficulties. Some of the research which has indicated the usefulness of this adaptation has been published by Adams, Kenny, and Canter (1973), Horine and Fulkerson (1973), and Pardue (1975). Sabatino and Ysseldyke (1972) have employed a similar procedure, called "extraneous background" with good results in differentiating readers from nonreaders.

Basic research and clinical investigation of perceptual–motoric phenomena have dealt with a variety of clinical phenomena other than those already considered. Some of these problems are in the areas of familial and nonfamilial mental retardation, effects of psychosurgery, effects of physiologic and pharmaceutical agents, manic–depressive psychoses, and relations to other clinical and psychological test phenomena. We shall consider these studies at various points in the book when they are relevant.

This brief summary and evaluation of the history of work done with perceptual–motoric phenomena suggests that the lode in this area is quite rich. Despite the large number of studies to date, only a start has been made in exploring this lode. It is easy to become overly optimistic about the possibilities and to overgenerlize the findings, but time and patient study will finally help us to make a better assessment of the possibilities in this area.

3
General Problems in Psychodiagnosis

In order to use a diagnostic tool properly the interpreter must possess a number of basic attributes. It goes without saying that he must fully understand the tool which he is employing: its underlying rationale; its methods of standardization; its techniques of administration; its clinical and experimental findings; and its values and limitations in assessing the particular phenomena it is designed to test. However, having all of these attributes for a particular test or for a series of diagnostic techniques does not qualify the interpreter as a clinician. Without much more he is merely a psychometrist, although he may be a very good one and he may contribute significantly along this line. We should not underestimate the function and value of the psychometrician, but, by the same token, we should not confuse them with the funtion and value of the clinician.

The distinction between the psychometrician and the clinician is important for both theoretical and practical reasons. The former, according to our definition, has developed the appropriate knowledge and skills to use and interpret one or more instruments or techniques. He is not necessarily well versed in general psychology, much less in psychopathology or even the psychology of personality. He has not been trained to relate psychometric findings to other aspects of the clinical history or to other clinical data, nor to make decisions concerning the management of and therapy for the patient. He is familiar with and respects the research findings concerning reliability and validity of the measures he employs, but he is not in a professionally appropriate position to go beyond these confines of his knowledge. As we shall see, clinical diagnosis, or, as we prefer to term it, *psychodiagnosis,* characteristically involves much more.

43

Psychodiagnosis includes the gathering and weighing of *all* relevant evidence concerning the patient, an analysis of the causative factors in the present condition, a description of the present condition in terms of the total syndrome which is evident, an evaluation of the dynamic characteristics of the present condition (under what conditions does a "cause" give rise to an "effect"), and prediction of those changes that may be expected from present and/or altered circumstances (Hutt & Gibby, 1957).

As we have indicated, the distinction between these two types of clinical workers is important for theoretical reasons. We are still in the stage of development concerning psychopathology in which we make the assumption that a given psychiatric syndrome constitutes a unique entity, separate and distinct from all other such entities. Some workers have begun to question this assumption and others have already rejected it. However, as long as the assumption is maintained, it is necessary to postulate that a given configuration of *behavioral characteristics* defines a particular clinical entity, with its own etiology, development, and final outcome. Thus, psychiatry arrived at the basic classification of "mental disorders" with the discovery that certain kinds of behaviors tended to belong to one set of etiologic conditions while others belonged to other conditions. This type of descriptive psychiatry had to assume a one-to-one relationship between behavioral configuration and underlying psychopathology. Almost all types of objective tests of personality make the same assumption—that there is a one-to-one relationship between measures of behavioral traits and psychiatric abnormality. Yet, clinical and research evidence has accumulated which challenges this fundamental assumption.

For one thing, it has been demonstrated that some patients who fall within one psychiatric category may later belong in other categories. For example, a group of patients originally diagnosed as manic-depressive were later found, in a follow-up study, to be more appropriately classified as manic-depressive in some cases, as schizophrenic in others, and as in still different categories in other cases, on the basis of the later development of their condition and their changing behavioral characteristics (Hoch & Rachlin, 1941). Increasing doubt has been cast on the essential homogeneity of schizophrenia as a distinct disease entity. Certainly, patients with simple and hebophrenic forms of this condition differ from others with paranoid and catatonic forms in certain important respects: amount of regression, susceptibility to treatment, spontaneous remission, etc. Similarly, many individuals who show, as a result of severe and acute trauma, reaction patterns which closely resemble essential psychoneurotic conditions differ significantly from the usual varieties of psychoneurotics. Clinical evidence gathered during the years of the Second World War amply substantiated these differences (Grinker & Spiegel, 1945). Finally, persons with neurotic character disorders are difficult to distinguish, on the basis of behavior syndromes alone, from other persons with classical neurotic disorders of the same type (Hutt & Gibby, 1957). All of these and related observations suggest that there is no one-to-one relationship between current psychiatric grouping and underlying psychopathology. Parenthetically, this is probably one of the important reasons that psychiatric criteria of psychopathology are relatively low in reliability.

If, then, there is no direct relationship between symptoms or behaviors and type of psychopathology, it follows that there cannot be a simple, unilateral relationship between a test sign or test measure and a psychiatric condition. On the contrary, a test sign or a test measure may acquire different meanings depending upon (1) the *constellation of which it is a part* and (2) the *conditions which give rise to it*. Qualification 1 may be tested statistically by evaluating the differential power of various configurations of signs. Indeed, this is the pattern which has been followed by a considerable portion of contemporary clinical research. Although this type of work has offered some promise, notably in some problem areas such as the differential diagnosis of brain pathology, the results have not been altogether encouraging. This outcome should not have been unexpected since configurations of behavioral measures can only (if done adequately) contribute to the accuracy of predicting configurations of behavior, i.e., psychiatric categories, and we have seen that psychiatric categories may be of limited value. The second qualification noted above, the condition which gives rise to the behavior, may, and on theoretical grounds should, give better results. For here we can begin to deal with *process phenomena* which have a certain independence of the resultant behavioral phenomena. Before we proceed to elaborate this point, let us note that we are not recommending abandonment of the use of configurational measures, for they do have important uses. Rather, we are emphasizing the value of process phenomena in differential diagnosis and the theoretical basis for their use.

By *process phenomena* we mean derivatives as directly related as possible to the underlying causative factors. We can further clarify this definition by comparing the usual behavior phenomena with process phenomena. An individual, for example, displays the behavioral trait of passivity. His passivity may be readily recognized as such, and techniques may be employed for measuring the intensity of this trait. But this behavioral trait in one person may mean something far different from what it means in another. In one case, it may be the direct expression of avoidance or withdrawal defenses. In another, it may signify the presence of some degree of conflict over dependency needs. In still another, it may represent a compromise reaction or a reaction formation to latent aggressive strivings. The accurate assessment of the trait, then, tells us little or nothing about the underlying processes which have given rise to the behavior. The trait may be conceived of as the indirect result of varying underlying process phenomena. Passivity may thus occur as the end product of various conflicting drives and their "resolution" in terms of the ego's resources in dealing with them in the context of a given cultural setting.

The same argument may be made concerning all such traits—which are more accurately described as *surface traits* (Hutt, Isaacson, & Blum, 1966). Traits are usually conceived of as more or less persistent behavioral tendencies. Most present-day objective tests of personality measure such surface traits, and evidence concerning them has considerable value in predicting the likely, overt, behavioral phenomena which an individual may manifest. However, to deal adequately with the person who has these traits, or even to understand him, we need to know something of the conditions which give rise to them. And to do this we have to understand, measure, and deal with the primary process phenomena which produce them (Carr, 1960).

Process phenomena, then, refer to the dynamics of the behavioral resultant. They are rooted in the latent tendencies which each individual possesses—in the drives which motivate his behavior. Rarely do drives manifest themselves directly in observable behavior, even in the most primitive of people. It may be said that the more civilized an individual is, the more indirect is the expression of primary drives. Civilization imposes the requirement that drives be socialized: they must be inhibited, delayed, and integrated in socially appropriate ways. Psychopathology, for different reasons, defensive in character, also requires that only the most indirect expression of drives be permitted. But in both types of instances, the overt behavior can only offer obtuse clues to the processes which give rise to them. It might be added that it is easier to infer the drives which motivate behavior in the case of a "normal," civilized individual than in the case of a psychopathologic individual; their expression in behavior is more direct in the former instance.

Projective tests, and clinicians employing projective hypotheses, probe for the underlying processes which give rise to a given form of behavior. When a person is asked to respond to a relatively unstructured stimulus, we assume that in the process of organizing his response to this situation, he will display some derivatives of the underlying drives, that he will project these drives into the "test" situation. If we obtain a number of samples of such projective behavior, we are then able to infer the presence and intensity of such drives. Note that we said *infer,* for projective behavior is still overt behavior and merely gives us greater access to underlying phenomena, not direct measures of them. There are two conditions, then, for effective use of projective behavior: a sufficient sample of such behavior under varying conditions, and an inference concerning the sample with respect to the kind of process which gave rise to it.

Now we are in a position to begin to understand the role of the clinician. He will wish to employ, like the psychometrician, those techniques and measures which will enable him to assess, with an appropriate degree of reliability and validity, the presence and intensity of the important traits that the patient manifests. But he will go one step further: he will try to relate these findings and the findings of the case history to the intrapsychic conditions which give rise to them. In this latter step he will employ, among other things, devices like projective tests in order to gain access to process phenomena. To do this he will need more than good instruments for eliciting projective behavior. He will need to know how to go about making certain kinds of inferences from the results of such "tests," and, if he is scientifically trained, he will carefully weigh the significance of the evidence, look for corroborating and constrasting findings, and integrate all of this data into the most parsimonious explanation he can offer for the problems which have been raised.

To play the role of the clinician appropriately, and not just to *play at* the role of clinician, the individual will have acquired certain kinds of training and be able to use this training effectively. In the first place, he will have secured training in general psychology so that he has sophistication about the findings relative to behavior in general. Among other things, he will know the following: something about the principles of scientific method; basic information concerning biologigical mechanisms; what has been learned concerning behavioral development, including sensory processes and perception, and patterning of behavior; the values and limitations of current theories of personality; the present state of knowledge concerning psychopathology; and theories and techniques relating to therapeutic process. Of these, perhaps of greatest importance for the clinician is his knowledge of personality theory and psychopathology, for without this he cannot make appropriate inferences about his observations and test findings nor can he check his initial hypotheses about a patient against other plausible, perhaps more plausible, hypotheses. With these assets in his training, he can, if he is not too rigidly bound in his *initial* speculations about a patient, begin to think through the possible implications of his data (Hutt, 1968).

The last point probably needs elaboration if its meaning is to be clearly conveyed to the reader. There are probably two great limitations in the work of a clinician that may interfere considerably with his effectiveness. One of these is an insensitivity to relevant data. This may come from inadequate knowledge about behavior, especially about psychopathologic behavior, or it may come from an inability to use function appropriately as an observer. Both of these may be improved by training, although there may be serious limitations as to what training can accomplish with some types of personality. The other limitation, also related to both training and personality, concerns the "freedom to speculate wisely" about a patient. The data, once they have been gathered, must be examined in such a variety of ways as to maximize whatever significance they may have. The clinician must be able to entertain relevant hypotheses about the patient, even when the evidence is at first quite tentative, check these hypotheses against all relevant findings, and reject or confirm the hypotheses on the basis of the evidence. Scientific training too often overemphasizes the checking of hypotheses and underemphasizes the ability to develop creative and frankly speculative hypotheses. Both types of creative thinking are essential in developing and checking hypotheses about a patient.

Projective tests offer access to data related to underlying process phenomena, and these data may then be manipulated in various ways to germinate and corroborate inferences concerning psychopathologic behavior. They are less useful in defining specific psychiatric syndromes which have been derived from an examination of clusters of overt behavior. The latter task may well be left to good history and case analysis procedures or to more exactly defined, objective tests of personality. Critics of projective tests who have pointed out that validation studies of such tests have not had great success are essentially correct. The criticism is valid but it overlooks another, at least equally important point. The designation of a particular psychopathologic syndrome tells us very little about the meaning of a particular patient's behavior.

Here, again, we must emphasize our contention that a psychiatric label has little significance when we are dealing with an individual patient. It defines the broad category of people who have the same designated, overt behavioral features, but it does not warrant the assumption that *all* the people with that label have the same conflicts, the same drives, or even necessarily the same psychopathology. To acquire knowledge about these matters requires more appropriate assessment of the nature of the drives, conflicts, ego resources, and other specific characteristics of the psychopathology. This is the clinician's task: describing or measuring the character structure of the individual, not merely designating the behavioral syndrome which is present. And this is the task with which the therapist must deal if he is to have meaningful data to manage effectively his interpersonal relationship with the patient. One might highlight this argument by stating that a psychiatric label offers information as to the general category of patients to which the individual belongs and is most useful for administrative reasons, while a psychodiagnostic evaluation of the patient offers information as to the specific features of the dynamic processes which a particular patient possesses and is useful in the appropriate management of the patient.

The HABGT is particularly useful in gaining access to underlying process phenomena. It can be used, as some studies have done, to derive scores based on clusters of perceptual errors in order to define psychiatric categories or severity of psychopathology (Bender, 1938; Gobetz, 1953; Pascal & Suttell 1951). As we have indicated, such a use is of limited value, and there may be other and more efficient ways of securing such results. Or the HABGT may be used to get at underlying process phenomena which give rise to the resultant behavior. Because the ways in which an individual perceives, organizes, and executes responses to a task of this kind maximizes the projective aspects of his behavior, this test offers leads to projective hypotheses about the patient.

We shall now elaborate on this aspect of psychodiagnosis and then present a sample of a projective analysis of a test protocol to concretize the discussion. Chapter 2 and Chapters 5 and 6, especially, offer more detail concerning this method.

When a person is asked to examine a simple Gestalt design, he may or may not percieve it accurately. Whether or not he does depends, first, upon the biological maturation of the organism. Without such maturation the organism is unable to perceive mature Gestalten (Wertheimer, 1923). If, in a particular instance, the individual is able to percieve some of the more mature Gestalt forms (more mature as determined on the basis of normative data) but is unable to perceive accurately some of the less mature Gestalten, we have prima facie evidence that some personality disturbance, and not inadequacy in general maturation, is responsible.

Now, assuming that discrepancies of the kind suggested above do appear, what can be inferred? There are several patterns of perceptual distortion, each of which is related to different kinds of defenses. If, for some idiosyncratic reason, the Gestalt is percieved as threatening to the individual, it may be defended against by *over-adient* or *over-abient* behavior. (See Chapter 7.) Abient behavior represents an attempt to withdraw from the perceptual stimulus. In extreme instances, the individual may "black out" the stimulus (or part of it) and not "see" it at all. Some cases of hysterical blindness manifest this kind of defense. Or he may see the stimulus as smaller than it is in reality. Some cases of micropsia represent this kind of defense. Or he may perceive some parts of the stimulus as relatively smaller than other parts. Some cases of withdrawal and repressive responses to curved portions of stimuli represent this kind of defense against the symbolic meaning of curved lines to some patients. On the other hand, he may show an over-adient response, probably a more mature and active type of defense, by increasing the perceptual size of the stimulus or of part of it. In such instances, the patient is able to deal more directly with the stimulus than when he "withdraws" by decreasing size, but he also makes some compensatory efforts in dealing with it.

In addition to gross distortion in size, another type of general defense pattern may be employed. The patient may show the type of distortion which we have called *retrogression*. In such instances, the patient substitutes a more primitive Gestalt for a more mature Gestalt, such as the substitution of a circular form for a diamond, or a substitution of loops for dots, or of nonoverlapping characteristics for overlapping characteristics.

Still another type of distortion is represented by perceptual rotation in which the figure is perceived as if its axis has been rotated to some degree. There are various hypotheses related to different degrees of rotation and to direction of rotation, but, in general, rotation appears to represent feelings of impotency in reacting to the stimulus and to the psychological characteristics which it represents.

These three examples of perceptual distortion may suffice at this point to indicate the projective possibilities of ascertaining relatively pure examples of defensive behavior. As we shall see, there are many other types and subtypes of perceptual distortion, many of which have been studied experimentally and clinically.

However, the HABGT involves not only perceptual but also motoric behavior. Here we can utilize examples of aberrant motor behavior as leads to underlying needs, defenses, and conflicts. For example, a very simple indication of anxiety is the inability to make a smooth, even, motor movement, resulting in incoordination and impulsive motor behavior. Another example is the tendency to exaggerate or to decrease movements in either the horizontal or vertical planes, tendencies which are related to conflict in dealing with authority figures and close interpersonal relations, respectively (Mira, 1939–1940, 1943). Still another is the difficulty in executing relatively simple motor responses involving the crossing of lines or the closing of figures, difficulties related to fear of or inability to maintain emotional cathexes with other people (Clawson, 1959; Story, 1960). Each of these behaviors may, of course, be the result of disturbances in the perceptual as well as the motoric sphere.

Finally, the HABGT involves the planning, organizing, and revising of plans in the successive phases of the *basic* method: the copy phase, the elaboration phase, and the association phase. The arrangement on the page (or pages) of successive drawings, the use of space, the use of margins, the ability or inability to modify or to correct discrepancies—these and many other features involving planning and organizing of successive responses give us projective evidence of characteristic personality styles employed by different patients. For example, the crowding of many drawings into a small corner of one page, or the need to separate each drawing from every other drawing, or the inability to shift the placement of the figure in accordance with the reality features of the drawing and the space available represent different kinds of needs and defenses that may be present in different psychiatric syndromes, yet these syndromes have basic underlying features common to all or to some. We shall defer to Chapters 5 and 6 a more detailed consideration of such features, but point out here that there are correlates in underlying personality features of such styles of organizing behavior responses (Hutt, 1949; Mira, 1943; Shapiro, 1965).

One feature of process diagnosis involves the *experimental modification* of test procedures so as to provide a better basis for inferring the factor or factors which help to explain the test behavior. This can be especially important in an individual case. We have indicated that any test phenomenon, no matter how bizarre, can usually be due to more than a single unitary antecedent or cause. The test phenomenon may clearly suggest organic brain damage, or mental retardation, or simply immature perceptual–motoric development. Although this analysis may prove to be true in most cases, the clinician may have reason to be suspicious of the usual conclusion in a given case. In such an instance he may explore the possibility of other explanatory factors by questioning the individual in order to uncover, if possible, what led to the specific test behavior, or by modifying the conditions of the test so as to expose the underlying cause or causes. I have called this procedure Testing-the-Limits (Hutt & Shor, 1946), but it is clearly an experimental–clinical method.

Suppose an individual produced the drawings which are shown in Plate 2. These drawings are taken from a record of a 13-year-old boy who had been referred for study because of delinquency and very inferior school work. The examiner had correctly noted that on design 1 (see Plate 1) the production clearly showed marked evidence of *perseveration* and some degree of *clockwise rotation.* On design 7 the drawings indicated *difficulty with overlapping, difficulty with angulation,* and *closure difficulty.* These and other findings led the examiner to suggest that there was the possibility of organic brain damage or mental retardation, or both. Yet there were inconsistencies in the record which suggested that some other explanation might account for the test behavior. Almost nothing was known about this boy's educational, social, and physical background; he had arrived in his present school only some 9 months before, and no school or medical records were available. The present writer, who was consulting on this case, asked why such information was unavailable and was told that the parents were uncooperative and the boy was uncommunicative! I suggested that we employ a clinical–experimental procedure to investigate some of the factors that might account for the abnormal test phenomena.

The boy was recalled for further examination and another attempt was made to establish better rapport—with some degree of success. Then the examiner presented the test card (for design 1) alongside the test produc-

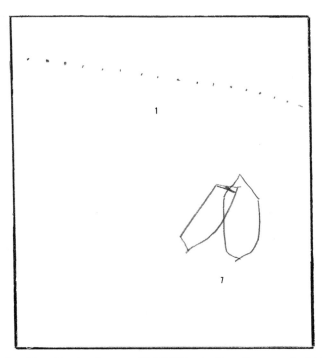

Plate 2. Two Productions on HABGT of a Boy Suspected of Having Organic Brain Damage or Mental Retardation, or Both

tion which the boy had offered on the initial test. He was asked: "Can you tell me whether these two are exactly the same?" When he responded that they were not, he was asked: "And how are they different?" He replied that his design had too many dots. He was asked: "Is there anything else that is different in your drawing?" And the boy stated that his drawing was "not straight." The examiner then gave the boy a new sheet of paper and told him: "This time, I'd like you to copy the drawing on the card so that yours is exactly like that one." In Plate 3, it will be seen that the boy's first new effort was much better than his original reproduction. Since the product was still inaccurate, the boy was again asked whether it was exactly correct, and when he noted that it was not, he was asked to try again. His second new effort resulted in a very fine reproduction, without any indication of psychopathological significance.

The same type of procedure was followed for design 7. Again it took two additional trials before a good production was achieved. It was also obvious from observation of the boy's behavior that he needed a great deal of encouragement and urging in order for him to exert sufficient effort to complete satisfactory drawings. It was clear that he did not suffer from

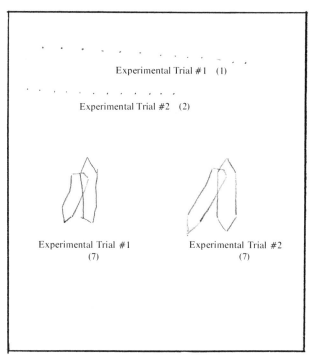

Experimental Trial #1   (1)

Experimental Trial #2   (2)

Experimental Trial #1   Experimental Trial #2
(7)   (7)

Plate 3. Clinical–Experimental Trials on HABGT for the Drawings Reproduced in Plate 2

any gross perceptual–motoric abnormality and that he had not had much previous experience in performing with great care on tasks such as these.

Subsequent interviews with the boy and his parents revealed that he had attended school for only short periods during his previous educational career, that his parents, who were illiterate and not very involved with their child, offered almost no motivation for schooling, and that the family had suffered from severe financial difficulties, was of very low socioeconomic status, and was, in other respects, seriously "disadvantaged." We shall not attempt to elucidate the picture further except to indicate that this boy, who had suffered from such deprivation, was apparently of about average intelligence but had a very low aspiration level, very limited educational skills, and little interest in coping with the very complex situation into which he had been moved when the family came to live in this new area. The "apparent" pathological indicators on the first HABGT were, rather than evidence of pathology, manifestations of his low level of involvement in the tasks he was given and indicative of his practice of doing things in the easiest way available to him. Perseveration and the slight rotation design 1 essentially resulted from a lack of adequate effort and involvement in the task. The difficulties on design 7 reflected the same factors, this design presenting an even more difficult task and requiring even greater attention and careful effort. The clinical–experimental procedures were instrumental in eliminating some of the tentative formulations suggested earlier, and they led to exploration and elucidation of some of the relevant factors.

At this point it would be useful to summarize a report on the projective analysis of an HABGT test (copy phase only, see Chapter 4). The analysis was based on the rationales and test factors available at that time,* and would be slightly different in the light of the newer evidence we present in later chapters of this book. Essentially, however, it is still valid.

We are told that Tom, one of a pair of identical twins, is heterosexual and is 27 years of age. We have no information, unfortunately, on his methods of work during the Bender test.

Taking a general overview of Tom's Bender reproductions (see Plates 4 and 5), we note that he has arranged the figures on two successive pages in correct sequence, and further that he has spontaneously numbered each of the figures from 1 to 9. The figures are considerably enlarged in size and this enlargement tends to increase with each successive drawing. (Note, for example, that Tom has drawn five of the figures on the first page, and has drawn four figures on the second page, using the entire page in each case.) Although he has utilized space liberally, the spacing of successive figures is appropriate to the size of the reproductions. With this initial information, we are able to offer some hypotheses based on Tom's general approach to this problem: These are: he tends to be outgoing, labile and assertive in his approach to a new and relatively unstructured situation, showing no essential evidence of overt anxiety in his test behavior (although we can infer that the increase in size is compensatory for some degree of latent anxiety); he tends to order his world, using external controls (the numbering) to gain some degree of mastery or self-assurance (a subhypothesis is that he uses the service of compulsive defenses to achieve this end-product); the appropriate, but liberal, use of white space suggests that his assertive drives are at least reasonably well socialized.

A second set of general observations may be made, taking note of the relatively heavy line drawings he utilizes and the generally *impulsive* or spontaneous (more probably the former) quality of his *motor executions*. These data reinforce our hypothesis that he is labile and outgoing and that he tends to act out rather than suppress the discharge of his drives. One

---

* This "blind analysis" was done entirely on the basis of the evidence presented herewith. It was originally reported at a symposium of the American Psychological Association, in Cleveland, Ohio, September 4, 1959. It was later published in the volume edited by Carr (Hutt, 1960).

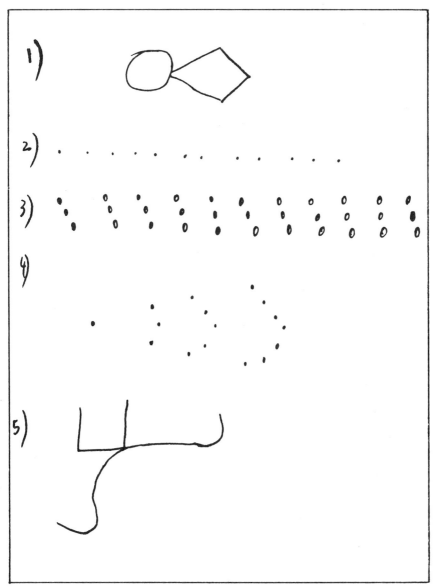

Plate 4.   Case Illustration: Tom (page 1)

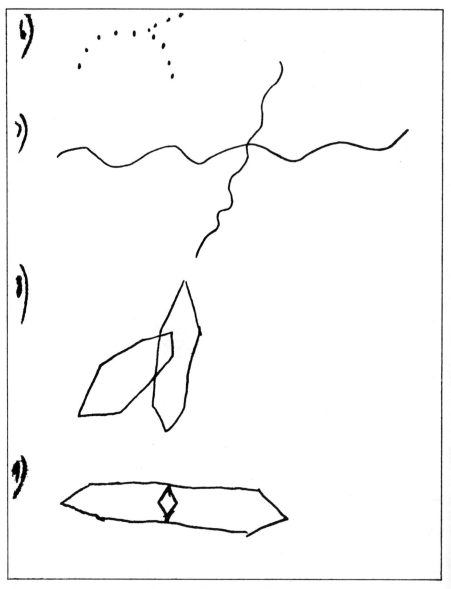

Plate 5.   Case Illustration: Tom (page 2)

can infer that his outgoing and assertive behavior may, perhaps, stimulate counterassertive behavior in others so that, in turn, he has more apparent external basis for his own assertiveness; hence, if this were so, he would tend to use rationalization to a pronounced degree.

Turning to an examination of the reproductions, we note that in figure A* (the circle and the square), he *reproduces the Gestalt adequately* (this will turn out to be generally true of the other figures); he places the figure in a *common position on the page* for figure A (slightly left, top portion of the page); *enlarges the square* in proportion to the circle, *markedly increasing its horizontal dimension;* shows *impulsivity* in the drawing of the circle (overlap in closure); shows *joining difficulty* of the square and circle; makes *no attempt to correct* or erase; slightly flattens the circle, the net effect of which is to *increase the total lateral or horizontal dimensions* of the figure. From these observations, we are led to the following hypotheses: he has good contact with reality, and has reasonably good ego cathexes; he tends to be conventional rather than unconventional in his social orientation; he is making considerable effort to establish or maintain interpersonal relationships (showing a need for such relationships); he tends to be fearful in authority situations; impulsivity, as a character trait, must be fairly marked; he is dissatisfied with the nature of his interpersonal relationships, and more specifically is concerned over his sexual adequacy; affect is outgoing but may lack depth and integrated qualities in his total behavior.

This exemplifies some of the methods of inducing hypotheses. Due to limitations of space, the remaining figures will be dealt with in less detail. Figure 1 does not have much to offer us. It is correctly reproduced, although there is some tendency toward paired grouping of the dots. The dots are made fairly heavily, but neatly (no sketching). These data support the hypotheses that Tom is in reasonably good contact with reality; he has good energy capacity which he expends in a centrifugal manner. The increase in the laterality of this reproduction emphasizes Tom's need to relate to others.

Figure 2 shows the following features: initially correct angulation of the first column of figures with a constantly increasing egocentric orientation of the successive columns (as if Tom were the pivot around which the columns were oriented); correct number of columns (if there were 11 columns in the original stimulus); circles drawn as good loops, but with some impulsivity and some closure difficulty. Inferences: good perceptual accuracy, but strong narcissistic tendency and generally forceful but impulsive behavior; some fearfulness in interpersonal relationships. The

* Tom numbered figure A as 1, and numbered the succeeding figures from 2 to 9. Thus, his numbering is always one digit higher than the "standard" numbering.

egocentric trend combined with the previously noted labile and outgoing qualities indicate that, as a second order inference, he is insecure but compensates rather well for his latent anxiety.

On figure 3 we note a radical, lateral, and overall expansion in the size of the figure but the Gestalt is preserved. However, this time the dots are heavily filled in (in contrast to figure 1). Thus, in an unclosed figure, Tom strives even more strongly in stressing his need for dependent interpersonal relations, but at the same time becomes more openly aggressive in his behavior.

Figure 4 gives us some additional clues to the underlying sources of Tom's problems and the residual behavior which he manifests. The unbalanced feature of this figure (with the curve at a 45 degree rotation from the horizontal) is relatively more upsetting to anxious, nonspontaneous adults than to others. In his reproduction, Tom makes two adaptations. First, he draws the curve in such a manner that the acuteness of the angle of the base and the upper curve is reduced. Second, he markedly increases the size of the curve, both absolutely and in relation to the open square. In addition, there is excessive, slightly fragmented looping on the end of the curve. Further, one of the vertical sides of the open square is made longer and more jaggedly than the other. The open square is slightly larger than the stimulus but reduced in proportion to the curved figure. The typical signs of rapid, impulsive work habits are clearly noticeable. The inferences are, respectively: he has an excessive need for control and conformity; he expresses hostile drives more openly in emotionally tinged situations. He is, once again, showing his fearfulness of authority figures. Possibly, he has a more pronounced feminine than masculine identification.

Tom's first real indication of fairly severe inner tension and conflict seems to be revealed on figure 5. Here some very striking modifications appear in his reproduction. In the first place, the hallmark of poorly controlled, impulsive drives appears: his figure collides with the upper edge of the page, and the vertical axis of the figure is thereby foreshortened. Yet, he makes no attempt to correct the figure or redraw it. He decreases the number or dots in both parts of the figure, but fills each dot in very heavily. Again, let us remind ourselves that this is an open, noncontinuous figure (less structured). We cannot be sure of the possible sources of this overt, obvious breakdown in controls, but the following suggest themselves. Possibly, the accumulation of frustrations involved in the test procedure has begun to have its effect. More importantly, the unstructured quality of the figure creates special problems for an individual attempting to assert control through acting out and overcompensation. Other possibilities are, of course, likely to account for these phenomena. In any case, planning and anticipation are now shown to be inadequate.

He is not the comfortable, confident figure he tries to present to the world. The tendency to edging of his figures, previously evident but not commented upon, is now reinforced by placement of the figure almost in the extreme, left-upper corner position. Strong compensatory efforts to ward off feelings of inadequacy and frustration are evident in the excessive effort devoted to filling in the very heavy dots.

On figure 6, an extreme expansion in size, in both lateral and vertical planes is noted. The size is more than doubled in both dimensions. The curves are flattened in the horizontal plane, and made irregularly and rectangularly in the vertical plane. The angulation of the figure is generally preserved, but the figure is rotated slightly in a counterclockwise fashion. The loops, particularly at the ends of the vertical curve, are reversed. The whole figure appears to have been drawn rapidly and no revisions or corrections attempted. Inferences: acting-out tendencies, under conditions of emotional stimulation, are very pronounced; egocentrism is a central feature of the personality; contact with reality is maintained, and social conformity is exercised despite marked tendencies toward impulsivity; the extroverted, non–self-critical features of the personality are highlighted. Aggressive tendencies, formerly kept under more adequate control, now assert themselves boldly.

Figure 7 shows the following features: simplification of the Gestalt (in that the two figures are made to overlap in the vertical segment of the vertical figure); closure difficulty; irregularity in line movement and line quality. We can now hypothesize that under the impact of progressive traumata there is a regressive tendency; despite initial tendencies to apparent confidence in interpersonal behavior, there is considerable conflict and fearfulness in such situations; underneath the armor of self-confidence there is considerable latent hostility.

The last figure, figure 8, is striking and unique in several respects. Despite his perceptual maturity, as revealed in previous drawings, he has considerable difficulty with this figure. The left-hand vertex of the lateral hexagon shows considerable evidence of motor incoordination and poor control; joining and closure difficutly are very noticeable; he has great difficulty with the internal diamond, doing some redrawings for the first time and making many false motor movements in the process. Despite the history of heterosexual adjustment which we are given, this analyst would question Tom's heterosexual adjustment. This reproduction is indicative of fairly marked conflict over homosexual tendencies. This problem probably lies at the core of his difficulties and insecurities in interpresonal relationships: he is really unsure of his sexual identity, and overcompensates with apparent masculine behavior to mask this problem for himself. The ambivalent quality of the internal diamond as a sexual symbol makes Tom's usual coping methods less adequate on this figure, and hence the redrawing and obvious uncertainties on this part of the reproduction. One can also hypothesize that if Tom is egocentric in orientation as we have suggested, problems centering around masturbation as a tension reducer are also present.

Our analysis has yielded several hypotheses concerning underlying source traits and several hypotheses concerning explicit and simplex examples of overt behavior. We have begun to understand Tom as an outgoing, labile, assertive individual with strong, overcompensatory characteristics. We have seen that he ordinarily holds on to an adequate perception of reality but that he shows considerable regression (neurotic in character) under specified conditions, namely, cumulative stress and, more specifically, emotional types of trauma. We have seen certain features of his attempts at control through compulsive conformity and external props. From these and other types of evidence we must try to understand why it is that he functions, at least on this test, in the unique ways that he does.

The core of his difficulties may be hypothesized to be in the problem of his sexual identity. Our inference is that he has dealt with the problem of latent homosexual tendencies by various mastery and compensatory techniques. Together with the hypothesis that he is egocentric but centrifugal in his orientation, we can point to an unsuccessfully resolved and repressed oedipal problem, with the likelihood that he was overprotected by a mother with whom he tended to identify. He had learned to perceive himself as more comfortable in a feminine role, but conflict resulting from the assumption of this role led him to assume more outgoing, assertive and masculine behaviors as a more secure mode of adjustment. Nevertheless, the underlying conflict remained and more compensatory mechanisms were necessary to maintain a heterosexual way of life. On the other hand, the heterosexual way of life had its own social rewards, and probably helped to differentiate him from his identical twin. Thus, the masculine ways of behaving were reinforced and, in turn, these ways produced secondary gratification. Underneath, infantile sexuality remained and fear of really close interpersonal relationships was fostered. Thus, his self-perception became ever more obtuse and he had to learn to bolster his own sense of self by more outgoing, masculine behavior. In the process, spontaneous affective response and capacity for mature fantasy behavior were diminished. This, then, is the neurotic character structure which is suggested by our data. Note that we are giving no attention to physical history and other biological factors which may be relevant and important in attempting to understand Tom. Were these available we could then proceed to correct and supplement our present formulation.

Assuming our basic analysis is substantially correct, what can we infer about overt behavior? Here, we are severely limited by not knowing the conditions of the testing and by not having observational data concerning Tom's methods of work, his verbalizations and the like. Nor does this accounting of shortcomings include other types of life-history and test data. However, given these limitations, what can we now infer—with, of course, lowered limits of confidence?

First, we can predict that Tom will function at least reasonably well in many, if not most, situations. He has considerable energy available for daily tasks. He gives the superficial impression of a likeable, fairly stable and assertive person. He is usually orderly and controlled enough not to be gauche and to be also a social asset in that his outgoing and apparently labile, responsive qualities make him rather attractive to others. He would particularly appeal to masculine-oriented women who would not see him as a threat to their own masculine strivings. He would generally tend to be expansive in mood and rarely reveal depressive reactions. He would not easily confide to others, however, his own gnawing feelings of inadequacy, nor would he be likely to reveal to others, much less to himself, his fearfulness of authority figures. He would be able to establish superficial relationships quite readily, and he would be a joiner and an active participant, but he would not develop intense relationships with anyone easily, if at all. Not only would he be assertive, however, but he would be self-assertive, whenever the situation permitted. One would also predict there would be apparently inexplicable periods of indecision, work reduction, and even more overt disorganization when he was unable to escape from repetitive emotional frustration. His own self-doubts and feelings of uncertainty would finally lead him to seek some form of therapeutic help.

4

Methods of Administration

To a very considerable extent the methods which are proposed for administering test stimuli depend on the author's previous clinical experience with the material. Usually, there is also a rationale based on broader clinical perspective and personality theory. It would be best if such clinical and theoretical biases were put to experimental test and those methods retained which *were most effective in terms of specified objectives for the test*. At this stage of work with the HABGT we still have to rely, to a large extent, upon clinical experience and theoretical rationale. Fortunately, there is some research evidence which can be adduced, and we shall refer to this where relevant. In the present discussion we shall first turn to some considerations of a general nature relating to test administration. Next we will discuss our own usual methods, consisting of the basic method or copy phase, the method of elaboration, and the method of association. Finally, we shall consider some other methods of administration and their probable values.

SOME GENERAL CONSIDERATIONS

There is considerable evidence that many factors can influence the results of testing. Among those which have received research documentation are: the expectancies of the examinee; the explicit test instructions; the "atmosphere" in which the examination is conducted; the personality

62

of the examiner; the sex, race, and color of skin of examiner and examinee; and the point in the diagnostic sequence (or diagnostic–therapeutic sequence) in which the particular test or procedure is administered. Some tests are much more sensitive to such influences than others, and greater care is needed with such tests in interpreting results; both advantages and disadvantages accrue from such sensitivity. In addition to these general factors is the general problem of the effect upon test results of prior social–cultural–educational experiences of the individual.

It has been reported (Tolor & Schulberg, 1963) that, as suggested by this author (Hutt & Briskin, 1960), the HABGT or other variations of this test could be used as a buffer test due to its nonthreatening and nonverbal characteristics. Although such a buffer use of the test is helpful in many ways, this does not negate the importance of obtaining proper rapport *before* the test is administered. Developing such rapport would seem to have two highly important functions. First, it would induce maximal motivation on the part of the examinee, thus helping to insure that the product more accurately represents his present, full capacity. Second, it would enable the examiner to understand the examinee's expectancies and motivations and thus provide a more adequate basis for interpretation.

In order to develop proper rapport, the test procedure must be considered as a task governed by the examinee's needs. The examinee should be given an explanation of the test's purposes in terms of *his* needs, rather than those of the clinic, hospital, or diagnostician. In other words, the examinee should develop some conviction that taking the test will really be useful to him. In many cases, this will not require extended discussion; even when it does not however, ample opportunity should be permitted for expression of feelings, fears and uncertainties. And when there is fear of reluctance to proceed with the testing, directly expressed or implied, great care should be taken to explore and discuss these issues—not in the spirit of conning the examinee into taking the test, but in the spirit of fully accepting his feelings as relevant and significant. Testing can proceed fruitfully only when such issues have been fully explored and accepted by the examinee in terms of his own needs and interests. If circumstances should arise when this is not feasible, and testing still has to be carried out, then this definition of the situation should be stated frankly and the results interpreted with considerably greater caution than would otherwise be necessary.

There is some evidence (see discussion on pages 80–82) that group administration does not, on the whole, significantly affect many aspects of the test results as compared with individual administration, but group administration cannot properly take into account the broad spectrum of the motivational factors we have been discussing and makes interpretation of individuals' results much more tenuous, to say the least.

ADMINISTRATION AS A PROJECTIVE INSTRUMENT

In order to maximize the projective properties of the test situation, certain features of the total situation should be kept as unstructured and as nonspecific as possible. On the other hand, to make results from the testing of different individuals comparable, other features of the testing should be kept constant. When these "constant" factors are modified, sometimes for very good clinical reasons, the deviation should be carefully noted so that subsequent analysis of the results may attempt to take this into account.

Test materials consist of: a number of medium-soft pencils (number 2–3 in hardness); a stack of white, *unlined* 8½" × 11" bond paper; a pencil eraser; the HABGT cards. The examinee should have a comfortable position for drawing and a stable, smooth writing surface on which to draw.

The *usual* process of administration consists of three phases: the copy phase, elaboration phase, and association phase.

Copy Phase

The examiner places the stack of bond paper *near* the examinee and also places the pencils and the erasers in a conveniently accessible position. He then places the 9 HABGT cards in front of his own body, on the table, with the designs in a face-down position. The backs of the cards are thus exposed, in a pile, so that the examinee may see that there is a number of them, but he is *not* told how many cards there are. The following instructions are then offered. (The language may be varied so as to make the meaning clear, as may be necessary for some children and for adults who have language problems, but the essential content is kept constant.)

"I am going to show you these cards (pointing to the pile of cards), *one at a time. Each card has a simple drawing on it. I would like you to copy the drawing on the paper, as well as you can. Work in any way that is best for you. This is not a test of artistic ability, but try to copy the drawings as accurately as possible. Work as fast or as slowly as you wish."*

Any questions by the examinee are answered by paraphrasing the above, but *no suggestions are offered* as to methods of work, or the like. When such questions are raised, they should be answered with some such noncommital phrases as: *"Well, that's up to you.; Do it the way you think is best."* One question that is asked frequently is: "How many sheets of paper shall I use?" The response is: *"That's entirely up to you."* If one is asked: "May I erase or correct it?," the response is, again, *"That's up to you."*

The examiner then takes a *single sheet* of paper from the stack and places it directly in front of the subject, with the long (or vertical) axis of the paper at right angles to his body. The first test card, Card A, is then taken from the stack of cards, and is placed in front of the subject with the base of the card (as indicated by the letter A on the back) toward him. The instruction, *"Copy this as well as you can,"* is repeated.

Each of the pertinent features of this method of administration needs some comment.

1. *The stack of bond paper.* Presenting the examinee with a stack of bond paper gives him a choice: to use a single sheet, to use two sheets, or to use a number of sheets, possibly one for each drawing. For reasons that will be discussed in later chapters, it is believed that the way in which the examinee structures this aspect of the task for himself reveals important aspects of his life space in general. Although the forced use of a single sheet of paper for all of the drawings has other advantages, it does not permit (encourage?) the maximum variance in the use of space. The single sheet of paper that is presented to the examinee, while the stack remains available, is simply to prevent his making impressions on the other sheets, in the course of his drawings, which might be used as guides in making the subsequent drawings.

2. *The stack of cards.* The stack of test cards is kept visible so as to enable the subject to make some anticipatory adjustment in his planning, if he wishes, in deciding where to place his drawings or even to decide how large or small to make them. If the subject asks how many cards there are, the response is, *"Just this stack of cards."*

3. *Placement of the single sheet of paper.* It will be noted that we start the subject off by presenting him with a single sheet with the long axis perpendicular to his body. This is done because it is the usual position when writing or drawing on $8\frac{1}{2} \times 11$ inch paper. However, the subject is *free to change its position,* so that he may decide to shift the paper and have the long axis, for example, parallel to his body. There are a number of issues involved in this matter. For one thing, it is probable that presenting the paper in the "vertical position" while the test card is presented in the "horizontal" position, as we have suggested, maximizes the frequency with which rotations will appear, especially in younger children. (See the related research: Griffith & Taylor, 1960; Hannah, 1958.) We shall consider the possibilities of modifying this and other features of test administration in the section titled "Testing-the-Limits: Experimental–Clinical Methods."

Another aspect of our suggested "standard" procedure is the meaning behind a subject's decision to rotate the test paper. One *possible* explanation is a tendency toward oppositional behavior. (Such a possibility needs to be checked and explored in various ways, as we shall see.) When the subject changes the position of the paper, a note should be made as part of the record.

4. *Placement of the test card.* The standard placement of the test card provides for a standard perceptual task. Shifting the position of the card may change its Gestalt quality. Hence, if the subject rotates the test card, the examiner should replace it in its standard position, with the added instruction, *"You are supposed to copy it this way."* However, if the subject insists upon having the card in a different position, make a note of this in the record, and then interpret the possible meaning of the reproduction on a different basis. (See the *HABGT Revised Record Form** for further instructions on this point.)

5. *Pencils and eraser.* The use of a medium-soft pencil helps to maximize nuances produced by varying pressures while drawing. Thus, the examiner can later examine the drawings for variations in pressure and consider such possible variations in terms of their meaning as indicators of anxiety, frustration with the task, etc.

The presence of the eraser is suggestive that corrections and erasures may be made, but no explicit directions are given. If the examinee asks whether he may erase or correct, he is told, *"That's up to you."* Some examinees may make more than one attempt at drawing a design. *This is neither encouraged nor discouraged.* Again, if asked about this, the examiner states, *"That's up to you."* When more than one attempt is made in reproducing a design, the examinee's choice as to which he considers best is used as the basis for later scoring. If no choice is made, then the best reproduction is used in later objective scoring (see Chapter 7). However, the several drawings may furnish important clues about the features of the design that are difficult or disturbing to the examinee.

Returning now to the remainder of the administration of the copy phase of the test, when the examinee has completed his reproduction of the design on Card A, the examiner removes this card from sight, with some appropriate comment such as *"That's fine,"* and then places Card 1 directly in front of the examinee with the comment, *"Now copy this drawing as well as you can."* As in the placement of all cards, the base of the card, indicated by the number on the back, is placed toward the examinee. Similarly, when Card 1 has been completed, it is removed and Card 2 is placed in position. This procedure is continued until all test cards have been administered.

The sequence in which the cards are presented is considered important. Although there is no adequate research evidence on this point, clinical experience suggests that variations in sequence influence results. For example, perseveration is more likely to occur on Card 2 when it follows Card 1. The sequence of Cards 4, 5, and 6 seems to maximize difficulties

---

* Packages of the *HABGT Revised Record Form, 2nd edition* may be purchased from the publisher, Grune & Stratton, Inc.

on curved figures, when such a tendency is present. Cards 7 and 8, the most difficult from the viewpoint of perceptual maturity, are given last and might adversely affect the performance of some subjects on later tasks if given earlier in the sequence.

As with any psychological task, the *behavior of the examinee* is sometimes as important as the test response itself. Especially in the early stages of the examiner's experience with this test, copious notes should be taken on all relevant aspects of the examinee's behavior. *His spontaneous comments should be recorded* and examined later for possible significance. Among various aspects of the examinee's methods of work to be recorded the following are the most important: (1) Does he preplan his drawings or does he proceed impulsively or even impetuously? (2) Does he count the number of dots, loops, or sides of figures, or does he proceed haphazardly? (3) Does he make frequent erasures? If so, on what figures and on which parts of these figures does he have difficulty or does he show extra care? (4) Which part of the figure does he tackle first? (5) In what direction does he proceed as he copies the figure? Does he draw from the top down or from the bottom up? Does he draw from the inside out or from the outside in? Does the direction of movement vary from figure to figure? (6) Does he use sketching movements? (7) Does he show unusual blocking on any figures?

The time taken by the examinee in reproducing the designs is not recorded. There is no evidence that this factor correlates significantly with important personality variables. However, *extreme variation in time* to make the drawings should be noted carefully, and clinical experience will soon indicate to the examiner when such extremes occur. Excessively long time is usually indicative of psychomotor blocking and thus can be an important clinical indicator of a number of types of pathology (e.g., latent catatonic blocking, brain damage, or extreme compulsivity). Unusually rapid performance may also be significant and may indicate one of a number of conditions (e.g., extreme anxiety with a need to "get out of the situation," psychopathic attitude, or strong oppositional tendencies). Hence, future valuable dividends may be gleaned from a manifestation of extreme variations in time.

The *HABGT Revised Record Form* contains space and directions for recording these and other features of the test performance.

Elaboration Phase

The elaboration phase is the second phase of administration of the test as a projective instrument. Its major purpose is to assist in maximizing those projective reactions to the test which will enable the examiner to offer tentative hypotheses about the particular examinee. This phase of the testing *further reduces the structured quality of the test situation* and thus requires the examinee to impose his own idiosyncratic meaning upon it.

After the copy phase has been completed, the examinee's drawings are *removed from sight*. Again, a stack of paper is provided and placed near the examinee. The examiner instructs something like: *"Well, that was very nice. Now, I'm going to ask you to do something else with these drawings. This time, I'd like you to modify the drawings, or to change them in any way you wish, so as to make them more pleasing to you. Feel free to change them in any way that you like. (They may even remind you of things.) You can change the drawings as little or as much as you like. Just make them more pleasing to yourself. Do you understand what I'd like you to do?"* Any questions are then answered within the framework of these instructions. The wording may be modified to clarify the meaning of the instructions. Thus, for a more sophisticated subject, the examiner might say, *"You might like to make them more esthethic in appearance."* To a young child he might say, *"Say if you can make them better looking."*

The examiner then presents each card in sequence with the instruction: *"Change this one in any way you like so as to make it more pleasing to you."* If the examinee states that he likes the drawing the way it is, he should be told, *"All right, but will you please copy it again the way it is."* This is done for two reasons. (1) Even when the examinee attempts to recopy the drawing, he may reveal aspects of his performance that were not clear the first time, or he may modify it involuntarily. In either case, further evidence becomes available that is useful in later interpretation. (2) The sequence of the drawings, and their placement on the page (pages) needs to be considered, especially if an aberrant placement (deviation in sequence) has occurred.

When time considerations are important, and it is thought to be important to reduce the total time for the testing, certain cards may be omitted from the elaboration phase. Cards A, 2, 4, 6, 7, and 8 will usually furnish a sufficient sample to make all of the necessary deductions. These cards present about all of the important Gestalt qualities found in the entire sample of cards, and can therefore be used for such an abbreviated procedure. Of course, sequence is then modified and may affect some of the possible findings. The saving in time is increased when a few cards are eliminated from this phase, because they are then also eliminated from the next phase, the association phase.

Again, as in the copy phase, notes are taken on the examinee's spontaneous comments and test behavior.

The degree of freedom the examinee exercises in the elaboration phase, the kind of individual creativity he displays, and the definition he imposes upon this ambiguous task all tell us something about the way in which his personality functions. Some subjects are quite anxious when they are asked to work without specific structuring of the task. They become overly defensive and are fearful of revealing unknown aspects about themselves. But these and other subjects often are led to modify the drawings in ways which they do not "consciously intend." Sometimes the very act of drawing the designs, with latent cues derived either from the drawing or their own distortions of the drawing, trigger important deviations in the elaboration phase that were hardly noticeable in the copy phase. Even compulsive individuals, intending only to reproduce the designs faithfully, find themselves modifying them in highly idiosyncratic ways. The relative lack of fantasy and creativity in other subjects is often highlighted. In still others, the need to conform or the excessive and neurotic fear of authority figures becomes evident as they strive only to reproduce the "standard" designs. In some cases, the disintegration or severe regression which occurs during the elaboration phase is highlighted. They "escape" from any reality controls and engage in "doodling," or present their drawings in a confused jumble, sometimes letting the figures collide or overlap. Occasionally, we see a peculiar fascination with a particular part of a design which intrigues the subject, and it is redrawn with elaborate and excessive care. These and other features sometimes become evident during this phase and provide important clinical leads to understanding the unique features of the individual. Of particular interest is the performance of some brain-damaged patients who struggle impatiently with some aspect of the design which troubles them and which they are unable to reproduce accurately either in the copy phase or in the elaboration phase.

A comparison of the accuracy of nosological predictions based on the copy phase alone as contrasted with a combination of both the copy phase and the elaboration phase (utilizing 130 male adult psychoneurotic subjects, 38 schizophrenics, 119 heterogenous cases with organic brain damage, and 25 hospitalized nonpsychiatric patients) indicated that the latter combination gave improved accuracy of predictions significant at the .05 level of confidence.

Association Phase

The chief function of the association phase is to elict the individual's associative content to *both* the original test cards and the elaborations which have been made of them during the elaboration phase. It is assumed that when an individual modifies the design, he is doing so, in part, be-

cause of implicit and unconscious cues which his perceptual–motoric behavior stimulated. The *contrast* between the original designs and his elaborations of them is believed—with considerable clinical evidence and
some research evidence (Story, 1960)—to increase the likelihood of evok-
ing significant associative material.

The method is quite simple. After the elaboration phase has been
completed, the examiner presents stimulus Card A *alongside* the elaboration the examinee has made of it. He then says: *"Now, look at the design
on the card and look at the modification you made of it in your drawing.
What does each of them remind you of? What could they be? What do
they look like or suggest."* The examiner records the association(s) to the
card and the association(s) to the elaboration. If the examinee offers an
association only to the card, he is then asked, *"And what does the one you
made look like or remind you of?"* Conversely, if an association is offered
only to the elaboration, the examiner asks, *"And what does the one on the
card look like or remind you of?"* The sequence in which the associations
are offered is numbered and a notation is made of the stimulus (*O* for
original stimulus card, and *E* for the elaboration stimulus) to which the
association is given. It is also advisable to ask, *"And what in the drawing
made it look like that?"*

A similar procedure is followed with each of the other cards; in each
case, the stimulus card is presented alongside the elaboration and the
examinee is asked, *"What does each of them remind you of?"*

SOME ADDITIONAL COMMENTS

When adminstration of the HABGT has been completed, the following data are available: (1) drawings made during the copy phase, together
with notes and observations concerning the examinee's comments and
behavior; (2) drawings made in the elaboration phase, together with comments on the examinee's behavior and verbalizations; and (3) associations
given to both the original stimuli and to the elaborations. All of these data,
taken together, constitute the material for use in projective interpretation:
two samples of perceptual–motoric productions together with the acces-
sory information concerning the sequence in which the drawings are
placed on the page(s); two sets of associative comments; verbal behavior;
comments on methods of work.

In order to score on the objective scales which are presented in Chapter 7, only the material from the copy phase needs to be utilized. In order
to develop projective hypotheses, all of the material will need to be considered first separately, and then in conjunction. In general, projective

interpretation follows principles derived from work with all projective instruments. However, there are important additions, as well as some modifications, dependent on the specific stimulus properties of the present test characteristics. These principles for projective interpretation are presented in Chapter 6.

TESTING-THE-LIMITS: EXPERIMENTAL–CLINICAL METHODS

In their original volume on the Rorschach, Klopfer and Kelley (1942) discussed some of the values and limitations of varying the testing procedure, after the formal testing had been completed, in order to clarify the meaning of certain ambiguous findings. Shortly thereafter, the present writer proposed a rationale for more regular use of some testing-the limits procedures (Hutt & Shor, 1946). One of the features of this proposal was to explore the "levels of response." It was assumed that the original responses made to the Rorschach cards represented the level of easily available potentials of the personality. But what were the hidden resources of the personality, and under what conditions could they become available? Thus, in testing-the-limits procedure, it was thought advisable to offer different degrees of suggestions to determine at what point previously unavailable resources could become available.

This, it would seem, would be a major function of any testing-the-limits procedure. Suppose, for example, we have the HABGT record of an individual who has shown tendencies in his test protocol that suggest the possibility of organic brain damage (let us say, trends toward rotation, collision, and regression). The question arises: To what extent are these features fortuitous or accidental, and to what extent are they reliable indicators? As we shall learn in our review of the relevant literature, many types of individuals with brain damage are unable to correct for such deviations, even when they are asked to attempt to do so, whereas emotionally disturbed persons can frequently make appropriate correction when attention is simply called to the deviations with such a comment as, "Is that exactly right?" (Smith & Martin, 1967).

Although the experienced clinician will be able to devise many kinds of ad hoc procedures to test and evaluate questionable responses on the HABGT, I should like to describe some basic methods which may be employed in the clinical–experimental analysis of test behavior. It is usually best to begin the clinical–experimental analysis directly after the copy phase of the test, but it can also be employed after other phases of the test have been completed.

Interview Analysis

If the clinician suspects that some peculiar or abnormal test phenomena have resulted from factors other than those which usually account for their presence, he may proceed by inquiring about the responses in question. Suppose, for instance, that the subject has given an inferior response to one of the cards and this is suspect because he has responded in superior fashion on another, perhaps more difficult test card. The examiner can then present the test card alongside the subject's drawing for that card and ask: "Are these two exactly alike?" If the subject indicates that they are not, the examiner can inquire how they are different. If the answer indicates that the subject perceives accurately how they are different, the examiner can proceed further by asking why the subject made it the way he did. Frequently, the subject will clearly elucidate why he performed the way he did. It may be a matter of carelessness, lack of attention to detail, fear of approaching what seemed to be a difficult task, fatigue, or lack of interest or motivation. The examiner may then ask the subject to try drawing "that one" again, this time taking care "to make your drawing exactly like the one on the card."

The fact that the subject was aware of his error and could clearly perceive what was wrong is important evidence in itself. It may be that the factors noted above were responsible for the "failure." However, it might turn out that the subject is able to perceive accurately but is unable to reproduce the design accurately. Observation may indicate that either gross or fine coordination is poor. The examiner can then proceed to test for coordination by appropriate methods. It might also turn out that the subject had difficulty with some feature of the design, such as making smooth curves, or executing the parts of figures which overlap. In such a case, special procedures, noted below, may be employed to tease out the particular feature which interferes with good performance.

However, it may also happen that the subject is unable to determine how his production differs from the design on the test card. He may be dimly aware that his production is inaccurate, but he may be unable to pinpoint the difficulty, or he may be unaware that his production differs from the design on the test card. These possible characteristics of the interview data may lead the examiner to do some further ad hoc testing with different, possibly simpler, designs to evaluate the nature of the perceptual difficulty. If perceptual problems seem to be associated with the overlapping feature of Card 7, for example, the examiner can present the subject with his own drawings of two overlapping elipses or two overlapping squares to test out the nature of the perceptual problem.

These and similar procedures, based on an interview about the subject's performance, are extremely important in the clinical analysis of test data. Their proper employment may enable the clinician to test out hypotheses about the subject's performance and assist in arriving at an adequate explanation of the nature of the difficulty. They are also very useful in offering a basis for recommendations for remedial or therapeutic assistance. If the subject cannot perceive the nature of his error or cannot correct it even with support and guidance concerning the nature of the error, one may clearly suspect that either perceptual–motoric inadequacy (or slow development), some organic brain damage (if the subject is mature enough for a given design), or mental retardation is present.

Test Performance Analysis

Some of the procedures under this heading overlap with those already discussed in the previous section. Here, however, we are addressing ourselves more explicitly to the question: "What aspects of the test stimuli are causing difficulty for this subject?" The subject may show some evidence of pathological indicators, such as rotation of the figures, severe angulation difficulties, fragmentation, and so on. (See Chapter 5 for definitions of these terms.) If the interview analysis has not offered conclusive evidence of the nature of the problem, the examiner may proceed to test out, through the employment of specific ad hoc procedures, the precise nature of the problem. Such procedures are especially relevant when the test performance is not internally consistent, i.e., when "mistakes" are made inconsistently, or when easy items are difficult for the subject while difficult items are done more adequately.

The types of questions that require clarification are as follows: (1) Are certain features of the test stimuli casing difficulty (i.e., curves, angulation, overlapping, open figures, etc.)? (2) Is the difficulty level of the item causing the problem? (3) Are motivational (and/or fatigue) factors responsible? The task now is to provide the subject with additional test items that will help to clarify the difficulty. If, for instance, the problem seems to relate to curves, the examiner may provide new test stimuli which he now prepares (or has ready), in which the same type of design is offered except that straight lines are substituted for the curves. If angulation seems to be the difficulty, then substitute figures with different angulation are presented. If overlapping difficulty is noted, the same figures, but separated, or simpler overlapping figures are now presented. If, on the other hand, motivational factors are suspect, the examination may be repeated on another occasion and better motivation may be encouraged. If fatigue seems to have been a factor, the test may be repeated with rest periods offered between "sections" of the test.

Some subjects show rotational problems because the test paper is presented in a vertical orientation while the test card is presented in a horizontal orientation (see above). To test out the effect of the discrepant orientations of test card and test paper, the items of the test that are involved may be re-presented, this time with both paper and card in the same orientation. The relation of paper–test card orientation to organic brain damage has been explored by a number of workers (Griffith & Taylor, 1960; Hannah, 1958; Verms, 1974).

Card Sorting

A useful procedure, in some cases, is to ask the subject, after the test proper has been completed, to sort the cards into two piles: one pile containing the designs which he loves or likes most; the other pile containing the designs which he likes least. When this has been done, the examiner may inquire about the first pile: *"What is it about these cards that you like?"* Similarly, he may ask about the other pile: *"What is it about these cards that you don't like?"* The physical characteristics of the sortings may be quite evident. For instance, the subject may place the "easy" items in one pile and the difficult ones in the other. Or he may group the cards on the basis of open versus closed figures, or curves versus straight lines. Inquiry about the choices may prove to be quite revealing, however. Sometimes the cards are grouped on the basis of their symbolic (or unconscious) meaning (Suczek & Klopfer, 1952; Tolor, 1960). If the elaboration and association phases of the test have been completed, the sorting and explanation may be checked against the material obtained in those parts of the test.

Procedures for Malingerers and Nonmotivated Subjects

Some patients are very antagonistic to testing even though the examiner has attempted to establish good rapport. Others have characterological problems which interfere with effective effort and may approach the test with a nonchalant or indifferent attitude, making little effort to comply with test directions. These and many other types of individuals who are "unwilling" subjects and those who are willful malingers may produce an HABGT protocol which does not reflect their true capacities. Subjects who are referred by courts or penal agencies present similar problems in testing. The sensitive and ingenious clinician will attempt to deal with such individuals in some appropriate, adaptive manner. Šěpic (1972) found that adults who attempted to malinger on this test have very little success.

The following suggestions may be of some help in such instances. After all testing procedures have been completed, and preferably after a few days have elapsed, the copy phase of the HABGT should be read-ministered. This may suffice to demonstrate the invalidity of the previous testing since, in some cases, with the passage of time the patient may have forgotten the deliberate distortions he attempted, and make none this time, or quite different ones. Or with the passage of time motivational factors may have changed, if they were simply concurrent with the situation. If, however, significant distortions still occur during retesting, the examinee can be shown the stimulus cards in contrast to his drawings and asked, *"Does your drawing look exactly like mine?"* His response is then taken as the cue for further prodding. For example, *"You say yours is different. Well, tell me how."* And, *"Now try to make one exactly like mine."* The examiner may make use of the discrepancies between the two sets of drawings by the patient to ask him which one is better, and then to say, *"Well I see you can do much better than you did. Now, try it again, and this time make it exactly like mine."*

Another variation in retesting may prove to be helpful. When read-ministering the test after an interval of time, the test cards may be presented in an inverse position. Most of the figures thereby take on new configurational properties. The malingerer will usually be unable, for example, to reproduce his "faked" responses in the same way he did originally and evidence of his malingering thus becomes available. The changes in his productions can then be used as a basis for further discussion about his attitudes and his "goals" in taking the test.

Other Methods of Administration

A number of additional methods of administration deserve consideration. Some of these have very special purposes, such as the tachistoscopic method, while others are more generally useful, such as the recall method. In all clinical work, special situations may arise for which there is no clear-cut answer; the creative and experienced practitioner will then devise ad hoc procedures to fit such occasions and make cautious use of the findings. It should be noted that what we have called the copy phase is regarded by most clinicians as the standard procedure, and the findings from this phase are those most frequently presented in research studies.

THE TACHISTOSCOPIC METHOD

In a previous volume on the HABGT (Hutt & Briskin, 1960), the tachistoscopic method of administration was suggested "when intracranial pathology is suspected." It was thought that this method would improve diagnostic differentiation of patients with organic pathology from other nosological entities. This judgment was made, in part, on the basis of clinical experience with adults, and in part on findings by Ross and Schilder (1934) that tachistoscopic presentation results in the production of more primitive forms. Up to the present, only limited research evidence has been available to substantiate such claims, but the method still seems highly promising.

The method is essentially similar to that employed in the copy phase, the main difference being in the time of exposure of the stimulus card. The patient is told in substance: *"I'm going to show you some cards, one at a time, that have some designs on them. I shall let you look at the cards for only a few seconds. Then I'll take the card away and ask you to draw the design from memory. Do you understand? Remember, I'll show you the card for only a few seconds. Study it carefully so that you can draw it from memory when I take the card away."*

Card A is then exposed directly in front of the patient for a period of five seconds. It is then removed and the patient is asked to draw the design from memory. The remaining cards are presented in similar fashion, each card being exposed for only five seconds. The patient is free to use as little or as much paper as he wishes, and he is free to erase and correct. If desired, after the patient has completed all nine drawings by tachistoscopic presentation, the regular copy phase of the test may be administered.

The tachistoscopic method may prove to be quite threatening to some organic patients. For this reason, great care should be taken to gain rapport, and ample reassurance should be offered when required. Aside from the reproductions, the patient's behavior during the test is most important. In particular, evidence of feelings of impotence should be closely observed, for such evidence is a compelling hallmark of organic pathology.

A specific test of our hypothesis that the tachistoscopic method would increase diagnostic differentiation of organic pathology has been reported (Snortum, 1965). This study went beyond the testing of this hypothesis in that the effect upon intergroup differences among normals, neurotics, alcoholics, and organics was also explored, but we shall concentrate our discussion on the organic group. A five-second exposure was used, followed by the regular administration of the copy phase. There were 25 subjects in each of the experimental groups: normal, neurotic, alcoholic, and organic. They were matched for age (mean age about 36–37 years) and for education (mean grade about 11th–12th). All were male military personnel. The organic group consisted of 13 cases of encephalopathy due to trauma, 5 cases of encephalopathy due to arteriosclerosis, 4 cases of cerebral thrombosis, and 1 case each of postencephalitic psychomotor epilepsy, cerebral–cortical atrophy, and brain abscess and craniotomy. The neurotic group was a mixed group, as was also the alcoholic group.

A comparison was made of the efficacy of the tachistoscopic versus the copy method in differentiating among the four groups. Scoring of the records was done by the Pascal-Suttell method. On both copy phase and tachistoscopic phase scores, the order, from poorest to best, was organics, alcoholics, neurotics, and normals. Both methods differentiated the organics from normals, the copy phase at the .01 level of significance, and the tachistoscopic phase at the .001 level of significance. The latter method also differentiated the organics from the neurotics ($p = .02$), whereas the copy phase did not. Thus, despite the limitations of this study (small and mixed nosological groups, scores only for the Pascal-Suttell method), the findings serve to indicate the probability that organics are more effectively differentiated by the tachistoscopic than by the copy phase score. Further exploration of this finding seems warranted, using other scores and other populations.

Two other studies offering some indication of the value of the tachistoscopic method may be noted. Lindsay (1954) showed that the method was of value in differentiating among normals, anxieties, and hysterics. Korchin and Basowitz (1954) felt that it was useful as an indicator of ego strength.

It should be emphasized that this method is intended primarily to increase the efficacy of some types of diagnostic differentiation, mainly that of organics. It should not be used alone, but it should be considered a supplementary device that can offer supporting data when needed. At least, for individual diagnostic study, it should be supplemented by the use of the copy phase. Qualitative indicators and configurational scoring, as well as observational data, should all enter the diagnostic picture. Of course, in any well-rounded psychological study, other kinds of psychological test data should also be available. In the author's opinion, in the present stage of our knowledge qualitative and configurational evaluation are more desirable for individual diagnosis than are objective scores. (See Chapter 6 for discussions of qualitative and configurational evaluation.)

THE RECALL METHOD

One of the variants in administering the Bender or the HABGT is the recall method. The usual procedure is to request the examinee to reproduce from memory the designs which he drew during the copy phase. If the copy phase is followed by the recall method, this would possibly affect results which might thereafter be obtained with such other procedures as the elaboration phase and the tachistoscopic method. Hence, a choice has to be made based upon the purpose of the testing, which guides the form of test administration. As we shall see, the recall method has some possible advantages over other methods of administration, mainly in the differentiation of organics from nonorganics. However, neither clinical nor research evidence indicates any overall advantages of this method. Possibly this is one of the principal reasons why only about 20% of psychologists who use the Bender also employ the recall method (Schulberg & Tolor, 1961).

We shall review briefly selected studies that have explored the utility of the recall method. It would be advisable to keep in mind that there is no single method for administration and that methods of scoring and evaluating the results also vary. These factors alone would account for much of the variability in findings. In addition, there are the usual problems of definition of nosological groups, experimental design, and validity criteria which influence all research work in this field.

The earliest experimental study of the efficacy of the Bender recall used sparse and simple critria (Hanvik & Andersen, 1950). Three groups were compared (on both copy reproductions and recall reproductions): cerebral lesions in the dominant hemisphere; cerebral lesions in the non-dominant hemisphere; and controls (consisting of surgical and general medical patients). The only significant differences that were obtained for intergroup comparison on the recall material was that brain-damaged patients showed more rotations than the control goups. The two scores that were used were the average number of designs recalled, and the number of rotations of 30 degrees or more.

In a later study, Tolor (1956) investigated the relative efficacy of the recall of digits and the recall of Bender designs with three groups: organic; convulsive; and psychogenic. The three groups differed significantly in the average number of Bender figures recalled, the means for the three groups being: organics 3.69, convulsive 5.5, and psychogenic 5.53. It was also found that Bender recall differentiated better than digit recall with respect to organicity, but it was not effective in predicting organicity in individual cases. Tolor (1958) did a cross-validational study, this time using groups of schizophrenics, character disorders, and organics. The groups were matched for intelligence and approximately matched for age. Using as his recall score the total number of whole and partly, correctly and incorrectly reproduced designs on recall, the organics did significantly more poorly on recall than the other two groups, and the two functional groups did not differ significantly.

Reznikoff and Olin (1957) also attempted to determine whether organics could be differentiated from schizophrenics on recall. Using three scores for recall, they found that organics did more poorly than schizophrenics on the "Good Recall Score." They also compared the recall scores of the convulsives with the nonconvulsives, and, unlike Tolor, found no significant differences. Another study used geriatric patients (over 60 years of age), and divided the population into three subgroups, matched in age, in terms of organics, doubtfuls, and functionals. It was shown that in both copy and recall phases there were significant differences in scores from the functionals (highest) through the doubtfuls, to the organics (poorest) (Shapiro, Post, Löfving, & Inlis, 1956). Test materials consisted of six simplified and enlarged Bender-Gestalt designs.

Olin and Reznikoff (1957, 1958) conducted two other studies designed to test the efficacy of the recall method in differentiating diagnostic groups, as well as to explore other factors such as the difficulty of the designs. In these studies they used a modified scoring system adapted from that developed by Pascal and Suttell. In the 1957 study, organics, schizophrenics, and student nurses were compared. An anlaysis of differences on scores for each design revealed that only on design 4 did the schizophrenic patients do significantly better than the organics. Normals did better than schizophrenics only on design 6, while they did significantly better than organics on designs 2, 5, 6, 7, and 8.

A sophisticated study, utilizing five diagnostic groups (organic, schizophrenic, depressive, neurotic, and character disorder) and scores based on both the Reznikoff and Olin and the author's own revised scoring system obtained highly promising results (Armstrong, 1965). The original number in each group was small (only 20), but the groups were carefully matched, especially in age, the mean age being 33.56 years. The author's revised recall scoring system was better than Reznikoff and Olin's, and it differentiated the organics from the nonorganics remarkably well. There was little overlap in the two groups and ". . . only 21% of nonorganic patients had as high or higher a recall score than the lowest recall score . . . obtained by any organic patient." In addition, it was found that the copy phase score differentiated organics from schizophrenics, from depressives, and from character disorders at the .001 level of significance.

These studies indicate that scores based on the recall reproductions can fairly well differentiate organics from nonorganics, as groups, and there is some evidence that refined scoring may achieve results that are applicable on an individual basis. It is questionable, however, how much better the differentiation is when made on the basis of recall scores alone in comparison with scores based on copy scores alone. Other studies (Stewart, 1957; Stewart & Cunningham, 1958) have proposed other scoring systems based on the recall material by itself. Still others have explored the relation of performance on the recall of designs to intellectual ability and to nonorganic conditions alone (Aaronson, 1957; Gavales & Millon, 1960; Goodstein, Spielberger, Peek & Olson, 1955; Williams, & Dahlstron, 1959).

Studies are needed in which the contribution of memory and of psychomotor versus visual memory are teased out in relation to performance under recall conditions. An especially interesting study along such lines was done by Schwartz and Dennerll (1969). They analyzed recall performance on the Bender of outpatient epileptics. They found that the poorest recall results were obtained with those patients suffering from both grand mal and psychomotor seizures. Results did not appear to be influenced by lateralizable EEG abnormalities, multiple seizure types, or continuing occurrences of grand mal seizures. They concluded that in those patients with grand mal and psychomotor seizures combined, the psychomotor element was crucial and that consequent impairment led to short-term visual memory defects. Another study, by Rogers and Swenson (1975), sought to evaluate the relative contributions of memory and distractibility on Bender-Gestalt recall performance. They used 65 patients who had been referred for evaluation of possible intellectual defects (age range 16 to 78 years), analyzing their performance on the Bender-Gestalt recall and the Wechsler Memory Scale. They were able to conclude that the Bender-Gestalt recall was a good screening measure of memory, whereas the factor of freedom from distractibility did not correlate highly with performance. The correlation of the Bender-Gestalt recall score with the Wechsler Memory Scale score was 0.74.

Many issues remain to be resolved. In order to evaluate the true significance of the recall method of administering the test, it is imperative to control for exposure time in presenting the test cards before recall is attempted. If subjects are first required to copy the designs before the recall aspects of the test is employed, unknown variations in "experience" with the test designs as well as uncontrolled exposure before recall can contaminate the findings. Well-designed studies in which these factors are evaluated are clearly needed.

GROUP METHODS

The usefulness of the Bender-Gestalt Test or the HABGT as a screening device has been noted previously. This function would seem to be especially important in screening young children in school for further study in connection with severe personality problems, perceptual immaturity, and weak ego development, as well as for possible organic disturbance. Another important function for group administration would be in research, since large numbers of protocols or related information could thus be obtained relatively easily. One study interested in exploring the meanings of the designs to college students obtained the association data to the designs by group administration, without however, requiring that the designs be reproduced (Suczek & Klopfer, 1952). As far back as 1945, this author suggested the possible use of group administration and offered proposals for minimal conditions for such administration (Hutt 1945a).

A number of approaches have been used in the administration of the test as a group procedure. In testing young, immature children, especially, 2–4 children are each given a set of cards arranged in the correct sequence. They are asked to copy the card on the top of the stack and when all have completed this they are then asked to turn to the next card. The remaining cards are copied in a similar fashion. Dinmore (1972), for example, has used this procedure in obtaining developmental scores for young children. This method has the advantage that the examiner can observe unusual behavior during the test and take this into consideration in making individual evaluations. The method is also useful with small groups of psychiatric patients.

More typical group procedures involves testing larger groups— perhaps 15–20 individuals at the same time. A method that has been employed fairly frequently involves the use of enlarged test cards— usually 3–4 times larger than the standard set. Such cards have to be specially prepared, of course, by the examiner or a draftsman. Keogh and Smith used this kind of procedure (1961), placing the test cards in a holder at the front of the room, in clear view of the primary grade children. Tiedeman (1971) utilized this method in a large cross-cultural study in which she examined 7-year-old children in 13 countries. Other investigators have employed special test booklets with the test designs reproduced, one to a page, at the top of the pages. Group testing has also been done by projecting the test designs, with an opaque or slide projector, onto a large screen. Correlations of between .75 and .87 have been obtained between sets of scores derived from individual and group administration with kindergarten children (Becker & Sabatino, 1971; Ruckhaber, 1964). Although this degree of correlation is fairly high, it indicates that considerable variation in results can be obtained in some cases. Keogh and Smith's (1961) study was quite comprehensive. They examined 221 kindergarten children assigned to one of three groups based on a stratified random sampling. One group was given the test individually, another was given the test with special booklets, and the third was shown the enlarged designs on special cards. Using the Pascal-Suttell method of scoring, no significant differences were found among the three methods in relation to average scores. However, no check was made for possible differences that might have been obtained for the same individuals if they had been tested by differing methods. A study done with adults also found no significant *group differences* between individual and group methods of administration (Blum & Nims, 1953).

Such findings suggest that group methods of administration are valuable. One should not conclude, however, that there would not be significant and important differences in individual cases. Of course, group administration loses a great deal of direct observational material which can be highly useful in clinical work. Moreover, we have no evidence, as yet, of the possible effects of group administration on psychiatric or emotionally disturbed individuals. Probably, the most important use of group adminstration is for screening purposes, especially with primary grade children. These findings can lead to further individual study when appropriate.

OTHER EXPERIMENTAL APPROACHES

Isolated attempts have been made to explore still other variations in adminstration. We have already referred to the study in which multiple-choice selections of test designs were employed (Niehbur & Cohen, 1956). In studying the relative contribution of perceptual and motoric factors in test protocols, a comparison was made of the performance on the standard task and one in which the subjects reproduced the designs by placing pieces of felt on a felt board (McPherson & Pepin, 1955). It was found, incidentally, that performance was influenced primarily by covert perceptual responses.

Other procedures have been employed, principally to increase the test's differential capacity for organicity. One worker employed figures reproduced in relief on plastic plates (Barker, 1949). In this pilot study it was learned that this method appears to be much more sensitive for such differential diagnosis than the conventional method, but no data were presented. Another worker used figures designed with partially raised thumbtacks (Parker, 1954), and also found that brain-injured patients were even more effectively differentiated from nonorganics by this tactual–kinesthetic method than by the standard method.

A simpler and potentially much more useful method, on both practical and theoretical grounds, has been offered by Canter (1966). In this study the results obtained under conventional administration were compared with those in which subjects were asked to reproduce the figures on paper with curved, intersecting lines, called "background interference." As can be expected when figure–ground problems are made more complicated, the organics showed greater decrements under the latter conditions than did a group of nonorganics. In a cross-validational study, almost no overlap was found between organics and nonorganics. In a later study, in which a modified scoring method was employed, Canter (1968) found that the Background Interference Procedure (BIP) did significantly identify brain-damaged patients. Interscorer reliability was high. Song and Song (1969) found that in a study with brain-damaged retardates and other mental retardates, the BIP procedure was effective in differentiating the organics from the nonorganics. Adams and Canter (1969) were able to show that "ability to cope with the BIP effect is fairly well established by age 13." It seemed to have little relationship to intelligence as measured. In a recent study, Pardue (1975) was able to show that the BIP with Pascal-Suttell scoring differentiated male brain-damaged patients from male schizophrenic patients.

Psychologists have been ingenious in their modifications of test administration and test interpretation. It is to be hoped that even more fruitful techniques and theories will gradually emerge from these efforts.

5

Specific Test Factors and Their Interpretations

We shall now present and discuss those specific test factors which have been found useful in interpreting responses to the HABGT. Wherever possible the interpretations are founded on experimental evidence derived specifically from the Bender Test or one of its variations. However, it must be noted that there is still a lack of fully adequate, empirical evidence for some of the statements which follow. In such instances we must rely upon extended clinical experience, checked against clinical criteria and behavioral evidence in a wide variety of situations: diagnostic, therapeutic, and consultative. Even when experimental evidence seems to confirm our impressions, we should not regard this as the final word. In some cultural–situational contexts*, and in some individual instances, the end-

---

* I do not believe that any test can be entirely independent of differences in social–cultural influences, although the HABGT is largely independent in such respects. Gillmore, Chandy, & Anderson (1975) found no significant differences between the scores of Mexican American primary grade children and the norms on the Koppitz test, although these children tended to make more errors than "normal" after 7 years of age. No significant differences were found between black and white brain-damaged patients, except in the nonepileptic group, where blacks scored better than whites (Butler, Coursey, & Gatz, 1976).

It should be clearly understood that visual–motor development per se can be affected by developmental experiences in visual–motor behavior. Deprivation of such experiences is particularly likely to retard this development. Marked differences in widely differing cultures can also have their effects on such development. Even such differences in early experience as living in mountainous regions versus living in a region of plains can affect both perception and motoric phenomena, as has been demonstrated by Segall, Campbell, and Herskovitz (1966). Research evidence indicates, however, that in modern urban societies such differences in visual–motor development have been fairly well equalized by about age 9 or earlier. (Greene & Clark, 1973; Sonoda, 1973; Taylor & Thweatt, 1972). Certainly, the kinds of

product proves to have a highly idiosyncratic meaning. It is assumed that the careful clinician will not seize upon any one, or even more than one, bit of evidence to make sweeping generalizations about the individual under study. Rather, each factor, which may have several meanings even for the same patient, should lead to an interpretation which is more in the form of a hypothesis rather than a conclusion. When hypotheses of this kind are used to *explore the possible meaning of the behavior,* and are evaluated against other pieces of evidence, especially against possibly conflicting interpretations, they will have served a useful and creative clinical function. The final clinical summary will then contain *probable* implications of the findings, together with *possible* implications. All clinical statements must be regarded as probabilities rather than as confirmed conclusions.

A number of introductory observations are in order. The interpretations that are offered for each of the test factors were derived, in the main, from clinical and experimental evidence with adults. In most instances, the same or similar interpretations would have comparable validity for children 7 years of age or older. However, two qualifications are needed. First, the level of intelligence, while reflected in perceptual–motoric functioning, is more likely to influence perceptual–motoric functioning in younger children than in adults. Hence, especially with moderately to severely retarded children, the meaning of test behavior may require considerable additional exploration. Second, when children are found to have some significant perceptual lag, their test behavior may be seriously influenced and thus require quite a different interpretation. Of course, in the case of any significant and relevant handicap—such as serious visual defect, gross muscular incoordination, severely limited visual–motoric experience—the results should be evaluated with great caution.

It should also be clear that certain kinds of distortions or deviations in the reproductions may be due to extrinsic factors such as a poor or rough writing surface, errors in the stimulus figures (which we have, unfortunately, observed in some instances), improper pencil for drawing, and hurried conditions of testing. It is assumed that the examiner will duly note such extrinsic factors, *recording them in detail on the Revised Record Form*.

Each of the factors discussed below is presumed to be related to specified personality processess or outcomes. The clinician begins by assuming that the factor has the meaning(s) attributed to it. He may suspect other possible meanings. He may also develop alternate or modified

---

phenomena this chapter deals with are usually attributable to personality rather than developmental differences in visual–motor experience. In any case, the HABGT used as a projective test, depends far more on such personality factors. (See Chapter 7 for other studies.)

hypotheses concerning the significance of a factor as it recurs under different circumstances or is present in a new configuration. (This kind of rein-
terpretation is especially likely to occur during analysis of the elaboration
phase material.) Thus, the *process* of interpretation is guided by (but not
limited to) the typical meanings of the several factors and is continuously
confirmed, modified, or rejected on the basis of new evidence. (In objective scoring, as in our Psychopathology Scale, we assume that the weights
represent the typical loadings which the factor represents, and that vari-
ances from such loadings tend to cancel themselves out.)

In addition to the listing, definition, and interpretation of test factors
which follow, we have added a listing of several other factors which have
been reported by other workers. Our own list of factors and their interpretation have been modified in the light of new evidence since the last
publication of this volume.

The discussion of test factors is presented under five major groupings:
organization, deviations in size, deviations in form, gross distortion, and
movement.

FACTORS RELATED TO ORGANIZATION

1. Sequence*†

DEFINITION

Sequence refers to the relative degree of regularity in the successive
placement of the drawings on the page(s) used in making the reproductions. The expected order of successive placements is either from *left to
right* or from *top to bottom*. Sequence is scored in terms of the number of
shifts which occur as a deviation from the order in succession which the
examinee has already manifested. When the examinee places his successive drawings in order from right to left or from bottom to top, this is
scored as one shift in sequence. Otherwise, *each time* the sequence is
altered it is counted as one shift. Thus, when an examinee has been
arranging his drawings from left to right and then places the next figure
above or below or to the left, this is counted as a shift in sequence. *The
score on Sequence is the total number of shifts.* Chart 1 illustrates examples and scores for such shifts. If an examinee places each drawing on a
separate page, this is considered an *irregular sequence* (see below) and is
counted as 2 shifts. (Note: allowance is made, and no score for shift in

* Refers to items used in the Psychopathology Scale, Chapter 7.
† Refers to items used in the Adience–Abience Scale, Chapter 7.

A 1	**A**		
2 ⓢ 3 ⓢ 4 5 6 ⓢ 7 8	1 2 3 ⓢ 4 5 6 7 8		
Example 1: 3 Shifts	Example 2: 1 Shift		
A 1 2 3 ⓢ 4 5 6 ⓢ 7 8	**A** 1 2 3 ⓢ 4 5 6 ⓢ 7 8		
Example 3: 2 Shifts	Example 4: 2 Shifts		

Chart 1. Examples of shifts in sequence. The circled S's indicate the point at which a shift in sequence may be noted. In example 1, the first shift occurs from figures 2 to 3, since previous sequence was from left to right; the same applies to the shift from figures 6 to 7. In example 3, no shift is counted from A to 1, since the general direction of sequence has not yet become manifest, but a shift does occur from figures 3 to 4 since the prior sequence had been from top to bottom.

sequence is counted, when the examinee reaches the edge of the paper and places the next figure in an appropriate space below.)

Sequence is characterized as: normal or methodical; overly methodical; irregular; confused or symbolic. The definitions and Psychopathology Scale values (PSV) for each characteristic are given below.

Confused or symbolic sequence (PSV = 10.0): Drawings are placed in a jumble on the page—that is, without any apparent plan—or some symbolic arrangement is evident. A symbolic placement may be a figure-eight pattern, spiral pattern, etc.

Irregular sequence (PSV = 7.0): More than one shift in sequence, but no obvious confusion or jumble can be detected.

Overly methodical sequence (PSV = 4.0): No shift occurs; the figures are placed in rigid sequence, without deviation.

Normal or methodical sequence (PSV = 1.00): Only one shift in sequence occurs.

INTERPRETATION

In addition to the research literature on organizational factors in spontaneous paintings, there is significant but limited research data on the significance of "sequence" on Bender reproductions (Byrd, 1956; Clawson, 1959; Mosher & Smith, 1965). Only one of these was done on adults (Mosher & Smith), and that study was concerned primarily with brain-damaged patients. We believe that the way an individual organizes his reproductions on the page (or pages) tells us something about his organizational and planning attitudes and skills. The highly compulsive individual is likely to arrange his drawings precisely in correct sequence, not even permitting the spontaneous adaptations to occur that are suggested by the objective features of the designs or space requirements. On the other hand, highly anxious neurotics and especially agitated schizophrenics tend to show irregularity to confusion in the sequential placement of the figures. Thus, the "style" of work, in this respect, is an important indicator of this aspect of personality "style" (Shapiro et al., 1965). It is assumed that the more rigid the personality the more rigid the cognitive style is likely to be. Thus, normal individuals, unless under severe stress, tend to use a methodological sequence, whereas neurotics tend to use either irregular or overly methodological sequences.

Donnelly and Murphy (1974) did a specific study of the relation between sequence and impulse control in psychiatric patients. An analysis of styles of sequence for 37 bipolar and 30 unipolar depressives revealed that irregular sequence was indicative of lack of control and was characteristic of bipolar depressives (manic–depressives), while overly methodical sequence was indicative of (overly) methodical impulse control and' was characteristic of unipolor depressives.

The way in which the ego controls behavior, making it overly rigid or spontaneous in functioning, is important in the total evaluation of the personality. For this reason, in *inferential analyses* of records (see Chapter 6), *sequence* is considered early in the development of hypotheses about the individual. A confused sequence is very likely to be indicative of a highly disturbed individual, and is frequently found in the records of anxious schizophrenics and patients with delirium, dissociative and toxic psychoses, and manic or hypomanic conditions.

Our own count of the frequency of three types of sequences in the records of 80 "normal" college students, matched individually for age and sex (40 males and 40 females) with 80 outpatient neurotics (mainly anxiety and mixed reactions), shows the following:

Sequence	Normal	Overly Methodical	Irregular
Normals	62	13	5
Neurotics	9	41	30

Another consideration in interpreting sequence is the point in the record at which a shift occurs. Possible hypotheses concerning causative factors in producing the shift may yield a harvest of important hypotheses about the individual. Was it the particular design which caused some upset? The data in the elaboration and association phases may be quite revealing. Was it the point on the page which had been reached? An example of shifts in sequence which occur on this basis is that of the individual who follows a regular sequence, lines up his drawings on one side of the page, then follows the same pattern on the other edge of the page, but suddenly finds himself out of room on the page and then crowds the remaining figures either at the bottom of the page, or indiscriminately in blank spaces left on the page. The lack of anticipatory planning and the borderline ego control which are thus made manifest may uncover an aspect of this individual's functioning which was not manifest in other areas of his social behavior, in other test situations or in interview. The examiner will observe the individual's behavior closely when shifts of this nature occur, in the search for evidence of anxiety, disorganization, or even regression. Psychological characteristics which may be related to such functioning include: low frustration tolerance, high latent anxiety, indecisiveness, excessive rigidity, covert feelings of inadequacy, and compulsive doubting.

Sequential progression in the placement of the figures from right to left may indicate negativistic or rebellious tendencies in the personality. The examiner should also check the possibility that cultural factors may have contributed to such functioning.

Placement of each figure on a separate page (usually in or near the

center) is likely to indicate egocentricity, as well as oppositional characteristics. In our sample of 80 neurotics referred to above, 6 of the 8
patients who were judged to be narcissistic showed this characteristic.

In general, patients use either a single sheet of paper or two sheets,
using only about half of the second sheet. The use of more than two sheets
should be regarded as unusual and occurs most typically among
psychopaths, egocentric individuals, manics, and schizophrenics with
ideas of grandiosity.

2. Position of the First Drawing*†

DEFINITION

This factor refers to the placement of figure A on the page, whether
the examinee uses a single page for all of the drawings or uses more than
one page.

Abnormal placement (PSV = 3.25): Any portion of the drawing is
within one inch of any edge of the page.

Normal placement (PSV = 1.0): The *entire figure* lies within the
upper one-third of the page, and *no portion* of the figure is less than one
inch from any edge of the page.

Other placements: These are not scored but will be considered in
terms of possible interpretive significance.

INTERPRETATION

We believe that this first placement choice of the individual in responding to the test situation is an important one, although its meaning is
not always unambiguous. Our own research data, especially with the
Abience–Abience Scale, support the use of this factor, as does our general
clinical experience with it. Unfortunately, we must note that there is no
other research evidence available which supports our position. The study
by Byrd (1956) did make a limited test of this factor, but defined differently
from our criterion, and did not find any statistically significant differences
between well-adjusted children and those in need of psychotherapy. With
the adult population of 160 cases which we have utilized in gaining empirical verfication, we found that 41 neurotics showed abnormal placement
while only 10 normals did. In individual clinical study of the neurotics,
there seemed to be great significance when abnormal placement occurred.
Highly abnormal placements, such as in the lower left-hand or lower
right-hand corners of the page, have, *without exception,* been correlated

---

* Refers to items used in the Psychopathology Scale, Chapter 7.
† Refers to items used in the Adience–Abience Scale, Chapter 7.

with highly abnormal personality adjustment. Thus, in 207 consecutive cases in which this occurred, during the author's clinical experience since 1944, such placements have always been associated with conditions such as: schizophrenia, highly anxious neurotic states (with borderline psychotic processes possible), extreme paranoidal reactions, and, in a fewer instances, malingering associated with a psychopathic state. It has never been noted in either cases of "good" adjustment or in confirmed cases with organic brain damage.

The general pattern of approach–avoidance of the individual seems to be associated with the type of placement. Timid or fearful people tend to place their first drawing in the extreme upper left-hand corner of the page, and frequently also reduce the size of the figure. On the other hand, narcissistic, egocentric, and blatantly psychopathic characters tend to place the first drawing in the center of the page, usually enlarging the size of the figure, and frequently employing a single page for each of the drawings. In developing hypotheses about the placement of the first figure, other phenomena associated with this drawing should be considered, such as size of the figure, distortions in the Gestalt, closure problems, and relative size of the two parts of the figure.

3. Use of Space, 1*†

DEFINITION

This refers exclusively to the spacing between *successive or adjacent drawings*. The criterion is *always* the preceding or adjacent figure, and space is judged in terms of the *relevant axis* of that figure. Thus, when space is judged in relation to two figures in the same horizontal plane, the *horizontal* axis of the drawing at the *left* is considered. When space is judged in relation to two figures in the same *vertical* plane, the vertical axis of the drawing *above* is considered. When the drawing is placed between two figures (either to the left or above), the relevant axis of the *nearer* figure is considered.

This factor can be either normal or abnormal. It is *abnormal* if the space between two successive drawings is either *more than half the size* of the relevant axis of the preceding or adjacent figure, or is *less than one-fourth the size* of that axis.

Abnormal use of space (PSV = 10.0): It can be abnormal and excessively constricted, or it can be abnormal and excessively expansive. In either case, abnormal space is scored when the phenomenon, as defined above, occurs on *two or more occasions*.

* Refers to items used in Psychopathology Scale, Chapter 7.
† Refers to items used in the Adience–Abience Scale, Chapter 7.

Normal use of space (PSV = 1.0): It is neither excessively constricted nor expansive, as defined above.

INTERPRETATION

Both this factor and the next factor (Use of Space, II) seem to be related to basic modes of personality adaptation as manifested in perceptual–motoric performance. There is considerable evidence concerning this relationship derived from studies of drawing and painting, especially in children, but also in disturbed adults. More directly pertinent to our use of these factors is the recent work on perception conducted by many investigators. Piaget (1950) had proposed that the tendency toward "centralization" is very pronounced in young children. This type of diffusion in perception causes size overstimulation. As children develop they decentralize attention and can "scan" more, so that this tendency decreases with age and by the adult level individuals do not make consistent estimation errors and veridical size perception appears. A recent study compared size estimation in emotionally disturbed children with that in schizophrenic adults (Davis, Cromwell, & Held, 1967). Using the Harris materials (Harris, 1957), which consist of pictures of a square, a dominance scene, an acceptance scene, a rejection scene, an overprotective scene, and a neutral scene, they were able to show: (1) children (mean age 11 years) tended to overestimate size; (2) there were differences in size estimation of withdrawn as compared with acting out and disturbed children; (3) paranoid and good premorbid schizophrenics underestimated size whereas nonparanoid and poor premorbids overstimated size. Such findings indicate that both perceptual maturity and emotional adjustment influence size estimation.

In our test factor we are dealing with the *relative* estimation–reproduction of successive figures. Thus we believe we are maximizing our measure of perceptual–motoric behavior in terms of adaptive factors more than in terms of perceptual maturation factors. Strong supportive evidence for this definition of our factor as a personality measure can be found in the studies by Byrd (1956) and by Clawson (Clawson, 1959). The specific interpretations we have previously suggested are "confirmed" in these researches. Moreover, our own data in connection with the Psychopathology Scale (differences between normal and neurotic and between neurotic and schizophrenic groups are significant at the .01 level) and with the Adience–Abience Scale (in which successive cross-validations supported the use of this factor) offer further support for the following interpretations. Additional support has been found in studies by Culbertson and Gunn (1966) and by Mlodnosky (1972).

An excessive amount of space between successive drawings tends to correlate with behavior that is characterized as hostile, "acting out," and assertive. Constricted use of space is related to passivity, withdrawn behavior, and schizoid tendencies. The possibility of repressed hostility and of masochistic trends may also be associated with constriction. In general, abnormal use of space is indicative of some form of emotional maladjustment, the precise nature of which may be more fully inferred from further analysis of this and other factors on the HABGT.

We believe that we can generalize to the assertion that use of space is one important indication of the individual's attitudinal orientation of himself in relation to the world. More specifically, whether hostile feelings are openly and appropriately expressed or whether they are suppressed and distorted can often be inferred from this stylistic feature of the reproductions. Actively paranoidal adults tend to use excessive space (in the Use of Space factors I and II), and tend to reproduce the figures as much smaller than the stimuli. Frequently they compress all of the drawings into less than half of a page, make them very small, and leave much space between figures.

4. Use of Space, II *(Compression Versus Expansion)*†

DEFINITION

This factor refers to the size of the reproductions in relation to the test stimuli upon which they were based. Table 1 indicates the "normal" limits

Table 1
Normal Height and Width Limits for
Factor 4 (in inches)*

Figure No.	Height Limits	Width Limits
A	0.67 to 1.00	1.18 to 1.97
1		3.11 to 5.20
2	0.27 to 0.40	2.94 to 4.96
3	0.67 to 1.10	1.14 to 1.89
4	1.10 to 1.81	1.00 to 1.67
5	0.79 to 1.34	0.79 to 1.34
6	1.02 to 1.76	1.97 to 3.31
7	0.97 to 1.53	1.10 to 1.81
8	0.35 to 0.59	1.85 to 3.07

* The package of Revised Record Forms contains a scoring template for these limits.

† Refers to items used in the Adience–Abience Scale, Chapter 7.

for each figure in terms of height and width. A reproduction is considered to be *compressed* if either of its dimensions is less than the limits in Table 1. It is considered *expanded* if either of its dimensions exceeds these limits. This factor is no longer included in the Psychopathology Scale but a variation of it is included in the Adience–Abience Scale.

INTERPRETATION

We have already referred to research evidence concerning this factor. Constricted use of space tends to be related to withdrawn, fearful, and covertly hostile modes of behavior. Expansive use of space is related to overly assertive, rebellious, and egocentric modes of behavior. Sometimes all figures are either constricted or expanded. In such instances the probability that the hypotheses we have advanced are relevant is very great. When only a few of the figures are constricted or expanded the probability should be regarded as less likely. When both constriction and expansion are present in the same record, it is likely that the personality is characterized by ambivalent modes of approach–avoidance behavior. We do not have precise figures to corroborate it, but the author's distinct clinical impression is that patients whom he has seen in the course of psychotherapy who have shown wide mood fluctuations have shown this ambivalent characteristic in their HABGT records.

5. Collision*

DEFINITION

Collision refers to the actual running together or overlapping of one figure by another. The perimeter of one figure must either touch or overlap the perimeter of another figure. If the line of dots or circles of one figure intrudes into the open space of an adjacent figure, but there is no actual touching or overlapping of the perimeter, this is *not* counted as collision; rather it is considered a collision tendency, and is so scored and interpreted.

There are seven subcategories of collision and collision tendency.

Collision, extreme (PSV = 10.0): Collision occurs more than 2 times.
Collision, moderate (PSV = 8.5): Collision occurs 2 times.
Collision, present (PSV = 7.0): Collision occurs 1 time.
Collision tendency, extreme (PSV = 5.5): Occurs more than 2 times.
Collision tendency, moderate (PSV = 4.0): Occurs 2 times.
Collision tendency, present (PSV = 2.5): Occurs 1 time.
No collision or collision tendency (PSV = 1.0).

* Refers to items used in the Psychopathology Scale, Chapter 7.

When the phenomena of both *collision* and *collision tendency* are present in the same record, the scores for both are summated, but in no case can the total score for this factor be more than 10.0.

INTERPRETATION

The author's major hypothesis with respect to this phenomenon, as stated in a previous publication (Hutt & Briskin, 1960), was that it was indicative of "a marked disturbance in ego function." Two qualifications must be added. (1) Collision and, especially, collision tendency are related to general developmental factors which govern motor control and perceptual acuity, so that one would expect such phenomena to appear relatively more frequently, even in normal cases, in very young children, say below 7 years of age. (2) These phenomena may also occur as a result of peripheral neurological impariment and muscular disturbances which affect motor control. We believe that when brain damage is accompained by loss in ego control, collision or collision tendency may occur on the HABGT. However, they may also occur without brain damage when there is a significant psychological disturbance in this area. Reflected in the phenomena are poor anticipatory planning, difficulty with figure–ground relationships (which shows up even more clearly on overlapping figures like design 7), and extreme degrees of impulsivity.

The phenomena do not occur with great frequency in any unselected population so that statistical tests of significance in comparisons of clinical subgroups are not readily obtainable. When the factor is present it is likely to have important, clinical significance.

In addition to our own data, we should like to refer to four studies which evaluated this factor, but not necessarily our criteria for scoring it. The study by Byrd (1956) utilized our former definition of this factor. He compared the frequency of the occurrence of the collision phenomenon in four age groups of 50 children in need of psychotherapy with 50 children who were judged to be well adjusted. In the 8–9-year-old group the frequencies were 11 and 7, respectively; in the 10–11-year-old group they were 11 and 5, respectively; in the 12–13-year-old group they were 5 and 6, respectively; and in the 14–15-year-old group they were 7 and 0, respectively. At the upper age level the difference was significant at the .02 level. When the age groups are combined, we find 37 instances of collision in the group needing psychotherapy and 18 instances in the well-adjusted group—a statistically significant difference (beyond the .01 level). Obviously, developmental factors may account for the greater frequency in the younger groups. More significant is the fact that the comparison of the oldest groups, in which we may assume considerable heterogeneity in severity of malajustment and in adequacy of good adjustment, reveals *no cases of collision* in the "normal" group, and 7 (out of 50) cases in the other group.

Clawson (1959) included this factor in an aggregate score called "use of white space." Her comparisons involved a "clinic" group (heterogeneous), and a "normal" group. Analysis of her data lend some indirect support to the validity of our hypothesis of the relationship between collision and ego control, especially in terms of congruent Rorschach data.

In terms of the capacity of this factor to assist in differentiating brain-damaged groups from other psychiatric and normal groups, two studies may be noted. In one, using a measure of "overlap designs," Hain (1964) found this factor to have a high, discriminating weight in terms of a total, successful differentiating score. The "test sign" was given a weight of 3, and only 3 other test signs (with weights of 4) out of 15 significant "test signs" had a higher weight. In a study by Mosher and Smith (1965) in which comparisons were made between 142 brain-damaged cases and 28 neurological cases (without brain damage) and 92 schizophrenics, collision was found to discriminate at the .05 level. We would expect that, at the adult level, collision would be found infrequently in a schizophrenic group such as was used in this study (acute schizophrenics who had been returned to active military duty), so that the finding of some significant difference is all the more impressive.

The author's data in which 80 normal college students were compared with 95 cases of confirmed brain damage (miscellaneous, adult group), yielded the following figures. Among the college group there was only one case of a collision tendency and one of actual collision (respective scores of 2.5 and 7.0). Among the brain-damaged group there were: 4 cases of collision, score 10.0; 5 cases of collision, score 8.5; 5 cases of collision, score 7.0; and 3 cases of collision, score 2.5. In terms of total groups, the difference in psychopathology scores on this factor is significant at the .001 level.

The use of this factor is recommended, therefore, with the provisos already indicated.

6. Use of the Margin

DEFINITION

This factor refers to the placement of any portion of a figure within one-half inch of any of the edges of the test paper. Abnormal use of the margin consists in the occurrence of this phenomenon on seven or more of the figures. Although we continue to favor the use of this factor in developing projective hypotheses, we do not include it in either the Psychopathology Scale or the Adience–Abience Scale.

INTERPRETATION

Excessive use of the margin is often indicative of covert anxiety and may represent an attempt to maintain control through the use of external support. In extreme cases of severe anxiety, and in some paranoidal conditions, all of the figures "hug" the margin very closely. It is sometimes found in the records of patients with organic brain damage and can possibly be interpreted in such instances as a compensatory attempt to maintain control and to reduce feelings of impotence. The author's clinical experience supports these hypotheses, but it must be noted that due to the relative infrequency of occurrence (in adults) and the absence of adequate criterion data there has not been a sufficient empirical foundation for inclusion of this factor in the Psychopathology or Adience–Abience Scales. However, we can furnish the following data. Among the "normal" college population ($N = 80$) only one case occurred which could be rated as abnormal use of the margin. Among the comparative neurotic group ($N = 80$) there were 4 such cases among 42 anxiety neurotics and 3 such cases among the remaining neurotics with miscellaneous syndromes. However, in a group of 50 comparable paranoid schizophrenics (active, process), there were 9 instances of this phenomenon. In the clinical work in which the author has had opportunity to observe psychoneurotic individuals in the course of long-term therapy, this phenomenon has occurred frequently whenever there was severe, covert anxiety.

Byrd (1956) found only one instance of excessive use of the margin among the 200 cases of children he studied, but it should be noted that his criterion was different from the one suggested here. On the other hand, Clawson (1959), using a composite of three criteria of "page cohesion" based on what she termed "edge tendency," "top tendency," and "bottom tendency," found 21 instances among the school population but 34 instances among the clinic population. Separately, none of these three elements in her composite reached statistical significance in tests comparing the two groups. Combining the three elements, the test of significance reached the .05 level. This finding lends support to the possible interpretation of the use of "edging" even in the case of children, but the power of the hypothesis must be considered weaker than in adults. Nevertheless, extreme instances of the use of the margin should be given careful consideration in terms of our hypothesis.

7. Shift in the Position of the Paper*

DEFINITION

This factor refers to the actual rotation of the test paper from the vertical position, in which it is presented, to the horizontal position (or a

* Refers to items used in the Psychopathology Scale, Chapter 7.

shift approximating 90 degrees). (This factor should not be confused with *rotation* or *perceptual rotation,* as defined in Factor 6, below.) Three degrees of paper rotation are considered.

> *Rotation of paper for all figures* (PSV = 10.0).
> *Rotation of paper for 3 to 8 figures* (PSV = 7.0).
> *Rotation of paper for 1 or 2 test figures* (PSV = 5.5).
> *No rotation of paper* (PSV = 1.0).

INTERPRETATION

There has been surprisingly little published comment on this factor although many clinical psychologists with whom the writer has spoken assert that they employ it in their interpretations. We have nevertheless retained it because of its apparent clinical usefulness and because original data from 1945 supported it (Hutt, 1945a). In addition, it turned out to have fairly good item validity in the construction of the Psychopathology Scale.

The specific meaning of this test behavior has been elucidated in diagnostic and therapeutic study of many adults over a period of almost 35 years. Although other factors may enter into it, there is almost always what may be described as a willfulness or even "cantankerousness" about patients who display it. In more precise terms, latent or overt passive oppositional qualities are present. In addition, there may be elements of egocentricity. Some pedantic or "fussy" individuals shift the position of the paper for each drawing, sometimes several times in the execution of a single design. Of course, prior experience, especially in drawing and sketching activities, may influence the style expressed in such behavior. In such instances simple questioning about this aspect of test behavior will usually indicate this. One should also note that children sometimes rotate the paper because of rotational tendencies (perceptual), either on a developmental or pathologically organic basis; and there is research evidence which indicates that fewer perceptual rotations occur when the card with the test stimuli and the test paper are aligned so that comparable axes are congruent (Griffith & Taylor, 1960; Hannah, 1958).

8. Shift in the Position of the Stimulus Card

DEFINITION

This factor refers to changing the position of the stimulus card from its "standard" position with the long axis parallel to the examinee's body to one approximately 90 degrees from this position, i.e., with the short axis parallel to the body.

INTERPRETATION

Some of the same conditions as those that cause the examinee to shift the position of the paper apply to this factor. There are no research data, other than those obtained by the author, to support this interpretation. A check of the two groups of individuals who were employed in testing other factors, 80 college students and 80 outpatients neurotics, showed the following: there were 7 instances in the college group in which the card was shifted at least once, according to our criterion, whereas there were 19 instances among the neurotics. Another check run on the author's own therapy cases in which oppositional trends were clearly evident indicated that in a group of 45 such cases, this phenomenon was present 32 times. Although there was no control group for this test, the data are consistent with the hypothesis, offering some indication of concurrent validity.

FACTORS RELATED TO SIZE

An individual may change the size of the reproduction without destroying its Gestalt quality and without other serious distortion. It would seem wise to consider both the changes in size and other types of deviation when refining the possible interpretative significance of changes in size. There are three useful measures of alterations in size: overall increase or decrease in size; isolated increase or decrease in size; progressive increase or decrease in size. Before commenting on these specific measures, a word is in order on expectancies concerning all of these measures.

Generally speaking, on the basis of the general experimental literature and clinical evidence on size estimation and distortions in the reproduction in size of stimuli, we should expect that anxiety and size deviation would be significantly correlated. However, there are many pitfalls in any attempt to establish such simple linear relationships between errors in size and anxiety. On the other hand, as the contradictory and tortuous research concerning the measurement of anxiety has demonstrated, anxiety has many overt forms and some covert forms. Different indices attempting to measure "anxiety" are often poorly correlated or not correlated at all. Often the measure of anxiety has no specific attributes other than that it measures some aspect of anxiety. Different writers speak of basic anxiety, chronic anxiety, test- or situation-specific anxiety, induced anxiety, and so on. On the other hand, deviations in size may reflect a number of different, and even uncorrelated factors. There is the developmental factor (Davis et al. 1967; Piaget, 1950), the emotional factor (as we shall specify), and the factor of brain pathology. Great care is therefore needed in interpreting a simple correlational study of aspects of anxiety and aspects of size deviation.

When some form of anxiety is present, it may not necessarily manifest itself in the phenomenon of size deviation. Whether or not it does so, assuming that there is a tendency for these phenomena to be related, will depend upon other aspects of the individual's style and his defensive repertoire. Some anxious people act out, others inhibit, still others somatize their anxiety, and others may show a wide variety of derivatives even in the perceptual–motoric sphere. Sometimes, when anxiety does manifest itself in the perceptual–motoric sphere, the resultant is expressed in only one of the 9 figures, but a highly significant change in size may occur in that figure or a portion of it. Hence, while our measures of change in size have some value, their contribution becomes more significant when they are considered in relation to other aspects of the total test performance. We shall have more to say about this issue in the following chapter.

9. Overall Increase or Decrease in Size

DEFINITION

This factor refers to the increase or decrease in the reproduction by one-fourth the size of either the vertical or horizontal axis of the corresponding stimulus figure. There is an *overall increase* when 5 or more of the figures meet this criterion for increase in size; there is an *overall decrease* when 5 or more of the figures meet this criterion for decrease in size.

INTERPRETATION

An overall increase or decrease is frequently a means by which anxiety manifests itself in the test situation. Children over the age of 9 years more frequently tend to increase the size of their reproductions. However, children with very high anxiety may, compensatorily, decrease the size, especially if they are also suspicious and withdrawn. Increases in size are often accompanied by feelings of inadequacy and impotence. Decreases are more often associated with covert anxiety of an intense nature. Patients with markedly disturbed ego functions, especially those whose ego functions have become "fragmented" (Hutt & Gibby, 1957), may sometimes show the phenomenon of *micropsia*, that is, extremely small reproductions.

At the overt behavioral level, increase in size appears to be correlated with compensatory, outgoing, assertive modes of performance, whereas decrease in size is related to withdrawn, passive, and inhibited performance.

There is research evidence on this test factor on the HABGT. Byrd (1956), using an older criterion measure proposed by Hutt, found that overall change in size was significantly different for well-adjusted children and children needing psychotherapy (ages 10–15), and the difference was in the expected direction. Clawson (1959) used three measures of modification in size (following Hutt) and found the measures differentiated school and clinic children at the .001 level. Surprisingly, her children ranged in age from 7 to 12 years; but her more pronounced differences, in comparison with Byrd's, may have been a function, in part, of more significant differences between her two groups. She also found that decreased figure size was significantly associated with the behavioral phenomenon of being "withdrawn" ($p = .01$). In addition, constricted figure size was related to a Rorschach measure of constriction ($p = .001$). All of the findings were in the expected direction.

On the other hand, a study of adolescents (Taylor & Schenke, 1955) compared an aggressive group with a passive group of a control group. The assignment to groups was made on the basis of responses to questionnaires by raters. The Bender protocols were scored using Peek and Quast's (1951) method. With respect to changes in size, the only positive finding ($p = .05$) was that aggressive individuals more frequently produced distortions in size than the other two groups. The differences in scoring methods, the nature of the criterion variables, and the methods of analysis may have had something to do with the generally negative results. In our view, meaningful results could not have been expected if, at the least, there were not significant differences in the anxiety levels of the groups. Another study (Gavales & Millon, 1960) with college undergraduates compared the size deviations of four subgroups: high anxiety (as measured by the Taylor Manifest Anxiety Scale) and experimentally induced anxiety; high anxiety without induced anxiety; low anxiety with induced anxiety; and low anxiety without induced anxiety. It was found that the groups with induced anxiety produced significantly smaller Bender reproductions and the groups high in anxiety tended to be different in a similar manner from those low in anxiety.

Both Kai (1972) and Naches (1967) found that increased size in the drawings of young children reflect emotional disturbances and acting out tendencies. The work of Elliott (1968) as well as that of Kai supports the use of this factor, when there is a decrease of size, as an indicator of other types of emotional problems (involving withdrawal and inhibition).

In the author's own data, the significance of anxiety is more clearly shown. When the neurotic group ($N = 80$) is compared with the "normal" group ($N = 80$) in terms of overall increase or decrease in size on the HABGT (as defined), the results are significant in the expected direction at the .05 level. Moreover, when the subgroup of anxiety neurotics ($N = 42$) is compared on this factor with the total college group, the difference is significant at the .001 level.

10. Progressive Increase or Decrease in Size

DEFINITION

This factor refers to the increase or decrease in the size of the reproductions relative to the stimulus figures. *Progressive increase* is said to
occur when there is a progressive increment in the size, by any measure-
able amount, over at least 6 figures. *Progressive decrease* occurs when the
same criterion is met but there is a decrement on at least 6 figures.

INTERPRETATION

This factor is tentatively being retained although there is little research evidence to support it. Clawson's (1959) data are supportive but
not definitive. Our own data have not lent themselves to an adequate
statistical test. However, clinical experience continues to support the following hypotheses, which may, at this time, be taken to have low
strength.

When a record clearly shows a tendency toward constant increase in
size of the figures, it is likely to be associated with irritability, tendency
toward loss of control, and acting out impulsively. Progressive decrease is
likely to be associated with tendencies toward withdrawn, inhibited, and
depressed reactions. Often psychosomatic complaints are present. In general, the phenomenon seems to be related to some type of low frustration
tolerance and poor ego controls. Although research data are needed, we
rely heavily upon our clinical impressions with respect to this factor.

11. Isolated Increase or Decrease in Size

DEFINITION

This factor refers to either an increase or a decrease in a portion of a
figure or of a single total figure in relation to the other figures. The criterion
which has been applied to changes in the sizes of parts of figures is that it
is one-third larger or smaller than other parts of that figure. The criterion
applied to a total figure is that it is about one-fourth larger or smaller than
the other reproductions.

INTERPRETATION

It is felt that isolated changes in the size of parts of a figure or of a
single total figure are clinically significant. Such meanings are likely to be
highly idiosyncratic, although changes in some individual figures (insofar

as size is concerned) may be more frequent than in other figures either because of their perceptual properties or because of their tendency to elicit symbolic associations (Sternberg & Levine, 1965; Story, 1960; Suczek & Klopfer, 1952; Tolor, 1960). Isolated changes in size may be regarded as "slips of the tongue" occurring in the perceptual–motoric area of behavior; although they may occur by chance, a much stronger hypothesis is that they are the result of some emotional disturbance and reflect an underlying personality process which is not easily and openly revealed by the individual.

In addition to the use one may make of the "general meanings" of the figures as adduced in research studies (limited as these may be), one should look for clues about the possible meaning of isolated shifts in size in terms of other "internal evidence." Of foremost importance in this regard are the associations that are obtained in the association phase of the test. These associations should be considered a beginning point if one wishes to explore fully the possible meanings of isolated size change. Further interview about this material can be helpful, as can other clinical data about the patient.

Isolated changes in size within figure A have been associated, frequently with comparative attitudes toward female figures (represented frequently by the circle) and male figures (represented frequently by the diamond). Similarly, such changes in figures 7 and 8 are often associated even more specifically with attitudes toward sexuality, and even more specifically toward phallic qualities (Sullivan & Welsh, 1947). In general, reduction in size is associated, we believe, with withdrawal or other repressive maneuvers, while increase in size is associated with approach and compensatory defenses toward sexual stimuli. But we must caution against "wild" conclusions based on tiny bits of evidence. On the other hand, such shreds of evidence, considered as leads for hypotheses, can be extremely illuminating and should not be discounted.

For instance, a recent study by Brannigan and Benowitz (1975) found that among adolescents uneven size of the figures was clearly related to acting out, antisocial tendencies as rated by housemothers.

The reader is reminded of Mira's (1939–1940) important findings which have led us to consider shifts in size in the vertical plane (especially if occurring on more than one figure) as indicative of conflicts in the area of relationship to authority figures, while shifts in size in the lateral or horizontal plane are considered as indicative of difficulties in forming or maintaining interpersonal relationships. The general relationship between constricted size of figures and constriction in other indices of personality functioning (Clawson, 1959), and between curves and emotionality (Breen 1953; North, 1953; Story, 1960) have already been noted.

FACTORS RELATED TO CHANGES IN THE GESTALT

The factors discussed in this section have to do with some degree of change in the quality of the Gestalt. The Gestalt is not destroyed or severely distorted, as may result from the operation of factors described in the next section, but it is altered in some qualitative way. Such changes are thought to represent psychological derivatives of a more specific nature than those discussed in the preceding section.

12. Closure Difficulty*†

DEFINITION

This factor refers to difficulty in "joining" parts within a figure or two adjacent figures which touch each other. The figures on which closure difficulty may occur are A, 2, 4, 7, and 8. Problems in "joining" may occur in connection with completing the circle or the diamond in figure A, in completing the circles in figure 2, in joining the sides of figure 4 or the junction of the curve and the open square in the same figure, and in joining the sides or connecting the adjacent parts in figures 7 and 8. The difficulty may be manifested in a number of ways: gaps at the point of joining; "overshooting the joining" (overlap at this point); erasures or corrections at the point of joining; and, noticeably, increased line pressure or redrawing at such points.

The *raw score* on this factor is the total number of closure difficulties which occur, but there are two special provisions: (1) no more than 2 closure difficulties may be counted on any one figure; and (2) on figure 2, count 2 closure difficulties as a raw score of 1, and 3 or more closure difficulties as a raw score of 2.

There are five subcategories of this factor: very severe, severe, moderate, mild, and absent.

Very severe (PSV = 10.0): Raw score is 9 or above.
Severe (PSV = 7.75): Raw score is 6–8.
Moderate (PSV = 5.5): Raw score is 3–5.
Mild (PSV = 3.25): Raw score is 1–2.
Absent (PSV = 1.0): Raw score is 0.

INTERPRETATION

Our major hypothesis relating to closure difficulty is that this phenomenon represents, at the visual–motor level, difficulty in maintain-

---

* Refers to items used in the Psychopathology Scale, Chapter 7.
† Refers to items used in the Adience–Abience Scale, Chapter 7.

ing adequate interpersonal relationships. Subhypotheses include the association between closure difficulty and fearfulness in interpersonal relationships, and the association between this phenomenon and emotional disturbance in general, in which there usually tends to be a problem in sustaining adequate and consistent cathexes with external objects. Of course, as with most phenomena, one should not expect anything like a near-perfect linear relationship with the complex end-product—some specific personality characteristic. Rather, it should be considered as *one part of a possible configuration* which expresses this linkage. Hence, our hypothesis would be supported if general trends in the predicted direction proved to be significant.

Apart from our own extensive clinical experience which supports these hypotheses, there are some research data which also lend some support. Byrd's (1956) study found that there were consistent and significant differences (at the .01 level) between well-adjusted children and children in need of psychotherapy in this test factor at age levels 8–15. If his age level data are combined, the significance of the difference is greater than .001. We would assume that this finding, while not a direct test of our major hypothesis, is consistent with the hypothesis. It should be noted that Byrd's analysis was performed with a measure of closure difficulty that is far cruder than our present measure. Clawson (1959) found that the symptom of interpersonal problems was significantly predicted by a rough measure of closure difficulty, and similarly a measure on the Rorschach was also predictable. Another indirect test was provided in Guertin's (1954b) research, in which factor analysis of Bender records of 100 adult psychiatric patients disclosed a statistical factor called ''unstable cloture'' (with a measure derived from Billingslea's scoring criteria). This factor, with a high loading among catatonics, was thought to be indicative of ''emotional imbalance.'' Additional support for a similar factor may be found in Hain's (1964) study. A much more specific test of the hypothesis was provided in Story's (1960) study of alcoholics. Using a comparison of alcoholics with a control group of nonalcoholics, he found that each of two derived measures of closure difficulty separated these groups at the .01 level of significance. In our own comparison of a neurotic group with a comparable college group, we found mean closure scores of 5.7 and 3.1, respectively, and the difference significant at the .01 level.

Thus, in a general way, we can say that closure difficulty seems to be an important indication of some form(s) of emotional maladjustment associated with severity of psychopathology, and, more specifically, there is some support for the hypothesis relating to interpersonal problems.

13. Crossing Difficulty*†

DEFINITION

This factor refers to difficulty in executing the crossing(s) which occur on figures 6 and 7. It is manifested by redrawings, sketching, erasing, or markedly increasing the line pressure at the point where lines cross. When figure 6 is drawn as two tangential curves, this is *not counted* as crossing difficulty, but two noncrossing curves *do count* as crossing difficulty. The raw score is the total number of times this difficulty occurs.

Severe (PSV = 10.0): Raw score is 3.
Moderate (PSV = 7.0): Raw score is 2.
Mild (PSV = 4.0): Raw score is 1.
Absent (PSV = 1.0): Raw score is 0.

INTERPRETATION

It is believed that this manifestation is an indication of psychological blocking and is correlated with such behavior as indecisiveness, compulsive doubting, and phobias. It is also likely to be represented in behavior at the level of difficulty in interpersonal relations, although perhaps not as specifically as in Factor 12.

In the author's clinical experience this factor is almost invariably present when some significant form of blocking is present, although the opposite is not necessarily true. The factor has also withstood the more general tests of significance in the item validation of both the Psychopathology Scale and the Adience–Abience Scale.

There have been two studies in which measures based on some aspect of crossing difficulty have been tested. In both studies (Clawson, 1959; Story, 1960), the results have shown some support for the contention that the factor is significant, but its more precise meaning awaits further research.

14. Curvature Difficulty*

DEFINITION

This difficulty refers to *any obvious change* in the nature of the curves in figures 4, 5, and 6. Such changes occur when: there is an increase or decrease in the amplitude of the curve; the curve is replaced by straight or spiked lines; the curve is flattened; the curve is made very unevenly or

---

* Refers to items used in the Psychopathology Scale, Chapter 7.
† Refers to items used in the Adience–Abience Scale, Chapter 7.

irregularly; the number of loops on figures 4 and 6 is either increased or decreased. The raw score is the total number of figures on which such changes occur.

Severe (PSV = 10.0): Raw score is 3.
Moderate (PSV = 7.0): Raw score is 2.
Mild (PSV = 4.0): Raw score is 1.
Absent (PSV = 1.0): Raw score is 0.

INTERPRETATION

Our own findings, both clinical and statistical, indicate that this factor is a highly sensitive indicator of emotional disturbance. Increases in curvature are thought to be indicative of increases in, or overly active responses in, emotionality, whereas decreases have a polar opposite meaning. Emotionally labile patients tend to produce increased curvature and depressive patients tend to produce decreased curvature. Irregularity in curve production is associated with irregularity in emotional behavior, and often, especially if associated with increase in curvature, with hostile acting out. On this factor, like all others, one should not expect there to be a simple linear relationship between curvature change and behavioral change, although such a relationship is probably more likely on this factor than on most other factors. It seems to be a rather direct expression of the pattern of internal emotional feeling.

Psychologists have long been interested in bodily and behavioral manifestations of emotional experience. Line movement, especially as represented in the drawing of curves, has been found to relate fairly well to this aspect of personality (Allport, 1937; Wolff, 1943). With respect to Bender reproductions, changes in curvature seem to reflect, rather clearly, shifting changes in emotional expression. In two separate studies involving factor analytic methods with psychiatric patients, it was found that propensity toward what is called curvilinear movements was related to "poor emotional control" (Guertin, 1952), and that curvilinear distortion was related to impulsiveness (Guertin, 1954). Byrd (1956) found curvature difficulty to differentiate well-adjusted from "poorly" adjusted children at all levels from 8 to 15 years. Clawson (1959) found, similarly, that "clinic children drew the curved line of figures out of proportion," and that "the deviation was in the direction of increased curvature." The frequency of occurrence, in her sample, did not permit an adequate test of the significance of the direction of shift in relation to specific personality manifestations. Story (1960) discovered that the nature of the change in curvature sensitively reflected such personality manifestations in al-

* Refers to items used in the Psychopathology Scale, Chapter 7.

coholics. Finally, in a subgroup of the author's experimental neurotic population ($N = 12$), increased curvature was significantly related to increased emotionality, while in another subgroup ($N = 15$), decreased curvature was significantly related to decreased emotionality. In both subgroups, independent clinical judgments were available concerning the criterion of emotionality, and changes in curvature were scored by means of the scale values on the Psychopathology Scale. Corroborative research supporting the usefulness of this factors may be found in the studies by Kai (1972) and by Brannigan and Benowitz (1975) for children and adolescents, respectively.

15. Change in Angulation*†

DEFINITION

This change refers to an increase or decrease, by *15 degrees or more,* of the angulation in stimulus figures 2, 3, 4, 5, 6, and 7. In figure 2, a change of 15 degrees or more in the angle the columns make with the horizontal rows is the criterion. In figure 3 it is a change in the angle made by the columns of dots. In figure 4 it is the angle of the curve in relation to the open square. In figure 5 it is the angle of the external dots in relation to a presumed horizontal line. In figure 6 it is the angle at which the two curves cross. In figure 7 it is the angle of intersection of the two figures. The score is the number of figures on which the defined degree of change is present.

> *Five figures* (PSV = 10.0).
> *Four figures* (PSV = 8.0).
> *Three figures* (PSV = 6.0).
> *Two figures* (PSV = 4.0).
> *One figure* (PSV = 2.0).
> *No figures* (PSV = 1.0).

INTERPRETATION

Our major hypothesis is that significant changes in degree of angulation reflect difficulty in dealing with affective stimuli, and in turn are related to problems in affective control and control of impulses. *Increased angulation,* by which we mean a change in the direction of rectangularity, is related to *decreased affectivity,* while *decreased angulation,* by which we mean a change in the direction of greater acuteness of the angle, is

---

* Refers to items used in the Psychopathology Scale, Chapter 7.
† Refers to items used in the Adience–Abience Scale, Chapter 7.

related to *increased affectivity*. We have also suggested that inaccuracy in reproducing angles is often associated with organic brain damage, and may be related to mental retardation, as well. The latter hypothesis is clearly related to the correlation between developmental and intellectual factors and accuracy in reproducing angles. The presence of angle difficulty in organics seems, however, to be attributable much more to difficulties with figure–ground problems and to primary disturbances in perception than to intellectual factors, per se.

There is substantial evidence that this factor assists in differentiating well-adjusted from poorly adjusted individuals. These findings could have been anticipated since the latter group is thought to have far greater problems in impulse control and in handling affectivity. A specific test of the hypothesis that alcoholics, who tend to suppress affect and have problems in handling affect, would perform adversely on this factor in comparison with nonalcoholics was made (Story, 1960). One measure of change in angulation was a shift in the angulation of the columns of circles in figure 2 toward the vertical position or even by a reversal of the "slant" of the columns. The other measure consisted of rotation of the upright hexagon in figure 7. On the first measure the level of statistical difference was .01, while it was .05 on the latter, both findings being consistent with the above hypothesis. Byrd (1956) found that, except for the 8–9-year-old group, children in need of psychotherapy did significantly more poorly than well-adjusted children. It is interesting to note that Byrd's data indicate that from age 10 through age 15, the relative frequencies of changes in angulation remain about constant, suggesting that age is not a significant factor above 9 years. Clawson (1959) found an even greater degree of significance in the difference between school and clinic children, the level of significance being .001. The fact that in both of these studies some children in the "good" groups showed difficulty in angulation may be indicative that some of these children also had emotional problems or that the measure, by itself, is insufficiently differentiating for such groups. In the authors' experimental groups of neurotics and college students ($N = 80$ in each group), the significance of the difference in angulation score (as defined) was above .001. A separate test was made of 14 individuals in the neurotic group who were clinically judged to be overly affective or bland in affect. Their combined angulation score was 6.7, while that of the college group was 1.9, the difference being significant at the .001 level. No test was made of differences between increased and decreased angulation.

Three other studies supply data on the efficacy of this factor in differentiating organics from nonorganics. In Mosher and Smith's (1965) study, angulation and change in slope, both rated by the criterion suggested by Peek and Quast (1951), were found to differentiate organics from nonorganics at the .01 level. Hain (1964) developed a score to identify brain damage in which 15 Bender-Gestalt signs were retained after item analysis. In the final measure for brain damage, difficulty with acute angles was retained and given a weight of 3, only three other signs having the greater weight of 4. The total score differentiated between organics, psychiatric patients, and controls. Wiener (1966) found that angulation difficulty significantly discriminated minimal neurological deficit in 8–10 year olds.

FACTORS RELATED TO DISTORTION OF THE GESTALT

The following seven factors are considered to be indicative of severe psychopathology. Although their occurrence may, on occasion, be attributable to factors other than psychopathology, their presence in a test record should raise the question of a severe disturbance. We would expect their occurrence to be only occasional in neurotic groups and significantly more frequent in psychotic and organic groups. They may also occur, however, as a consequence of transient and severe trauma, but would not be expected in such cases after recovery from the immediate effects of such trauma. Distortions typically represent loss of some aspect of ego control and are therefore to be regarded as serious.

16. Perceptual Rotation*†

DEFINITION

This factor refers to the reproduction of the test figure with a rotation of its major axis *while the stimulus card and the test paper are in their normal, standard positions*. This factor is called "perceptual" rotation to distinguish it from factor 7, Shift in the Position of the Paper. This factor is *not* scored if only a segment of the figure is rotated (as when there is a shift in the position of the external line in figure 5). Similarly, change in only some of the columns of figure 2 is *not* scored as rotation. *The score is the highest score obtained.***

> *Severe rotation* (PSV = 10.0): Rotation of 80–180 degrees on any figure.
> *Moderate rotation* (PSV = 7.0): Rotation of 15–79 degrees on any figure.

* Refers to items used in the Psychopathology Scale, Chapter 7.
† Refers to items used in the Adience–Abience Scale, Chapter 7.
** The package of Revised Record Forms contains a scoring template for degree of rotation.

Mild rotation (PSV = 4.0): Rotation of 5–14 degrees on any figure.
No rotation (PSV = 1.0): No rotation on any figure greater than 4 degrees.

INTERPRETATION

In evaluating the possible meaning of perceptual rotations, consideration needs to be given to both the degree of rotation and the frequency with
which it appears. Although we do not score for frequency of rotation in
our Psychopathology Scale (for empirical reasons in connection with that
scale), clinical interpretation will be more meaningful when this factor is
also considered. It should also be noted that rotation is an end product in
behavior and that many factors may contribute to it: e.g., age, intelligence, nature of the stimulus, degree of congruence between axes of test
figure and test paper, and type of pathology. What this really means is that
such factors should properly be taken into account in evaluating the possible significance of rotation as indicative of psychopathology. But, of
course, such considerations are important in all individual psychological
evaluations.

Severe perceptual rotation is usally indicative of profound disturbance in some aspect of ego functioning, unless accounted for by some
other clearly defined factor. In an earlier publication (Hutt & Briskin,
1960) we stated: ". . . it is most frequently found in the records of individuals who are psychotic, have intracranial pathology, or are mentally
defective." Commenting on this allegation, Tolor and Schulberg (1963)
say ". . . the multiplicity of diagnostic interpretations assigned to some of
the test factors clearly diminish their value for making specific diagnostic
judgments and . . . some type of ego impairment represents the only
common denominator. . . ." Such despair is not warranted; human behavior and tests of human behavior turn out to be complex things, and to
seek an overly simplified view of such phenomena is to demonstrate a
relatively naive view of the science of psychology.

The fact is that diverse groups show relatively high frequencies in
rotations, but there appears to be a commonality underlying this—a disturbance or inadequacy in some aspect of ego functions. For example,
Fuller and Chagnon (1962) found that, as they measured them, there were
significant differences in frequencies of rotations from normal children
(1.90), through emotionally disturbed children (15.00), to schizophrenics
(24.62). Griffith and Taylor (1960) found significantly more rotations
among organic patients than among nonorganic patients, and they also
found the following percentage frequencies for rotations (defined as angular displacement of 45 degrees or more): mental defectives, 55.9%; organics, 40.8%; and, schizophrenic, neurotic, organic, "other," and
character disorder, 22.8%. In a later study (Griffith & Taylor, 1961), they
also reported that intelligence was correlated with frequency of rotations.

Such findings as these seem to indicate that frequency of rotations is complexly related to type and severity of psychopathology; and that low level of intelligence may contribute an inordinate share of rotations. But if one is analyzing an individual record in which intelligence level is at least average and both severity and frequency of rotational difficulty are noted, psychopathology becomes highly suspect and other test (as well as clinical) indicators can be utilized to elucidate the specific meaning of the phenomena.

A considerable amount of research work has been devoted to the problem of rotations, some of which has been summarized in Chapter 2. In an analysis of the significance of rotations in connection with abnormal EEG's of children, Chorost, Spivack, and Levine (1959) shrewdly conclude that, despite problems of base rates in such populations, children who produce rotations are more likely to have abnormal EEG's than children who do not make such rotations. Hanvik and Andersen (1950) had found that, compared with a control group, organics produced more frequent rotations. Moreover, Mark and Morrow (1955) found that organics had significantly more rotations than a nonorganic, psychiatric comparison group. Hain's (1964) scoring scheme gives the highest weighting to rotations as an element in his score for identifying brain damage.

It should be emphasized that the position in which the test paper is presented, viz-a-viz the test cards, is important in relation to the phenomenon of rotation. As indicated, we prefer that the test paper be presented in a vertical orientation (with the long axis in a vertical position). The discrepancy between the axis of the paper and that of the test cards (which have the long axis in a horizontal position) maximizes the frequency and degree of rotations. Developmental studies indicate that rotations, particularly on designs A, 3, 4, and 7, tend to occur more frequently among very young children, but by age 9 years normal children rarely show rotational difficulties (Black, 1973; Weiss, 1971). These findings obtain with the test paper in the "normal" orientation. Frequency of rotations occurs more often with the paper presented in a vertical orientation. Verms (1974) found that among psychiatric patients without organic brain damage, presentation of the test paper in the vertical position produced significantly more frequent rotations than when the test paper was presented in a horizontal position. However, this study, which involved a large number of patients ($N = 349$), showed that the position of the paper was not significant with brain-damaged patients; presumably, the neurological deficit was, by itself, sufficient to induce the rotation phenomenon.

A comparison of heroin users with nonopiate psychiatric patients indicated that the users of heroin tended to rotate the designs more frequently than the nonusers (Korim, 1974).

It has been found that gifted children like to rotate the position of the paper to a horizontal position and rarely show the phenomenon of rotation of the drawings (Bravo, 1972). The reasons for the preference in having the paper in a horizontal orientation is unknown, but one can speculate that gifted children tend to be more creative, individualistic, and oppositional.

There is little doubt that ability to reproduce the designs without rotations is, in part, a function of the development of cognitive capacities. Rock (1974) has demonstrated that accurate perception of form involves, to some extent, the recognition of the concepts of "top," "bottom," and "sides." When cognitive functions are immature or when they have been disrupted, rotational phenomena tend to occur.

In work with children, we should like to cite again the studies by Byrd (1956) and Clawson (1959). The former found that the factor of rotation significantly differentiated the well adjusted children from those in need of psychotherapy at all age levels, 8–15. The incidence of rotations among the oldest group (14–15 year olds) was only 1 in a population of 50 well-adjusted children. The latter study found that when rotation was counted whenever the degree of rotation was equal to 15 degrees or more, this differentiated the school from the clinic population at the .001 level of significance. Surprisingly, "School and clinic children made about the same amount of rotation (90° to 180°)." A possible explanation for this finding is that large rotations in children often are more indicative of oppositional trends than of severity of pathology. Our own data with adults does not support the hypothesis that larger degrees of rotation are less significant diagnostically. Using our revised scale for measuring rotation we found the following: a mean score of 7.9 among 95 heterogeneous organic cases; a mean score of 7.2 among 100 heterogeneous cases of schizophrenia; a mean score of 4.3 among 80 neurotic cases; and a mean score of 1.5 among the 80 college students. Chi square tests for intergroup differences indicated that the only intergroup difference which did not reach the probability level of .01 was that between organics and schizophrenics.

The author's clinical experience suggests that mild degrees of rotation in the clockwise direction are often associated with depressive reactions. Counterclockwise rotations, especially but not necessarily mild in degree, are indicative of oppositional tendencies. Story (1960), testing the hypothesis that mild degrees of counterclockwise rotation were indicative of oppositional tendencies, and using only rotations on figure 7 in which the degree of rotation was in the range 5–20 degrees, found that this measure differentiated alcoholics from nonalcoholics at the .05 level of significance.

An important characteristic of the phenomenon of rotation concerns the degree of awareness of the patient of his rotational error. In general, there is clinical and experimental evidence to suggest that awareness of the patient of his rotation is indicative of transitional difficulties in the

perceptual area. Regressed schizophrenics and organics are usually unaware that their reproductions show rotation. Thus, when rotation occurs,
it is advisable to check the protocol on the elaboration phase for similar
rotations and to test for degree of awareness during the testing-the-limits
phase of the procedure.

Another important "limits" testing in connection with rotations, suggested in a previous publication (Hutt, 1960), is the capacity to correct
rotations when they are pointed out by the examiner. When the individual
is unable or not easily able to make a correct, nonrotated reproduction,
even when asked to "correct the drawing so that it looks just like the one
on the card," there is confirmatory evidence of the probability of either an
organic condition, or a severely regressed psychotic condition. A recent
test of this hypothesis was made by Smith and Martin (1967). They compared a group of 25 neurologically impaired patients with a group of 25
non–neurologically imparied patients. The impaired group made a significantly greater number of rotations and required a significantly greater
number of cues to correct rotations. These workers felt that the ability to
correct rotations is a more discriminating index of neurological impairment than frequency of rotations.

In clinical work, the clinician will wish to make use of all the factors
we have discussed in evaluating the significance of rotations: degree of
rotation; frequency of rotation; awareness of occurrence of rotation; and
ability to correct rotation. In addition, related data from the test will assist
greatly in reaching a more precise formulation of the meaning of the rotation in terms of the context in which it occurs. Of course, developmental
level and intellectual level will influence the interpretation of the meaning
of the rotation.

17. Retrogression*

DEFINITION

Retrogression refers to the substitution of a more primitive Gestalt
form for the more mature Gestalt of the stimulus figure. The most common forms of retrogression are as follows: substitution of impulsive loops
for reasonably well-formed circles (as in figure 2); substitution of dashes
for dots (as in figures 1, 3, and 5); and substitution of dots for circles (as in
figure 2). The criterion for counting such phenomena as retrogression is its
occurrence *at least twice on any given figure*. The psychopathology scale
value then depends upon the number of times this criterion of retrogression is met.

* Refers to items used in the Psychopathology Scale, Chapter 7.

Severe retrogression (PSV = 10.0): Present in more than 2 figures.
Moderate retrogression (PSV = 7.0): Present in 2 figures.
Mild retrogression (PSV = 4.0): Present in 1 figure.
No retrogression (PSV = 1.0): No retrogression, as defined, occurs in any figure.

INTERPRETATION

Strictly speaking, retrogression should be differentiated from developmental immaturity in the perceptual–motoric sphere, for by this term we are implying some form of reversion to an older mode of behavior rather than simply a present inadequacy. In clinical evaluation of retrogression on this test we should consider whether there is evidence of higher levels of functioning, and only when such discrepancies occur should we consider the phenomena under question to be an instance of retrogression.

Our general hypothesis is that retrogression occurs under conditions of relatively severe and chronic defense against trauma and is indicative of some degree of failure in ego integration and functioning. We expect that *some types of schizophrenic adults* would manifest this phenomenon. Such types would be characterized by disorganization of the personality and inadequate compensation for chronic conflict. However, neurotics with intense anxiety and ineffectual defenses should also be expected to display it. The problem of evaluating retrogression in children is much more complicated because developmental factors intrude much more significantly in performance, especially below the age level of approximately 9 years. It should also be noted that the points in the testing at which retrogression appears may be of considerable significance: whether in the copy phase or the elaboration phase; whether on difficult figures or on easy figures; whether in "open" designs or in "closed" designs. The possible significance of these associations requires clinical analysis, as we have indicated in previous chapters, and as we shall illustrate with case material in Part II of this book.

Various investigators have studied retrogression (or regression) on the Bender records. It is difficult to integrate the meaning of their findings because quite different definitions of retrogression have been utilized and quite variable criteria of suspected regression in behavior have been chosen. However, our analysis of these findings suggests that, generally, they consider retrogression to be indicative of some major disruption in functioning. There is not any consensus as to whether this is the result of regression in the usual sense or whether it is some form of malfunctioning. Thus, for instance, Suttell and Pascal (1952) compared the functioning of schizophrenics with both neurotics and normal children, using items from their own scoring scheme (based, in part, on previous suggestions by Hutt). They concluded that disruption of learned, regulatory responses sometimes accounts for the "regressive" phenomenon, and at other times maturation is the important factor. In this study schizophrenics and neurotics could not clearly be differentiated. One suspects that their criteria of regression accounted for these ambiguous results. On the other hand, studies by Guertin (1954c, 1955) indicate that, at least in the case of what is termed "disorganized hebephrenics," retrogressive phenomena occur significantly more frequently than in other "forms" of schizophrenia. Clawson (1959), using five criteria of Bender regression similar to our own, found that 23 of 80 school children and 57 of 80 clinic children, varying in age from 7 to 12 years, showed this phenomenon. The difference in frequencies was significant at the .001 level. She believes: "The so-called regressive signs . . . are evidence of lag in maturation rather than reversion to earlier modes of behavior," although it is difficult to learn on what basis she reaches this conclusion. However, it is interesting to note that, in agreement with this author, she believes that ". . . judgment of regression is warranted only if there is evidence of more mature forms . . . in the record."

Ames (1974), in a study of 92 older subjects between the ages of 57 and 92, separated these individuals on the basis of Rorschach data into normal adult, intact presenile, medium presenile, and deteriorated adults. The Bender records provided differentiation among these groups at a highly significant level ($p < .001$). Retrogressive features of the Bender records contributed to this differentiation. The regressive substitution of dashes for circles, especially, and for dots, has been found to be associated with emotional problems in children, particularly with aggressive behavior (Brown, 1965; Kai, 1972). Of course, regression in children is far less significant than the same phenomenon in adults.

Our own research data, utilized in the construction of the Psychopathology Scale, indicates that our measure of retrogression contributes to the differentiation of groups with greater psychopathology from those with lesser psychopathology. Although we find the score to have some value, we are even more impressed with the qualitative and clinical analysis of this factor.

18. Simplification*†

DEFINITION

Simplification refers to the reproduction of the stimulus as a simpler figure or one which is much simpler to draw. The following are examples of simplification: drawing the two parts of figure A as noncontiguous;

* Refers to items used in the Psychopathology Scale, Chapter 7.
† Refers to items used in the Adience–Abience Scale, Chapter 7.

reducing the number of elements in figures 1, 2, 3, and 5, by *at least 3 less* than in the stimulus; reducing the number of curves in figure 6; and reproducing the parts of figures 7 and 8 as rectangles or crude elipses. Simplification is *not scored* when either fragmentation or retrogression is involved; i.e., only one phenomenon is scored per drawing.

> *Severe* (PSV = 10.0): Present on more than 2 figures.
> *Moderate* (PSV = 7.0): Present on 2 figures.
> *Mild* (PSV = 4.0): Present on 1 figure only.
> *None* (PSV = 1.0).

INTERPRETATION

At the psychological level, simplification seems to represent a decrease in cathexes to external objects or tasks, or, in more behavioral terms, it represents an attempt to reduce the expenditure of energy required in completing a task or dealing with a situation. Although it sometimes occurs as a result of deliberate decrease in effort on the part of the examinee, primarily related to oppositional tendencies or a need to malinger, it usually seems to be related to difficulties in impulse control and the executive functions of the ego. Simplification does not, necessarily, reflect a profound disturbance in ego functions, but it may be present as a derivative of such disturbance. Hence, one expects to find it in organic cases and it is often associated with feelings of impotence in such cases. When other test indications of profound ego disturbance occur, the presence of simplification can then be regarded as confirmatory evidence of such disturbance.

Surprisingly little specific research evidence has been directed to this test factor, whether because of lack of confidence that this seemingly simple phenomenon is important, or because of lack of clarity about its meaning and definition. Our own hypotheses concerning it were derived, in the first place, from clinical observations of the relationship of this factor to other personality manifestations. Later, some statistical evidence was gathered. For example, this factor withstood the tests of item validation in the construction of the Psychopathology Scale and the Adience–Abience Scale. More specifically, we found the following frequencies of occurrence of some degree of simplification in our experimental populations: 1 of 80 college students; 6 of 80 neurotics; 8 of 100 schizophrenics; and 13 of 95 organics. Thus, there is a significant difference between the occurrence of this phenomenon in both organics and schizophrenics and that in "normals." However, simplification does not occur with high frequency in any subgroup, so that while it may add to the meaning of a total score in psychopathology, it does not by itself constitute a reliable differentiator. As we have noted, clinical evaluation of the phenomenon, together with other related phenomena, may add to its importance in a given record.

In two of Guertin's (1952, 1954a, b, c) factor analytic studies there is some evidence that is related to the significance of the factor we have defined as Simplification. The data indicate that "careless execution" (which is measured by factors related to our own) is a factor found in chronic schizophrenic Bender records, and that "minor inaccuracies" (again related to simplification) are especially frequent in the chronic undifferentiated group.

19. Fragmentation*†

DEFINITION

Fragmentation refers to the essential destruction of the Gestalt. It can be manifested in a number of ways. The most common are as follows: the reproduction is obviously unfinished or incomplete; or the Gestalt is drawn as if composed of separate parts, i.e., the parts are grossly separated so that the Gestalt is lost.

Severe (PSV = 10.0): Present on more than 2 figures.
Moderate (PSV = 7.0): Present on 2 figures.
Mild (PSV = 4.0): Present on only 1 figure.
None (PSV = 1.0).

INTERPRETATION

Fragmentation represents a severe disturbance in perceptual–motoric functioning and seems to be associated with decrement in the capacities for abstracting and synthesizing. It should therefore be expected to occur in diverse types of pathology in which the individual suffers damage in these functions. Although its absolute frequency of occurrence is not very great in the total clinical population, as has been demonstrated in many studies of neurotic, psychotic, and brain-damaged individuals, its appearance in a given record is highly significant of profound impairment. Various workers have defined and measured this type of distortion in diverse ways, so that results are not directly comparable. However, what Peek and Quast (1951) call "major distortion," what Pascal and Suttell (1951) call "distortion" and "part of design missing," and what Hain (1964) calls "distortion" are all closely related to our factor. Almost invariably in these and other studies this factor is shown to have high differentiating power between psychotics and normals and between or-

* Refers to items used in the Psychopathology Scale, Chapter 7.
† Refers to items in the Adience–Abience Scale, Chapter 7.

ganics and nonorganics, and is therefore given considerable weight in scores presumably measuring severity of psychopathology. Our own analysis of this factor also led to its inclusion in the Psychopathology Scale. One example of its efficacy may suffice: a comparison of mean scores on Fragmentation of the neurotic group with the heterogeneous psychotic group yielded a score of 1.1 for the former and 7.2 for the latter, the difference being significant at the .001 level.

Fragmentation, as measured, rarely occurs in the records of young children. For example, in one study of 400 cases ranging in age from 8 to 15, only 8 instances of fragmentation were noted (Byrd, 1956). Below age level 10 one would suspect that it has quite different meaning than above this age level and might be more closely related to developmental factors than to psychopathology. However, qualitative analysis of this factor may be rewarding, even in young cases.

20. Overlapping Difficulty*

DEFINITION

This factor refers to the specified types of difficulty with overlapping (figure 7) and contiguous figures (figures A and 4). This type of difficulty involves: gross overlapping where none exists in the stimulus figures (A and 4); failure to reproduce a portion of the overlapping (in 7); simplification or distortion of portions of either figure at the point of overlap (in 7).

Severe (PSV = 10.0): Overlapping difficulty on more than 1 figure.
Moderate (PSV = 5.5): Difficulty on 1 figure.
None (PSV = 1.0).

INTERPRETATION

Our present definition of this factor deviates considerably from previous definitions which we have offered and distinguishes it more clearly from Closure Difficulty, on the one hand, and Simplification and Fragmentation, on the other. Our experience had suggested that this difficulty was most closely associated with some types of diffuse brain damage, and that this factor was extremely sensitive to such damage. The work reported by Hain (1964) and by Mosher and Smith (1965) seem to support this contention. We do not yet have adequate tests of the hypothesis, and probably adequate tests would have to involve a greater sampling than the material the HABGT offers. However, we do have convincing evidence of the power of this factor to distinguish the organic group, in general, from the nonorganic (with $N = 95$ and $N = 180$, respectively) in our ex-

* Refers to items used in the Psychopathology Scale, Chapter 7.

perimental population. The former group attained a mean score of 5.6, whereas the latter group attained a mean score of 1.3, the difference in means being significant at the .01 level. With such heterogeneous groups, which would tend to attenuate the significance of the difference, such results are promising.

21. Elaboration or Doodling*†

DEFINITION

This factor refers to doodling or elaboration on the reproduction in which the form is markedly changed. The elaboration can include the addition of loops or curlicues, or the addition of lines or curves which change the Gestalt. This factor should be differentiated from Factor 22, Perseveration.

Severe (PSV = 10.0): Present on more than 2 figures.
Moderate (PSV = 7.0): Present on 2 figures.
Mild (PSV = 4.0): Present on 1 figure only.
None (PSV = 1.0).

INTERPRETATION

Anyone who has had occasion to examine the HABGT records of agitated patients will have noticed the presence of this phenomenon. It appears to be associated with problems in impulse control and intense, overt anxiety. However, we must also note that we have observed its presence in the records of some mentally retarded individuals as well as some organics. Hence, we suspect that the phenomenon is the complex and indirect end product of a number of intervening processes. The author has never observed this phenomenon in well-adjusted adults or in the records of compulsive neurotics. We should, however, be careful to distinguish doodling and elaboration, as defined, from minor or occasional embellishments of the figure *which do not essentially distort the Gestalt.* When the phenomenon does involve distortion of the Gestalt it is very likely to be indicative of some severe disturbance in ego control. It appears to be a significant contributor to measures or judgments of psychopathology, but not all types of psychopathology necessarily manifest it. Item validation in connection with both the Psychopathology and Adience–Abience Scales confirmed its contributory role in these measures. Qualitive analyses of clinical records have also demonstrated its clinical usefulness.

* Refers to items used in the Psychopathology Scale, Chapter 7.
† Refers to items used in the Adience–Abience Scale, Chapter 7.

The Pascal-Suttell scoring method (Pascal & Suttell, 1951) contains a number of examples of scores which involve phenomena very similar to this Elaboration factor. The scoring method developed by Hain (1964) also contains a "sign," called "added embellishment," which is given a medium weighting in this scheme. In Byrd's (1956) study of children's records, the phenomenon appeared infrequently, but it *never* appeared in 200 records of well-adjusted school children, only in those children needing psychotherapy. The contrast in frequency of occurrence in adult schizophrenic records is marked: it occurred in 12 of the 100 records of our chronic schizophrenic population.

In her recent work Koppitz (1975a) has added "spontaneous elaborations or additions to design" as another "emotional indicator." Her experience shows that this phenomenon is "rare and occur(s) almost exclusively on Bender Test records of children who are overwhelmed by fears and anxieties. . . ." The occurrence of the same phenomenon in adults is more likely, however, to be even more serious, and is indicative of some loss of control over reality factors or retreat into fantasy.

22. Perseveration*

DEFINITION

Perseveration refers to either of two types of perseverative phenomena: (a) perseveration in which elements of a previous design are utilized in a succeeding design when they are not present in the stimulus figure; and (b) perseveration of the elements present in a given figure beyond the limits called for in the stimulus. An example of perseveration of type (a) is the use of dots in figure 2 (instead of circles) perseverated from the dots used in figure 1. An example of perseveration of type (b) is the presence in figure 1 of 14 or more dots instead of the 12 dots present in the stimulus design. Another example is the presence of 12 or more columns of circles in figure 2 instead of the 10 columns present in the stimulus design. The criterion for scoring the presence of perseveration is the *occurrence of 2 or more* of the perseverated elements in the case of type (a), or the *addition of 2 or more elements* (perseverated) within the same figure in the case of type (b).

Severe (PSV = 10.0): Present in more than 2 figures.
Moderate (PSV = 7.0): Present in 2 figures.
Mild (PSV = 4.0): Present in only 1 figure.
None (PSV = 1.0).

* *Refers to items used in the Psychopathology Scale, Chapter 7.*

INTERPRETATION

Perseveration, as defined, seems to represent either an inability to shift "set," or a rigidity in the maintenance of an established "set." In either case it represents a markedly decreased degree of spontaneous and adaptive ego control. It is probably reinforced by a decrease in reality test functions. We had originally suspected that perseveration of type (b) was more significant than type (a) in persons with organic insult, but additional findings suggest that both types are about equally significant in organic damage. A mild degree of perseveration, however, such as the infrequent addition of a single element (like adding a single dot in figure 1) probably has quite a different kind of significance. It may, for example, represent some degree of carelessness in execution or some degree of inaccuracy in counting in the case of children. *Severe perseveration,* as defined, is almost always pathognomic in adult records and is most frequently associated with the records of organics and deteriorated schizophrenics. It should also be noted that severe mental retardates of almost all types frequently manifest this phenomenon, as the author's study of such cases (see Chapter 6) indicated.

The apparently opposite phenomenon, namely the *reduction* in the number of elements from the number in the stimulus designs, seems to represent an entirely different kind of phenomenon, and we have therefore included it in the Simplification factor. Pascal and Suttel (1951) combine these two phenomena in a single score and call it "number of dots (or circles)." They find that this score adds some weight to their general measure of psychopathology.

Perseveration is found most frequently in connection with figures 1, 2, and 5. It may be found less frequently on figure 3, and still less frequently on figure 6. Perseveration, type (a), is found most frequently on figure 2, perhaps because this figure is immediately preceded by figure 1, and in both figures the examinee is required to repeat the element a large number of times.

The author's research data yielded the following mean scores: college students, 1.04; neurotics, 1.90; schizophrenics, 4.70; organics, 5.97. Tests of the significance of these differences show that both organics and schizophrenics, as groups, are differentiable from the "normal" and neurotic groups (.01 level), but there is no significant difference between "normals" and neurotics, although there is a trend indicating neurotics to be inferior. Clinical observation suggests that highly anxious neurotics tend to perform differently from other types of neurotics.

Mosher and Smith (1965) found that perseveration of type (a) differentiated organics from controls at the .01 level of significance. The factor of perseveration, as measured by Hain (1964), was given the highest possible weight in the score that was used to discriminate organics from both controls and other psychiatric cases. In 300 cases, ranging in age from 10 to 15 years, Byrd (1956) found seven cases showing perseveration (as measured) in the psychotherapy group, and only one case in the well-adjusted group. Obviously, frequency of occurrence is not sufficiently great to make this measure useful in a score for such groups. He also reported that in the 8–9-year-old group more cases with perseveration (6) occurred in the well-adjusted than in the psychotherapy group (1). Although the usefulness of this factor is especially limited with clildren below 10 years of age, *severe perseveration* still warrants serious consideration as a pathognomic indicator, in our judgment, and should be evaluated clinically when it occurs.

Other data pointing to the usefulness of this factor may be found in Wurst's (1974) study, which extracted perseveration as one of the basic factors in visual perception, and that of Korim (1974), in which heroin users were found to manifest this phenomenon significantly more often than nonopiate subjects.

23. Redrawing of the Total Figure*

DEFINITION

Redrawing refers to a second attempt to reproduce a figure when the first attempt (which may not necessarily include reproduction of the total figure) is left without complete erasure or is simply crossed out. On rare occasions more than two attempts may be made to reproduce a figure.

Very severe (PSV = 10.0): Present 4 or more times.
Severe (PSV = 7.75): Present 3 times.
Moderate (PSV = 5.5): Present 2 times.
Mild (PSV = 3.25): Present 1 time.
None (PSV = 1.0).

INTERPRETATION

Scattered references may be found in Bender research literature, but surprisingly little systematic research effort has been devoted to this factor. We believe that one of two conditions generally produces Redrawing. One is the absence of adequate anticipatory planning and the other is an overly self-critical attitude, usually combined with the former condition. When this phenomenon is marked (i.e., occurs more than once) it is probably significant. A single occurrence, while scored, may only indicate a high degree of current anxiety.

* Refers to items used in the Psychopathology Scale, Chapter 7.

Table 2
Data for Various Groups on Redrawing

Category	N	Mean Score	SD
Normals	150	1.05	1.04
Outpatient neurotics	125	1.73	1.95
Chronic schizophrenics	155	3.12	2.10
Organics	98	3.94	2.14

Some scoring schemes which have been published for Bender-Gestalt protocols include this item. Pascal and Suttell (1951) give it considerable weight in scoring method. Koppitz (1975a) includes it as one of the factors in her list of "emotional indicators." The phenomenon probably occurs more frequently in the records of young children than in older subjects. We have reanalyzed our own data, using the scoring indicated above, and have obtained the findings indicated in Table 2. Significant differences in mean score are found between groups of organics and schizophrenics on the one hand ($p < .01$), and neurotics and "normals" on the other.

FACTORS RELATED TO MOVEMENT AND DRAWING

24. Deviation in Direction of Movement

DEFINITION

This factor refers to deviation from the expected direction of movement in drawing the lines and curves in the test figures. The usual directions of movements fall into three classes: counterclockwise (especially for "closed" figures such as a circle, hexagon, etc.); from the top down; and from the inside of the figure to the outside. Examinees who draw with the left hand are a possible exception to these expectancies.

INTERPRETATION

We have not included this or either of the two following factors in either the Psychopathology Scale or the Adience–Abience Scale. There are some supporting research findings which indicate these factors may have some value, but codification is inadequate and the infrequency of occurrence makes statistical treatment inadvisable at this time.

As will be noted on the *Record Form,* the examiner is requested to observe direction of movement as the examinee draws each figure, and to make appropriate notation of the direction. Direction of movement, as well as the end products in drawing, have been studied by several investigators (e.g., Mira, 1939–1940; Wolff, 1943). The significance of the fantasied movement response has also recieved clinical and research evaluation (e.g., Klopfer, Ainsworth, Klopfer, & Holt, 1954). There is some consensus that centrifugal movement, in comparison with centripetal movement, represents personality trends toward assertion and autonomy; whereas centripetal movements indicate some degree of egocentrism and oppositional quality. Similarly, difficulty with movement in the vertical plane seems to be associated with interpersonal difficulties with authority figures, and difficulty in the horizontal plane may suggest difficulty in maintaining adequate, interpersonal relationships with peers. Counterclockwise movements are suggestive of normal personality adaptations, whereas clockwise direction of movement suggests (passive) oppositional trends and ogocentricity.

The author's clinical observations support these hypotheses. Particularly in the case of regular clockwise movements there is a strong tendency for oppositional and egocentric qualities to be present in the personality.

A study by Peek (1953) suggested that, in a limited test of this general hypothesis, psychiatric patients who drew the diagnonal secant of figure 5 from the top down, rather than in the more usual manner, from the bottom up, tended to be more immature, depressive, and less well adjusted than the control population that was used. Peek felt that one could interpret the "inward" drawing of the secant as indicative of fear of being overwhelmed by external forces. This interpretation warrants further investigation. Clawson (1959) reported that the same phenomenon (she called it drawing the spike inward) differentiated school children from clinic children in the expected direction ($p = .05$): 66% of her well-adjusted group drew the spike outward, whereas only 30% of the heterogeneous clinic group did.

In a study of the drawing characteristics of 65 college students, Lieberman (1968) found that these subjects did not typically draw closed figures in a counterclockwise manner, nor did they always draw vertical features from the top down. It may be that college students are somewhat atypical; they may also be more oppositional than other groups. More data on this phenomenon could be very useful.

25. Inconsistency in Direction of Movement

DEFINITION

This factor refers to any shift from the previously established "typical" direction of movement. Such shifts in direction can usually be observed easily by the examiner, for they are often accompanied by other indications of some form of tension, both on the test and in behavior.

INTERPRETATION

Shifts of the kind we are referring to are usually sudden and unexpected. The examinee has already established his style on previous reproductions, then suddenly shifts on the next design or part of the design. Such inconsistencies tend to be indicative, we believe, of psychic blocking, oftentimes associated with the idiosyncratic and symbolic meaning of the design for the patient, and may be indicative of ongoing attempts to act out strongly conflictual trends in the personality. Sometimes such evidence may have a favorable connotation because the patient is actively struggling to work out a more reasonable solution to his conflicts.

26. Line Quality

DEFINITION

This factor refers to the quality of the lines used in making the reproductions. We identify 6 major types of abnormal line quality: excessively heavy lines; excessively heavy lines accompanied by poor coordination; excessively faint lines; excessively faint lines accompanied by poor coordination; poor coordination; and sketching. Poor coordination is manifested by irregularities, unevenness in line quality, and tremulousness. We have used, as a rule of thumb, a definition of *coarse coordination* in which the irregularities in line quality exceed one-sixteenth of an inch. Sketching refers to retouching of a line, or of a joining. It should be distinguished from the type of art sketching which results in a reproduction that is well controlled and well executed. Rather, sketching, as we have defined, it, refers to productions that are inferior and sometimes result in distortion of the Gestalt.

INTERPRETATION

Based primarily upon clinical observations, line quality appeared to be important in a great many cases of diffuse brain damage, in diverse cases showing intense anxiety, and in cases showing high degrees of feelings of personal inadequacy. In a previous publication (Hutt & Briskin, 1960), specific hypotheses were offered concerning each of the types of deviations in line quality defined above. The specific hypotheses have not been borne out by any systematic research, although there is some supporting evidence. For example, coarse incoordination was shown by Mosher and Smith (1965) to differentiate organics from controls at the .01 level of significance. Heavy line pressure discriminated clinic from school children at the .10 groups of significance (Clawson, 1959). The relative heterogeneity of both groups as well as the relatively low-order power of this factor may have reduced the significance of these results. Peek and

Quast (1951) have included tone of line quality in their scoring system, and Pascal and Suttell (1951) give fairly high weights to a sign they call tremors (both fine and coarse). On the other hand, "line tone" was not found to be differentiating among groups of aggressive individuals, passive individuals, and a control group (Taylor & Schenke, 1955). This negative finding is not surprising in view of a questionable rationale for expecting to find such differences and because of their definition of the three types of groups.

On the other hand, careful analysis of the records of hostile and aggressive children has demonstrated that line quality, particular heavily reinforced lines, is a significant feature of such records (Brown, 1965; Handler & McIntosh, 1971).

Inconsistency in line quality may be even more important than the line quality itself, for it is probably indicative of disturbance stimulated by idiosyncratic reactions to the specific designs. Tremors, whether fine or course, suggest difficulty in motor control and are either indicative of a high level of anxiety or some neurological problem. Generally, heavy lines are an expression of anxiety being directed outwards, while faint lines are suggestive of anxiety which is being internalized or the expression of which is inhibited. Sketching is likely to be indicative of feelings of inadequacy with some attempts at compensation. All of these indicators should be considered suggestive, but should lead to more intense analyses of other concurrent indicators, either in test reproductions or in other clinical behavior. Used in this manner, they may offer important leads to significant understanding of the individual.

SOME OTHER FACTORS

Although we have tried to incorporate in our presentation of factors those test signs which have received clinical and research support from other workers, we have been biased in our selection by our own clinical experience, our own research, and our own rationale for test interpretation. Doubtless, other factors than those we have discussed may have great importance, and still others, or new integrations of factors, may finally turn out to be more sensitive and discriminating indicators than those we have thus far presented. In order to give some idea of the scope of creative suggestions which have been offered by others, we list below a sampling of some factors which are not included in our own listing.

Hain (1964) has found the following additional factors to be important in a total score designed to identify brain damage: "concretion," "unit line separation," "acute angle difficulty," and "added angles." (All receive high weighting.) In addition, "omission of elements," and "absence of erasures" receive low weighting. Pascal and Suttell (1951) include such items as "workover," "asymmetry," and "guide lines" in their scoring scheme, but these are given relatively small weights. Guertin (1952) factor analyzed 41 test variables selected from Billingslea's work (Billingslea, 1948) and extracted five oblique factors: propensity to curvilinear movements; careless execution; poor reality contact; construction; and poor spatial contiguity. Although Clawson (1959) based her study on Hutt's suggested factors, she also analyzed some aspects of performance in her own way. For example, she scored for "scalloping," "dog ears," "the use of arcs instead of clear-cut angles," and "erasures." Kitay (1950) approached the problem of scoring by measuring size deviations by means of graph paper. Koppitz (1960, 1975a), whose work has been found to be so valuable in the analysis of children's Bender records from a maturational rather than a projective viewpoint, has offered a number of other innovations in her scoring scheme, originally presented in 1960. Since this approach is so fundamentally different from ours, the interested reader is referred to her research article.

Cross-cultural studies are also urgently needed. In addition to the works we have already cited, some useful findings may be found in studies by Fanibanda (1973), who suggests that cultural differences occur in elaborations, and by Money and Newcombe (1974), who indicate the usefulness of such studies.

6
Principles of Inferential and Configurational Analysis

In this chapter we shall discuss two types of separate but complementary studies of the HABGT. We shall first deal with problems of inferential analysis, and then discuss the findings of interpretation of configurational analysis. The latter type of analysis lends itself more easily to statistical treatment since it implies that different types of configurations of signs or factors mean different kinds of things, and the differences between or among various sets of configurations may be subjected to tests of statistical significance. All that is needed are clear specifications of the various configurations and clear statements of criteria of the differing phenomena which each configuration supposedly predicts. The former type of analysis may involve a whole series of sequential inferences that may or may not be precisely replicable in different cases and therefore involves a more complicated validation problem.

INFERENTIAL ANALYSIS

Inferential analysis depends, in the first instance, on the presence of discrete phenomena which already have a substantial body of data for validation purposes. However, this type of analysis goes beyond the simple statement of a correlational relationship between each phenomenon and each "trait." It assumes, on the contrary, that the successive productions of a given sequence of events are uniquely determined by the interaction of multidetermined events over a span of time so that the final product on the test represents the idiosyncratic resultant of the *given constellation of events operating over time.* Morover, it involves the postulation of not one but several alternate hypotheses during the process of developing inferences, until the analysis of sequential findings tends to confirm one or several of these hypotheses and simultaneously reject others. To illustrate in a general way what we mean by these latter two phases in sequential inference we may refer once again, as we did in Chapter 3, to the problem of passivity.

Suppose that our test results indicate that, as one of the plausible hypotheses, the patient in question shows passivity. We may have come to this inference on the basis of such evidence as: light line drawings, reduction of the Gestalten in the vertical plane, increased size of the figures involving curved lines, and difficulty with intersecting figures. Assuming that passivity is indeed present, we are now confronted with questions as: "Is the passivity a reaction formation to pronounced aggressive drives?" "Is the passivity part of a feminine orientation on the part of the patient?" "Is the passivity part of a general withdrawal of cathexes or of some other type of withdrawal?" At this point we have to examine the test data before and especially after those points at which the passive phenomena appeared. We may then find that the patient responds only to certain figures by passive withdrawal, that during the elaboration phase of the test, when he is offered greater freedom, passive characteristics do not occur, and that during the association phase he offers a number of marked but covert responses (symbolic) of aggression, like "hitting," "tearing," "cutting," and "disintegrating," In the light of the total response repertoire, and particularly in the light of successive sequences during which passivity occurs or fails to occur, we may be led to some final inference concerning the meaning, intensity, and etiology of the phenomenon of passivity.

General Stylistic Qualities

There are many ways in which to start the process of inferential analysis. One might begin with the first figure on the test, "speculate" concerning the specific features of the reproduction of this figure (or, more precisely, list the separate hypotheses which all of the features of the reproduction might suggest), and then move on in sequence to each of the subsequent figures, following this, in turn, with a similar type of analysis of the material from the elaboration and association phases. However, this type of procedure fails to take into account the general stylistic qualities of the total set of drawings, and we believe it is generally desirable to begin with this feature of the test. The major argument for this proposal is that the general style of the patient, as revealed in the overall organization and arrangement of the drawings on the page (and the repetition or modification of this style in the various phases of the test) reveals the most general and pervasive qualities of the patient's personality at the time of the test, and thereby offers some important and convenient parameters within which to organize the several separate and successive inferences from each of the drawings.

Let us contrast one aspect of "style" in two patients in order to make this point more meaningful. Suppose that we had the records of two adult patients, one of which showed a crowding of the nine figures within the confines of the upper one-third a single page, while the other showed a "distribution" of the figures over three pages. We could infer from the first patient's record a reaction of extreme withdrawal, perhaps suspiciousness, as well as marked anxiety in the face of a relatively nonthreatening test situation. Similarly, we could infer from the other record, a reaction of an extratensive individual, perhaps manic in quality, perhaps egocentric and the like, with relatively little overt anxiety or suspiciousness. Having offered such general hypotheses about each patient, we could then go on to test them, add to them, or modify them in the light of the several features of each of the separate drawings.

We shall begin, then, with features concerning the general style of the patient's drawings. The following suggestions may be applied separately to the drawings obtained from each phase of the test (or each method). When these several and separate analyses have been made from the data obtained in each phase, they may then be integrated into the most parsimonious set of explanations and predictions for the entire set of drawings.

The first question which confronts us is how much *space* the patient used for all of the drawings. Was it excessive, constricted, or normal (in terms of the criteria listed in Chapter 5)? The amount of space used tells us something concerning the patient's self-percept vis-a-vis the rest of the world. Furthermore, the ways in which he uses space as he moves through the total test tells us how adaptable he is with respect to this general orientation. It is highly useful in analyzing this portion of the data to try to emphathize with the patient's actual performance so that, in addition to the hypotheses we have offered in Chapter 5 concerning the use of space, we can derive tentative, alternative hypotheses concerning the specific ways in which this particular patient used space as he proceeded through the successive portions of the test.

Next, having extricated all of the possible inferences we can from the patient's use of space, we may turn our attention to the problem of *sequence*. Here, we start again with the criteria listed in the previous chapter, noting all of the hypotheses which the data suggest concerning sequence. These are noted, first, without regard to whether or not they appear to be in conflict with the hypotheses derived from the analysis of space. Moreover, any idiosyncratic features of the sequence are noted and hypotheses are developed. An example of this would be a generally orderly sequence with an outstanding exception, say, on figure 6 (the sinusoidal curves), in which a marked change in sequence appears, followed by an orderly sequence for the remaining figures. One would want to consider the possible difficulties which figure 6 might impose upon this or any patient, and the possible reaction to the previous figure in the light of what is known about these figures (see later discussion in this chapter). Having formed these two general sets of hypotheses, from the use of space and from sequence, it would be well, next, to attempt to reconcile them, being sure not to discard any hypothesis which cannot clearly be rejected. In this process, hypotheses of a higher, more integrated order might appear, or additional, alternative hypotheses, not deducible from either space or sequence alone, might be formed.

The next step in the general analysis of style concerns the *placement of the first figure*. Here again, as with the problem of the use of space, the patient's initial stylistic adaptation to his life space can be inferred (see Chapter 5). Does he, for example, place his first figure (i.e., himself) in the middle of the page, suggesting a highly egocentric orientation with respect to the world? Does he squeeze the first figure into the upper left-hand corner of the page, suggesting extreme withdrawal and fearfulness? Of course, the nature of the reproduction of the first figure (figure A) will enter into the speculative hypotheses which may be offered, but we shall leave until later the discussion of the separate figures. Once again, having made whatever hypotheses seem plausible on the basis of this stylistic feature, we attempt to integrate these with the previous hypotheses we have derived.

Next, we note whether any *collision or near collision phenomena* are present. Such data are indicative of loss of anticipatory controls and are most frequently associated with either marked anxiety (basic or transitional) or with intracranial damage and possible loss in psychological or motor control. In either case, there is an impairment of ego functions, and we carefully note the adaptation made during and following the figures on which collision tendencies occur. For instance, collision tendencies involving curved figures differ from those involving straight-line figures: the former are more likely to be associated with difficulty in expressive aggressive drives; the latter are more likely to be associated with passive drives. As another example, collision involving more complex figures, such as 7 and 8, but not simple figures like 3 and 4, are more likely to relate to loss in cognitive rather than emotional factors. We also examine the drawings to determine whether the patient is aware of or attempts to correct his collision phenomena. Such behavior indicates at least marginal awareness of the perceptual–motoric problem and, when corrected placement occurs after collision, is indicative of modifiability of response pattern—a highly useful finding in terms of therapeutic management and prognosis.

Another general stylistic feature refers to the *use of the margin*. We have already noted the most probable hypotheses associated with this phenomenon (see Chapter 5). We can offer a number of hypotheses based on the general use of the margin and others based on the use of the margin for some of the individual figures alone. (See Chapters 9, 10, and 13 for examples.) If, by this point in our analysis of a particular record, consistent hypotheses have been derived from the several sources of data concerning general style, we can be reasonably certain that these are strong hypotheses. Further indication of their strength may be derived from subsequent analyses of the separate figures, and then again from analysis of the data obtained during the elaboration phase of the test.

One other general source of hypotheses derived from stylistic features is that of *rotation of the test paper and the test cards*. Hypotheses related to egocentricity and/or rigidity are based on rotations of 90 degrees to about 180 degrees, while those related to oppositional qualities are based on rotation of 180 degrees or more.

All of the inferences derived thus far are based upon the overt behavior shown by the patient during the test and in his responses. To the extent that the behavior has obvious meaning to the patient, as, for example, when he rotates the cards despite the structuring of the test in opposition to such placement, or when he places his first figure in the center of the page, we can assume that the phenomena in question are at the conscious or preconscious level. To the extent that the behavior has only latent meaning, such as, for example, when the sequence is changed because a particular figure has some symbolic threat for the patient, we can assume that unconscious factors are operating. Not only can we therefore make a rough categorization of the level of meaning of the behavior to the patient (from conscious to unconscious), but by virtue of our general knowledge of phychopathology and the operation of defenses, we can begin to infer some specific types of dynamics (nature and severity of conflict) for the patient. Such dynamic inferences, especially as they are reinforced or confirmed in the light of evidence associated with the distortions on the several figures and with data from the elaborations and associations, are powerful tools for predicting the nature and significance of unconscious processes for the patient. When these are integrated with the overt behavior of the patient they enable us to extend our clinical analysis to cover a wider variety of contingencies than when they are limited to only one source of data (see Chapter 3).

Individual Figures

Now we shall turn our attention to the separate Gestalt figures, commenting simultaneously on the other test factors as they are likely to emerge on these figures.

Figure A has several features to commend it as the initial figure in the test presentation. In the first place it is a relatively simple figure, requiring only a mental maturity corresponding roughly to about 7–8 years of age for its successful reproduction. It is therefore useful to compare relative success on this figure with performance on the other simple and on the more complex figures (i.e., figures 1, 2, 3, and 4, on the one hand, and figures 6, 7, and 8 on the other). It can usually be assumed, for example, that consistently greater difficulty on the simple figures in comparison with the more difficult ones is due to intrapsychic difficulties rather than maturational problems.

Another feature concerning figure A is that it consists of two well-structured, closed, simple, and *tangential* figures. The tangential aspect makes the figure particularly useful in detecting difficulties in interpersonal cathexes (joining and closure factors). Still another feature is the presence of two figures which have well-nigh universal symbolic meanings: the circle represents the female object and the square represents the male object. (It is, of course, important to test the applicability of these symbolic meanings for a particular patient. The patient's responses during the association phase of the test furnish one basis for such verification.) It is possible to infer that relative increases in the size of one figure as compared with the other refer to problems in the patient's self-percept. Thus, for example, a patient who reproduces the square as greatly enlarged in proportion to the circle can be assumed to be attempting unconsciously to identify with a male role; the relative discrepancy in size is therefore indicative of difficulty in this identification, for otherwise both figures would receive equal emphasis. This type of hypothesis can be checked against the elaborations and the associations in the other two phases of the basic method of administration. Patients who wish unconsciously to see themselves as more masculine will be likely to exaggerate the square during the elaboration by some such method as placing the circle within the square or by producing a number of squares around the circle as a pivot.

Another feature of figure A is that is consists of a curved and a straight-line figure. From clinical and experimental evidence we know that difficulty in expressing aggressive drives is associated with difficulty in reproducing curved figures, whereas corresponding difficulty with passivity is associated with straight-line figures (Breen, 1953; North, 1953). We have already commented on the problem of placement of the first figure.

We can also add that, since this is the first figure in the test, whatever transient factors are associated with initial adaptation to the test situation are likely to be projected into some aspect of the performance on this figure. Hence, careful examination of all of the features in the reproduction of this figure is recommended. Comparison with the subsequent figures may make it possible to deduce which features are associated with problems in initial adaptation and which are more probably characterological in nature.

Figure 1 consists of 12 equidistant dots. Because it is an unstructured figure (i.e., it has no clearly delineated boundary), it presents difficulties to some patients. Patients with organic problems find this figure more difficult than its inherent structure justifies (because of figure–ground perceptual problems associated with organic deficit). Patients with intense, diffuse anxiety also find the figure difficult for similar reasons. Patients with severe aspiration problems have difficulty in leaving this figure, as simple as it is; they spend a great deal of energy in filling in the dots or in emphasizing the circularity of the dots. To some patients with traumatic anxiety the dots are suggestive of bullets or pellets coming directly at them and, as a consequence, they may produce a very wavy line of dots. Some schizophrenic patients with high ideational and paranoid qualities elaborate the dots and may ''extend'' them into birds or symbolic figures or ''doodles'' (some anxious neurotics do the same thing). Finally, a word may be said concerning obsessive–compulsive patients who spend an inordinate amount of time completing this simple figure because of their perfectionistic needs and frequently count and recount the number of dots.

The relative placement of figures A and 1 also deserves some comment. It is interesting to note the directional orientation which the patient takes after completing figure A. Does he move to the right, or does he move to a position directly below figure A in beginning figure 1? Preferred direction of movement is a stylistic feature which we have already commented on in the preceding chapter. Preferred movements in the lateral or horizontal plane, for example, are likely to be associated with unresolved needs for interpersonal cathexes, while movements in the vertical plane are related to difficulties in dealing with authority figures. Some patients, moreover, draw the line of dots in such a way that it represents an arc (sometimes barely discernible) with themselves as the pivot—indicative of an egocentric or, possibly, narcissistic orientation. Others draw the line of dots with a slight clockwise rotation, which is indicative of depressive trends. These and other general characteristics of the drawing of this figure are worth noting for the rich harvest of hypotheses which they may offer.

Again, we wish to emphasize that the contrast in performance and in general behavior which may be noted for the first two figures—or the consistency which is evident—is important for still other hypotheses which may be derived. Contrast may occur in size, in spacing, in directional orientation, in relative amount of time and energy expended in completing the task, etc. One may lose sight of the sequential production of such phenomena if specific attention is not directed to this phase of the analysis. As a consequence of this, only discrete hypotheses which can be summated in a score of deviations or distortions would remain.

Turning now to *figure 2*, we note that it consists of 10 angulated columns of circles. Because there is a shift from the dots of figure 1 to the circles of figure 2, we wish to attend particularly to the occurrence of perseveration which may first be manifest on figure 2 (although another type of perseveration may occur on figure 1). Some patients reproduce figure 2 with dots instead of circles, perseverating the dots of figure 1. This phenomenon is most characteristic of patients with severe ego impairment, such as psychotics, but it may occur when transient anxiety is very intense. The open character of this figure (like that of figure 1) with no clear indication of the boundary, is threatening to some patients. Organics and those with severe problems in interpersonal relationships sometimes have difficulty with this figure. When the figure is elongated in the lateral plane but the number of columns of circles is correct, we can infer that the problem is likely to be one of difficulty in interpersonal relations. When perseveration of the dots of figure 1, or perseveration of the columns of circles is present, some organic hypothesis is more likely.

Another feature of importance on this figure is any change in the angulation of the columns of circles. In general, reduction in the acuteness of the angulation (or "increased angulation" as we have defined it) corresponds to reduction in the affectivity of the patient, while increase in acuteness corresponds to increase in affectivity. Sometimes, the patient has difficulty in perceiving or in executing the angulation feature: for example, when he reproduces the columns as perpendicular to the base of the paper but rotates the whole figure in a counterclockwise manner to achieve some semblance of angulation. This kind of difficulty is associated with the feelings of impotence experienced by some organics; occasionally it may be present in the production of psychopaths. Still another phenomenon is the tendency to produce a figure with shifts in the angulation of the columns so that those at the left are produced with a relatively correct angulation but, as the other columns are drawn, the position of the columns tends to become more and more reversed, so that the whole figure describes an arc with the patient at the center or point of origin. As on figure 1, this phenomenon is indicative of egocentrism or narcissism. Some patients manifest a progressive and regressive shift in the angulation of the successive columns, an indication of compensatory attempts to maintain interpersonal cathexes.

Some patients draw the figure with a clockwise orientation or rotation, an indication of depressive trends. If depressive features in the personality result in clockwise rotation, this feature is usually present in all three of the first three figures and the hypothesis is thus strongly supported. Moreover, other test features may be associated with depression, such as light pressure in line movement and difficulty in completing any of the tasks. This combination of characteristics is usually associated with depression in a highly dependent and passive personality. When strong masochistic features are present, line pressure tends to be heavy. Another feature associated with masochism is the placement of dots within each of the circles. We have noted only some of the most important characteristics associated with the drawing of this figure. Many others are present and correlated hypotheses may be deduced.

Figure 3, the arrowhead constructed of dots, is another open figure. Some patients who have managed to maintain some degree of control with the previous open figures finally begin to break down on this figure. (Organics usually show their ego impairment before they have reached this figure.) For other patients the aggressive qualities of this figure, or its symbolic meaning to them, is threatening. For such patients we may expect that some compensatory effort will be made to reduce the apparent threat. This may be done by compressing the figure, thus destroying its essential Gestalt, or by reducing the angularity of the angles in the figure. Another fairly frequent characteristic of the reproduction of this figure in the case of regressed patients is a simplification of the figure (by reducing the number of dots or by reducing the number of component parts). Depressive trends are also frequently manifest on this figure in the form of rotational difficulties of a minor degree. Patients with strong anal fixations tend to be overly careful with this figure, counting the dots again and again, but sometimes losing the general Gestalt in the process because of their overconcern with minutiae. The specific associative meanings of this figure for the patient can frequently be easily inferred from the material in the elaboration and association phases of the test.

Figure 4, like figure A, presents two symbols which frequently are associated with sexual identification: the open square representing the male object and the curved figure representing the female object. It therefore has some of the same values as figure A. Confirmation of hypotheses dealing with identification can frequently be obtained by a comparison of the distortions on these two figures. Since figure 4 is more difficult than figure A, some problems usually emerge on this figure that have not been noted on figure A. The relative size of the curved portion of the figure in relation to the open square is particularly important in this respect. The tendency to flatten the curve or the tendency to produce an extra or excessive loop at the end of the curve is also important: the former is associated with emotional "flattening," the latter with impulsivity and poor emotional control.

Some patients have difficulty with the vertical sides of the open square, indicative of difficulty in authority relationships. This difficulty may be shown in a number of ways, such as sketching on the vertical sides, successive attempts to increase or extend these sides, or an increase in the dimensions of these sides. Other patients show fairly marked closure problems on this figure. Still others fragment the figure or separate the two components. The latter is associated with the severe ego impairment occurring in regressive states and in problems associated with organicity. The production on figure 4 should be compared with productions on other figures in which either straight lines or curved lines or both are present, in order to derive suitable hypotheses, and with the elaboration and association data for confirmation of these hypotheses and the development of new hypotheses to account for all of the data. A great variety of relevant inferences can be derived from this figure alone as well as from a comparison with the patient's productions on preceding figures. Note, for example, how this is done with some of the cases presented in Chapters 8–13.

Figure 5 is another open figure composed of dots. Several of the most pertinent phenomena associated with this figure will be discussed briefly. Rotation frequently occurs for the first time because of the perceptual valence of the secant, which forces some patients to rotate the entire figure; they are unable to resist the inertia created by the angulated secant and consequently rotate the entire figure. Another feature is the tendency to complete the circle by extending the circular portion of the figure. This phenomenon is usually associated with feelings of insecurity and dependence. Simplification may also occur as still another defensive maneuver. Obsessive–compulsive patients frequently count the dots over and over again, sometimes losing the Gestalt while trying to reproduce the number of dots accurately. The relative size of the secant should be examined for the deduction of any of a number of hypotheses, such as: paranoid features (elaboration or overextension of the size of the secant—because of its phallic characteristics); authority problems (decrease in the vertical dimension of the total figure with foreshortening of the secant); passivity as a reaction formation to hostile wishes (decrease of the secant together with a wavy line quality). Simplification of the figure may be attempted by reducing markedly the total number of dots, by substituting a curved line for the semicircle of dots, or by using lines in place of dots for the entire figure (see Chapter 9).

Figure 6, coming as it does after a succession of previous figures and representing such a direct portrayal of emotionality, is another important figure in sequential and inferential analyses. Not only does the curvature present problems to some patients, but the intersection of two sets of curves in a nonsymmetrical manner aggravates the problem for many. Patients who are able to maintain a facade of appropriate affectivity but whose affective behavior is not spontaneous have great difficulty here. The various phenomena which may result are highly revealing. Are the curves flattened (reduction of the emotional value of the stimulus), are they spiked (difficulty in holding aggressive drives under check), or are they reduced in number or amplitude (affective withdrawal)? Again, are the two curves made to intersect at right angles or are the curves drawn with considerable evidence of motor incoordination (inability to handle the "hot" emotional meaning of these stimuli)? Some patients draw the two curves not as intersecting but as two tangential "U" curves—an important indication of marked fearfulness in interpersonal relations. Depressive features sometimes appear for the first time on this figure (mild clockwise rotation, light wavy lines, and similar features). Paranoid characteristics sometimes become evident (the elaboration of the curve as the profile of a face, or the insertion of a dot for an eye, as examples). Patients with markedly impulsive characteristics will frequently increase the size of the curves greatly and will use excessive line pressure. The highly anxious but intact patient may, on the other hand, diminish the size of the curves and draw them with light pressure and sketchy lines.

As is well known by now, *figure 7* offers the most clear-cut evidence of the presence of organicity in the patient (difficulty with overlapping) but it offers many other leads as well. With respect to the problem of intracranial damage it should be emphasized that overlapping difficulty may be evidenced in very many different ways. The most obvious of these is the failure to reproduce the overlapping Gestalt. There are also other, less obvious ways: sketching at the point of overlap of the two figures; severe rotation of the figures; marked difficulty with some of the angles (especially if none was noted on such figures as A and 4); simplification of either or both parts of the figure; overlap at an incorrect point; marked overshooting in the closure at any of the apexes; substitution of curved for straight lines; and total destruction of the Gestalt.

The phallic quality of this Gestalt, and the threat it poses to some types of homosexuals, should not be overlooked. This type of reaction to the symbolic meaning of the stimulus figure can be checked against the reaction obtained with figure 8, discussed below. When the phallic quality is too threatening to the patient he may defend against this in a number of ways, such as rounding off any of the upper or lower apexes of the figures, decreasing the length of the figures or increasing their width, or shortening the extreme sections of the figures. Sometimes patients with severe superego problems and guilt over fantasied sexual perversions or excesses separate the two figures or simplify them; in such cases the evidence of overt anxiety noted in this and other figures will help to differentiate this type of difficulty from that of organicity. Figure 7 also lends itself to rather clear manifestations of other types of anxieties and difficulties in interpersonal relations, evidenced by such phenomena as closure difficulties, crossing difficulties, variations in line quality, difficulties with angles, rotational problems, and the like.

Figure 8 is also reacted to, very frequently, in terms of its sexual, particularly its phallic, qualities (Sullivan & Welsh, 1947). One of the interesting findings is that individuals with conflict over homosexuality (and young adults or adolescents with conflict over masturbation) have difficulties with the extremities of this figure. The most common distortions involve: production of the two extremities in markedly different sizes; difficulties with the angles in the extremities; substitution of curved lines for the straight lines in the extreme portion of the figure; and excessive sketching.

Another feature to which special attention should be given is the production of the internal diamond. Difficulty with this portion of the figure may involve: reduction in size; misplacement in position (off center); or difficulty in closure or joining of either parts of the diamond or the diamond with the sides of the hexagon. Such difficulties are usually associated with conflict with the female sex and fearfulness in connection with intercourse. When such distortions occur it is instructive to note whether similar difficulties have been experienced in connection with the square (or diamond) in figure A. It will sometimes be noted that no significant distortions occur in figure A but they are quite marked in figure 8. There may be many reasons to account for this, but the two most common explanations are that figure 8 is the last in the test and reflects the cumulative anxieties which have been built up in the course of the examination, and that figure 8 seems to evoke more directly some of the conflicts related to sexual relationships. Confirmation of either of these (or other) explanations for this figure may often be obtained during the elaboration and association phases of the test.

Elaboration and Association Phases

If the clinician has been following our suggestions for developing inferences from the responses to the copy phase of the test he will have developed many explanations and hunches concerning the patient, he will have revised and extended some of these, and he will have rejected others in the light of a more parsimonious explanation that became available. Further, utilizing his knowledge concerning personality theory and psychopathology, he will have developed a general personality conceptualization concerning the specific patient. On the basis of such leads a number of second-order inferences can then be developed. However, if data are available from the elaboration and association phases of the test, it would be advisable to examine these data before attempting to integrate these second-order hypotheses.

We have already discussed the rationale for the procedures of the elaboration and association phases of the test in Chapters 3 and 4. At this point we wish merely to emphasize certain features of these rationales.

In the first place, the motoric activity involved in the process of elaborating the Gestalt figures (especially since ego controls are relaxed somewhat by the instruction to ''modify the figures . . . so as to make them more pleasing'') tends to produce both exaggeration of underlying and relatively more unconscious processes, and associations and material (traumatic) related to the anal and oedipal phases of development (the periods of ''socialization''). Consistencies in distortions first found in the copy phase and later exaggerated in the elaboration phase are therefore of special interest. Also of interest are new types of distortions which occur only on the elaboration phase. These consistencies and new types of evidence can be evaluated more completely in terms of the associations given by the patient to both the copy phase and the elaboration phase material. Although we have stressed the capacity of these procedure to elicit material from anal and phallic phases, other phases of development may be projected in these materials—for example, such obvious ''oral'' associations to figure 6 as ''a fountain'' or ''sucking movements.''

Sometimes patients will reveal ''sudden insights'' concerning material they have produced during the elaboration phase. They will verbalize with surprise that they didn't know just what they were doing, or they were just ''doodling,'' but now it is very clear that the figure means ''such and such.'' Often, they will insist that no other explanation is possible; i.e., because of the intensity of the projection, they will have ''lost distance'' from their productions and can entertain no alternative explanations. Sometimes they will exclaim that the association is something they had forgotten or had never thought about before. Such kinds of verbal behavior are important evidence of the intrinsic validity of the productions—although, of course, any clinician will realize that sometimes the most apparently valid recollections are but screen memories.

In analyzing the elaboration data, it is suggested that the general rules offered for developing hypotheses in connection with the copy phase data be followed. First, it is desirable to analyze the general stylistic features of the total set of elaboration productions, and then it is advisable to analyze the separate productions in the sequence in which they were offered. Also, the same general procedures should be followed for entertaining apparently contradictory hypotheses until the evidence forces a selection or integration of the explanations. Only after the elaboration material has been analyzed in this manner is it desirable to compare the implications of the elaboration with the copy phase hypotheses in detail.

CONFIGURATIONAL ANALYSIS

We shall now discuss the approach utilizing configurational analysis. As we have noted previously, we should not expect to find perfect agreement between any configuration of test signs and a particular nosological category. The presentation of certain configurational patterns which are frequently associated with certain psychiatric categories is intended, rather, to indicate *commonly occurring, associated conditions*. The utilization of such configurations should *not*, therefore, lead to automatic diagnostic designations of individuals. They can be highly useful for group comparisons and for further analysis of individuals who are suspected of having a particular psychiatric condition. In the case of individuals, configurational analysis leads, rather, to an inference that this individual, who shows test behavior commonly associated with a particular psychiatric category, *may* also belong to that category. However, since each nosological category is, itself, quite heterogeneous, and since even configurations of test phenomena may result from varying causes, the clinician will wish to explore the basis for the particular configurational finding in the light of case history, current behavior and adjustment, and other clinical findings.

The essential test of the validity of any configurational pattern in discriminating between nosological categories is not whether all individuals who show that configuration fall within a given psychiatric group, but whether groups of individuals classified within a given psychiatric category are significantly distinguishable from other psychiatric groups in terms of that configuration. There have been many studies attesting to the great diversity within the category of so-called schizophrenia. There is considerable evidence that individuals with the same or similar organic brain damage differ in their behavior responses. Neuroses and character disorders are even more heterogeneous in terms of underlying pathologies. Nevertheless, if nosological categories have any merit, it is because they manifest, in each instance, some common attributes. The configuration on test phenomena assumes that, *as a group,* people are distinguishable from other people who show another configuration on the test. The configurations which we shall present serve this function. They have met the tests of clinical experience and research validation.

The following sets of configurations constitute a second revision based on reported findings in the literature and further validation against the author's own research data. The normative groups, matched for age and sex, consisted of the following: outpatient neurotics ($N = 125$); chronic schizophrenics ($N = 155$); unipolar depressives ($N = 68$); and organic brain-damaged patients ($N = 98$). The mean age for the total population was 31 years and 4 months. The groups varied somewhat in highest mean educational grade level, the lowest being the schizophrenic population (with a mean grade of 7.8) and the highest being the outpatient population (with a mean grade of 11.3). Our research findings indicate that grade level in adults is not significantly correlated with psychopathology score (Hutt & Miller, 1976).

It will be noted that each factor in the configuration is given a weight of either 1 or 2. These weights were assigned empirically on the basis of the discriminatory capacity of the component. The score for a given configuration is simply the total of the scores obtained on the relevant components. We also indicate the *marginal* and *critical* scores for each configuration. If an individual's score for a given configuration falls within the marginal range, his assignment to that nosological category should be regarded as questionable even though further clinical study may, indeed, indicate that he belongs to that category. If, on the other hand, his score falls within the range of critical scores for that configuration, his *statistical* placement in that category is quite probable. Even so, as we have indicated, the clinician will wish to test the significance of the findings by means of what we have called Testing-the-Limits. This procedure is especially relevant with subjects whose configuration scores suggest that they have organic brain damage. Not only will such procedures help to validate the diagnostic categorization, but they will assist in defining the nature of the organic defect; i.e., difficulties in spatial perceptions are related to defects of the parietal area of the brain; difficulties in motor coordination are related to defects in the motor or frontal area.

Previous studies that have attempted to evaluate the effectiveness of configurational analysis and of the relative merits of clinical versus actuarial analysis of Bender-Gestalt records have been inconsistent in their findings. An older study (Goldberg, 1959) showed that clinicians were better able to differentiate organic from nonorganic Bender records than chance expectancy, but that the Pacal-Suttell scores gave better differentiation. There were two interesting aspects to this study. One was that more experienced raters were less confident in their judgments than less experienced raters, but obtained better (more correct) results. The other was that the most experienced rater (the present writer), who was the least confident, but who took the most time in examining and evaluating the records, obtained better results than any of the other judges or the Pascal-Suttell scores, obtaining a "diagnostic hit rate" of 83%! The probable reason for this finding is that the "expert" was not only more experienced, but took into careful consideration both the "signs" of organicity and the inconsistencies in the records, thus tending to eliminate false positives of "doubtful" organics were classified as organics when the configuration showed some strong, but insufficient organic characteristics. In other words, configurational analysis can be improved in effectiveness when it is buttressed by careful, painstaking evaluation of the nature of the findings. The author feels quite sure that success in differentiating organics from nonorganics could be significantly improved if Testing-the-Limits were included in the total procedure.

Another study, by Bruhn and Reed (1975), posed the problem of differentiating 20 nonorganic college students who attempted to simulate brain damage in their Bender records from 33 organic patients. In this study the Pascal-Suttell score did not differentiate the two groups, but a certified clinical psychologist was able to do so with 89% accuracy. In a cross-validation study by the same authors, they found that clinicians, utilizing the findings from the pilot study, were able to identify all of the malingerers correctly.

In contrast, there is the study by Lyle and Quast (1976). Their subjects were in the age range 15–20 years. Using recall scores, they investigated their efficacy in separting three groups: those subjects who were showing symptoms of Huntington's disease ($N = 21$); those subjects who developed Huntington's disease after the Bender-Gestalt Test had been administered ($N = 22$); and those subjects whose parents had had Huntington's disease but who were themselves free of such symptoms ($N = 46$). Clinicians were also asked to separate the records into the three groups. In general, successful placements by the two methods were about the same, both methods achieving only about 67%–68% accuracy of placement. It should be noted, however, that the rationale for separating the three groups is quite questionable. Moreover, clinicians were not told to look for signs of Huntington's disease, but were asked to evaluate for organicity. The study leaves many unanswered questions, such as how much experience did the clinicians have with organic Bender records, how much did they know about Huntington's disease, and how different were the three groups, in actual fact, with respect to organicity? Finally, recall scores, as derived and used in a global fashion (i.e., simply the number of correctly recalled designs) are not necessarily related to organicity, much less to finely differentiated nuances between subjects who would later develop Huntington's disease, but had not as yet manifested the disease, and those who were already showing overt symptoms of the disease.

The fact that configurational scoring can be quite effective in differentiating *some groups* was demonstrated in two studies. Bilu and Weiss (1974), using a configuration involving seven components, were able to differentiate 81 inpatient psychotics from 81 outpatient nonpsychotics with reasonable accuracy and effectiveness. Johnson (1973), using configurational indicators of depression, was able to find significant results with this method. Even a single specific indicator can sometimes be used to highlight a particular psychiatric condition, as Donnelly and Murphy (1974) did in finding that irregular sequence was associated with lack of impulse control in bipolar depressives, while overly methodical sequence was associated with overly methodical impulse (or constriction) in unipolar depressives.

Keeping the reservations we have noted in mind, we can not return to our own configurational findings. Our findings indicate that if one utilizes what we have called the critical scores, neurotics can be differentiated from both organics and schizophrenics at a high level of significance ($p < .001$), while the differences of depressives, schizophrenics, and organics from each other are also fairly high in significance ($p < .01$).

Organic Brain Damage

In utilizing the following configurational phenomena, it should be emphasized that such factors as age at the time of the injury or disease, severity of brain damage, degree of localization, and laterality of the damage, as well as the personality of the individual, will affect the findings. The relevant factors and their weights are listed below.

Factor	Weight
Marked difficulty with angulation:	2
Severe perceptual rotation:	2
Collision or collision tendency:	2
Severe fragmentation:	2
Perseveration, types (a) and (b):	2
Overlapping difficulty:	2
Simplification:	1
Line incoordination (fine and severe):	1

Critical scores: 9 and above
Marginal scores: 6–8

There are other test indicators of possible organic brain damage. One of the most important behavioral manifestations is the subject's manifestation of impotence or great difficulty in perceiving or executing the design. He may also show evidence of this characteristic by redrawing part or all of the figure one or more times. Other subjects will begin to doodle or produce elaborations. Still others will "concretize" the drawings by making them into a real object rather than a design. However, none of these indicators showed adequate power to differentiate this group from other groups on a statistical basis.

The Schizophrenias

Our criterion population on which this configuration is based consisted of 155 chronic (process) schizophrenics. The vast majority of these *hospitalized* patients were categorized as either paranoids or as mixed types of schizophrenias (79%). There were 92 males and 63 females in the group.

Factor	Weight
Confused or symbolic placement:	2
Retrogression:	2
Highly abnormal placement, first figure:	2
Severe elaboration:	2
Very severe closure difficulty:	1
Severe curvature difficulty:	1
Moderate fragmentation:	1
Moderate perceptual rotation:	1
Simplification:	1
Either excessive use of margin, or crowding of figures into one-third of the page:	1

Critical scores: 7 and above
Marginal scores: 4–6

The Depressions

This particular configuration was derived from a population of 68 hospitalized patients diagnosed as having unipolar depression. The configuration for bipolar depressives is not presented at this time since our sample of such patients is limited. Moreover, many bipolar depressives subsequently develop some form of schizophrenia, and in our experience are not clearly distinguishable from that category. There were 32 females and 36 males in our sample.

Factor	Weight
Overly methodical sequence:	2
Severe compression of space on at least four figures:	2
Severe curvature difficulty (flattening):	2
Severe angulation difficulty (increased):	1
Severe crossing difficulty:	1

Critical scores: 6 and above
Marginal scores: 4–5

Essential Psychoneuroses

Neuroses differ markedly in severity and type. Our sample population is based on nonhospitalized or outpatient neurotics of whom 67 were females and 58 were males. Patients with clearly diagnosable character disturbances were excluded. The test protocols of these patients only infrequently showed gross disturbances such as destruction of the Gestalt or elaborations. Rather, they presented an accumulation of relatively minor changes in some aspects of the designs or their placement.

Factor	Weight
Irregular or overly methodical sequence:	2
Isolated changes in size (marked):	2
Crossing difficulty:	2
Inconsistent or uneven line quality:	2
Severe constriction of size:	2
Mild curvature difficulty:	1
Mild angulation difficulty:	1
Excessive use of margin:	1
Abnormal placement of first figure:	1
Markedly inconsistent direction of movement:	1

Critical scores: 8 and above
Marginal scores: 5–7

Mental Retardation, Moderate and Severe

Mental retardation at these levels may be the consequence of many interrelated factors, including genetic and constitutional factors, severe social–cultural deprivation, and severe emotional maladjustment. Unlike cases with profound mental retardation, organic brain damage is less likely to be evident (Hutt & Gibby, 1976).

Factor	Weight
Increasing difficulty with more difficult figures, especially 6, 7, and 8:	2
Irregular sequence:	2
Markedly irregular space between figures:	2
Perceptual reversal:	2
Fragmentation in figures 7 and 8:	2
Severe closure difficulty:	2
Overlapping difficulty:	2
Collision tendency:	1
Excessive size of figures:	1

Critical scores: 7 and above
Marginal scores: 5–6

It might be added that moderately and severely mentally retarded adults rarely execute figures 7 and 8 successfully. Adequate completion of these designs should make the clinician wary of concluding that the individual is, in fact, mentally retarded. A special problem which the clinician will wish to take into account in evaluating HABGT records is the quality of motivation. Sometimes subjects will do less well than they could because of low aspiration level.

7

The Measurement of Psychopathology and Adience-Abience

Despite our caveats and reservations about objective measurements, we have also noted that they possess important attributes. They are replicable, they can be utilized for comparative purposes, and they can be the foundations for normative analyses. If objective measures are utilized with full awareness of their inherent limitations, they can contribute significantly to clinical application. It is largely when they are taken literally at face value, without recognition that they are based on assumptions which do not necessarily hold in the individual case, and particularly in the individual clinical case, that their use may be inaccurate if not hazardous.

In this chapter we shall present two scales which can be utilized in the clinical study of indivdiuals. They can also be utilized for many other purposes, including group comparisons and many research functions. Both scales rest on the general assumption that global measures based on the projective characteristics of test behavior are of value. Human behavior is quite complex and can best be understood, in the author's view, if the total, complex response is not broken down into atomistic, meaningless units. The complex response contains a unique quality; the single elements into which this response may logically be reduced no longer define this quality, nor can they be reconstructed by logical means into the end product by some arithmetical construction. The complex response may, on the other hand, be evaluated in terms of its necessary antecedents and consequences; the separate, atomistic elements do not necessarily, and usually do not, manifest the same relationships.

THE PSYCHOPATHOLOGY SCALE

The Psychopathology Scale attempts to provide a global measure of the degree of psychopathology manifested on the HABGT. Psychopathology is considered to vary from a very small amount, which may characterize the so-called "normal" individual, to a very great amount, which may characterize the very disturbed individual. The degree of psychopathology varies on a continuum and is assumed to possess a linear quality, so that a higher score on psychopathology represents a higher degree of psychopathology.

The Psychopathology Scale is derived from the copy phase of the HABGT. Work on this scale was begun in 1958–1959, and a preliminary form of the scale was published in 1960 (Hutt & Briskin). It was called The 19-Factor Scale, since it was then based on the scoring of 19 factors, each of which contributed to the total score. Based on an analysis of comparisons of well-adjusted controls and two groups of patients, it was found that the scale differentiated the controls ($N = 50$) from psychiatric patients ($N = 20$) and from hospitalized deaf, mentally retarded patients ($N = 169$) ($p < .001$). These crude analyses seemed promising and led to further refinement and study of the scale.

The present Psychopathology Scale represents the culmination of a number of research studies. It consists of 17 factors, each of which is defined in objective terms. Sixteen of the factors are scored on a scale from 1 to 10; the other factor is scored on a scale from 1 to 3.25. Scores may range from a minimum of 17.0 to a maximum of 163.25, the total range being 146.25 points. In the following discussion we shall present the scale, then offer our present normative findings and summaries of research studies, and finally discuss some uses to which the scale may be put.

As noted earlier, the Psychopathology Scale is based on scores derived from the subject's productions in the copy phase. Each factor is given a raw score (where applicable) and a scaled score, based on the definitions of each factor as presented in Chapter 5. The Psychopathology Scale Score is the sum of the scaled scores.

The Psychopathology Scale

Factor	Raw Score	Scale Value
1. Sequence		
Confused or symbolic		10.0
Irregular		7.0
Overly methodical		4.0
Normal		1.0

The Psychopathology Scale (continued)

Factor	Raw Score	Scale Value
2. *Position, 1st Drawing*		
Abnormal	(See criteria)	3.25
Normal	(See criteria)	1.0
3. *Use of Space, I*		
Abnormal	(See criteria)	10.0
Normal	(See criteria)	1.0
4. *Collision*	(See directions)	
Extreme	Occurs more than 2 times	10.0
Moderate	Occurs 2 times	8.5
Present	Occurs 1 time	7.0
Tendency, extreme	Occurs more than 2 times	5.5
Tendency, moderate	Occurs 2 times	4.0
Tendency, present	Occurs 1 time	2.5
No collision		1.0
5. *Shift of Paper*		
On all figures		10.0
For 3-8 figures		7.0
For 1-2 figures		5.5
No rotation		1.0
6. *Closure Difficulty*	(See criteria)	
Very severe	9	10.0
Severe	6-8	7.75
Moderate	3-5	5.5
Mild	1-2	3.25
Absent	0	1.0
7. *Crossing Difficulty*		
Severe	3 or more	10.0
Moderate	2	7.0
Mild	1	4.0
Absent	0	1.0
8. *Curvature Difficulty*		
Severe	3	10.0
Moderate	2	7.0
Mild	1	4.0
Absent	0	1.0

The Psychopathology Scale (continued)

Factor	Raw Score	Scale Value
9. *Change in Angulation*		
On 5 figures	(See criteria)	10.0
On 4 figures	(See criteria)	8.0
On 3 figures	(See criteria)	6.0
On 2 figures	(See criteria)	4.0
On 1 figure	(See criteria)	2.0
None present		1.0
10. *Perceptual Rotation*		
Severe	80–180 degrees	10.0
Moderate	15–79 degrees	7.0
Mild	5–14 degrees	4.0
None	Less than 5 degrees	1.0
11. *Retrogression*	(See criteria)	
Severe	On more than 2 figures	10.0
Moderate	On 2 figures	7.0
Mild	On 1 figure	4.0
None		1.0
12. *Simplification*	(See criteria)	
Severe	On more than 2 figures	10.0
Moderate	On 2 figures	7.0
Mild	On 1 figure	4.0
None		1.0
13. *Fragmentation*		
Severe	On more than 2 figures	10.0
Moderate	On 2 figures	7.0
Mild	On 1 figure	4.0
None		1.0
14. *Overlapping Difficulty*		
Severe	On more than 1 figure	10.0
Moderate	On 1 figure	5.5
None		1.0
15. *Elaboration*		
Severe	On more than 2 figures	10.0
Moderate	On 2 figures	7.0
Mild	On 1 figure	4.0
None		1.0

The Psychopathology Scale (continued)

Factor	Raw Score	Scale Value
16. Perservation	(See criteria)	
Severe	On more than 2 figures	10.0
Moderate	On 2 figures	7.0
Mild	On 1 figure	4.0
None		1.0
17. Redrawing, Total Figure		
Very severe	4 or more times	10.0
Severe	3 times	7.75
Moderate	2 times	5.5
Mild	1 time	3.25
None		1.0

Scoring for the Psychopathology Scale is greatly facilitated by the use of the Scoring Template which is included in each package furnished with the *HAGBT Revised Record Forms,* 2nd edition, by the publisher, Grune & Stratton, Inc.

Normative Findings

We have accumulated norms for several well-defined groups of adults. Experience has indicated that, above age 10 years, age is not a significant factor in the Psychopathology Scale score (see later discussion). Table 3 presents these normative data for adults.

Table 3
Revised Normative Data for the
Psychopathology Scale

Group	N	Mean	SD
Normals*	140	32.8	4.9
Outpatient neurotics	125	53.5	9.6
Inpatient neurotics	55	61.7	8.7
Unipolar depressives	68	66.2	6.4
Outpatient schizophrenics	60	78.3	11.8
Chronic schizophrenics	155	97.1	12.1
Organic brain damage	98	100.3	14.3

* This group consisted of 80 individuals who were "screened" for evidence of disturbance and 60 "unselected" college students.

A few comments may be in order concerning the nature of these normative groups. The outpatient neurotics were selected from both the author's own practice and that of other clinical psychologists. It is not assumed that they are typical of a random selection of neurotics. The inpatient neurotics were hospitalized for a variety of neurotic syndromes, mostly severe anxiety or depression. Similarly, the unipolar depressives were hospitalized for a very severe depressive condition. The outpatient schizophrenics were being treated by clinical psychologists and psychiatrists (43 and 17, respectively). The chronic schizophrenic population was drawn from state mental hospitals and probably represents a larger proportion of indigent psychotics than may be found in psychiatric hospitals in general. All of the organic brain-damage cases were selected on the basis of clinically verified examination and represent cases with chronic disease processes or traumatic brain injury.

An analysis of the differences among means reveals the following. Differences between means are significant at the .001 level or better, except in two instances. The difference between inpatient neurotics and unipolar depressives reaches the level of only .01. The difference between chronic schizophrenics and the organic brain-damaged group does not quite reach the probability level of .05. Thus it may be said, on the basis of these findings, that the Psychopathology Scale scores provide significant differentiation between most groups of patients. The questionable difference between the depressives and the inpatient neurotics may be due to the fact that there was much overlapping in clinical pathology between these two groups. The organic group is a very heterogeneous group and is not claimed to be representative of typical organic cases. Moreover, it is likely that some of the patients in the chronic schizophrenic group suffered from some form of brain dysfunction.

It should be emphasized that although these data indicate the value of the scale in differentiating groups, they do not indicate that individual cases can be "defined" in terms of the scale score alone. We have emphasized the hazards of utilizing any clinical score, no matter how high its putative value, in making clinical diagnoses; much more information is necessary in the individual case.

Now let us examine the findings for children. Table 4 presents these tentative normative data.

The "normals" reported in Table 4 are unselected cases, the only restriction in their sampling being that they had not been referred for special study by the school psychologist or clinic. All of the "disturbed" cases are individuals who had been reported by their teachers as showing problems in their personal or social adjustment. It will be noted that the means for the disturbed children at these ages are very similar although slightly higher than the norms reported in Table 3 for outpatient neurotic

Table 4
Normative Data for the Psychopathology
Scale: Children

CA (years)	Type of Group	N	Mean	SD
10	Normals	28	43.8	6.2
	Disturbed	40	59.7	10.0
11	Normals	35	41.2	7.3
	Disturbed	43	58.4	10.2
12	Normals	39	42.3	7.6
	Disturbed	36	57.1	9.8

adults. We have reason, therefore, to assume that children who are disturbed in these age ranges do not perform very differently from outpatient neurotics on this scale. The means for the normal children are, however, significantly higher than the means for the normal adult population ($p < .001$). Apparently our scale is somewhat affected by the maturation factor although these differences are not striking. In the main, our data indicate that very high scores on the Psychopathology Scale, for these age groups, can differentiate disturbed from normal children ($p < .001$) and can be interpreted in much the same manner as is done for adults. Again, we caution that in the indivdiual case more than a high Psychopathology Scale score is needed before reaching the conclusion that an individual child is disturbed. The Psychopathology Scale score, rather, should be taken as suggestive, only. It is also interesting to note that, both for "normal" and "disturbed" children, there is no discernable trend, between the ages of 10 and 12 years, of any significant change in mean scores. Thus, although there is a slight difference between the means for children and adults, the maturation factor does not appear to operate significantly within the 10–12-year-old groups. We assume that this is also the case above 12 years of age.

We do not yet have adequate data for children below 10 years of age, although our extensive clinical experience with this procedure for such children indicates that the scale is "roughly" applicable for nonretarded children down to about 8 years of age. We shall discuss this problem more fully in Part II of this volume.

Research Findings

A number of studies have been completed with the Psychopathology Scale, some of which have been referred to in earlier chapters. Let us consider separately a number of topics which have been researched.

First, as to the question of objectivity in scoring, or *interjudge reliability*. As reported in our earlier edition of this work (Hutt, 1969a), the correlation between the total scores on the Psychopathology Scale for two "experienced" scorers for 100 schizophrenic cases was .96, indicating adequate objectivity. The reliabilities for the 17 factors of the scale ranged from a low of .76 for the factor of Simplification to a high of 1.00 for Shift of Paper. Only three of the 17 factors yielded a reliability coefficient of less than .81 (Perceptual Rotation, Simplification, and Overlapping). A series of subsequent studies (Miller & Hutt, 1975) showed that only slightly lower interscorer reliabilities were obtained when one scorerer was relatively inexperienced and the other experienced. The rho obtained was .895 for a population of schizophrenic patients. Moreover, in the latter publication it was shown that the three major components of the scale (Organizational Factors, Changes in Gestalt, and Distortions of the Gestalt) were also separately reliable.

A study of *test–retest reliability* with 40 hospitalized patients over a two-week period yielded rho's of .87 for the males and .83 for the females (Miller & Hutt, 1975). Further analysis indicated that both patients who obtained high Psychopathology Scale scores and those who obtained low scores obtained high test–retest reliability.

Data concerning the possible *relationships between Psychopathology Scale scores and chronological age, sex, and intelligence* have also been obtained. All of our data indicate that, at least above 15 years of age, Psychopathology score and age are not significantly correlated (Research Report #43, 1964; Hutt & Miller, 1976). Data presented in Table 4 also suggest that the relationship is not important, at least down to age 10 years for children who are not retarded. Neither does there appear to be a significant relationship between sex and Psychopathology score, as revealed by study of the data in the same publications. The question of the relationship between intelligence and Psychopathology score is a more complicated matter. It would appear that at lower age levels (below 10 years of age) and for mentally retarded individuals at even higher age levels, there is a small but significant relationship between the two variables. In our study of deaf–retarded individuals, the r reached the level of .55, which would indicate about 30% of commonality between the two variables. This conclusion is very tentative, however, since the measure of intelligence used in that study (Research Report #43, 1964) was quite unreliable and since the population studied was quite exceptional. Our evidence suggests, however, that at the adult level, intelligence and Psychopathology score are *not* significantly correlated. Using highest school grade reached as a rough estimate of intelligence, for a population of 100 outpatient individuals, an r of .004 was obtained between "intelligence" and Psychopathology score (Hutt & Miller, 1976).

Implications for Use of the Psychopathology Scale

There appear to be many possible uses for the Psychopathology Scale. In the research area there are many interesting issues which can be investigated. Aside from replication and extended study of some of the issues we have already discussed, the scale can be used in studying various clinical populations and in analyzing the contribution of degree of psychopathology to clinical and therapeutic improvement. VandenBos (1973), for instance, utilized the scale in research on the problem of "focusing" in relation to therapeutic improvement. The scale should be useful in comparisons among various cultural and social groups as well as in cross-cultural studies. Of course, the interrelationships between the Psychopathology Scale score and other criteria of psychopathology would be a fascinating area of exploration. These are but a few of the possibilities.

At the clinical level of application, there are also many possible uses. Since nonprofessionals can be trained quite quickly to score this scale, use of the scale in screening programs is quite feasible. The clinician who deals with a great variety of clinical problems should also find the scale useful as another way of discovering the degree of psychopathology of the patient, especially of the illiterate and language-handicapped patient. It should be remembered, however, that this one measure of psychopathology, like any other single, objective measure of the phenomenon, is limited in validity. A high Psychopathology Scale score should be taken as the *starting point* for the evaluation of probable psychopathology, not as the conclusion. High scores are more likely to be significant than low scores, however. The clinician will also wish to consider both the normative scores for a particular population against whom the patient is being compared, and the standard deviations in scores for those populations. For instance, let us say that a patient's Psychopathology Scale score is 75. In judging whether the patient is more likely to be properly categorized as a neurotic or a schizophrenic, one would consider that while this score places him slightly below the mean of outpatient schizophrenics (78.3), and thus is presumptive evidence that he may belong in that category, his score is still within 2 sigmas above the mean of inpatient neurotics (61.7). Thus, from a statistical viewpoint one could say that, judged on the basis of this criterion alone, he has a much higher probability of falling within the psychotic population than the inpatient neurotic population. The probability of "correct" categorization would be increased by the utilization of a configurational analysis. Clinical assessment would be greatly enhanced, of course, through inferential analysis.

THE ADIENCE–ABIENCE SCALE

The Adience–Abience Scale represents an attempt to measure a basic characteristic of the individual's perceptual orientation toward the world. The concept of adience–abience, and its preliminary measuring device, were first introduced by the writer in 1960 (Hutt & Briskin, 1960). The concept was further elaborated in a research study some years later (Hutt and Feuerefile, 1963) and in the earlier edition of this book Hutt, 1969a).

Perceptual adience–abience is conceived as a primary defensive operation of the personality. People differ markedly in their perceptual "openess" or "closedness" (perceptual approach–avoidance) to the world. It is believed that as a consequence of favorable perceptual contact with the world, on the one hand, or of unfavorable or traumatic experience, on the other, the young infant, and later the child, tends to develop either an approach-oriented position or an avoidance-oriented position, respectively, in his perceptual interactions with the external and his internal world. This aspect of perceptual style is thought to be the primary mode of a mediating experience and serves as a foundation for the later development of other defensive and coping operations of the personality. Is is assumed that once such a style has begun to develop, it tends to become self-reinforcing. Therefore, it persists unless dramatic circumstances cause it to change. It is inferred that adient individuals are more likely to be open to new varieties of learning experience and can profit from them more than others, whereas abient individuals tend to block out new experiences and profit less from such exposures. This perceptual, personality style is *not* assumed to be cooordinate with other aspects of approach–avoidance behaviors, such as extroversive tendencies or aggressiveness in overt behavior.

Although we expect that other aspects of defensive behavior may be correlated with abient tendencies, we also see significant differences. Perceptual vigilance (Postman, 1953), for example, is conceived to be a defense by the person which enables him to alter his behavior *after* he has perceived a "danger," whereas perceptual abience blocks the person's awareness from receiving perceptual input. Field dependence (Witkin, Dyke, Faterson, Goodenough, & Karp, 1967) may also be related to perceptual abience, but it defines a defensive style of being overly reliant on the visual field, whereas abience, agian, is a blocking of that visual field. Other defensive, perceptual concepts have been proposed by Sullivan (1953) (selective attention), Jung (1939) (introversion), Guilford (1959) (experimentally derived measures of introversion), Schachtel (1959) (autocentrism), Gardner and Long (1960) (leveling–sharpening), and Petrie (1967) (augmentation–reduction). All of these have in common some defensive operation manifested in the perceptual response after the stimulus has been perceived. In contrast, the concept of adience–abience relates to a *failure of the organism to process the visual input,* i.e., unawareness (more or less) that a visual stimulus is present (VonBékésy, 1967). Based on our view of present knowledge concerning the other types of defenses, we believe that these are secondary phenomena, i.e., reactive. In contrast, our conception of perceptual adience-abience is perhaps closest to the concept of Schneirla (1959) who in an intensive review of the development of what he terms underlying "biphasic" processes of aproach-withdrawal in behavior stated: "Much evidence shows that in *all* animals the species-typical pattern of behavior is based upon biphasic, functionally opposed mechanisms insuring approach or withdrawal reactions according to whether stimuli of low or high intensity, respectively, are in effect."

We have sketched the probable significance of adience–abience phenomena in relation to child development (Hutt, 1976a) and mental retardation (Hutt, 1976b), and in our review of the research evidence, below, we shall comment about this.

The derivation of the items of the Adience–Abience Scale came from extensive experience with the HABGT with a great variety of clinical patients. It was observed that certain types of test behavior were related to certain types of personality constellations. The first scale developed for the purpose of measuring adience–abience rested on these observations and on test factors that were being employed in the Psychopathology Scale. However, the definitions and measuring units of the Adience–Abience Scale were *differentiated from and weighted differently than* similar items of the other scale. Based upon further clinical experience, tested through various research studies, the scale has been revised so that we now have the Scale for Perceptual Adience–Abience, 2nd revision. We shall now present this scale and then discuss normative findings, research evaluations, and implications for use.

Scale for Perceptual Adience–Abience

2nd Revision*

General Directions

1. Use the Copy Phase test protocol based on the HABGT test cards, and score the drawings for each of the following factors by circling the weight that is appropriate for that factor.† When none of the definitions apply, the weight of that factor is 0.
2. When scorable, each factor is assigned a weight from +2 (high adience) to −2 (high abience).
3. The uncorrected score is the algebraic sum of the circled scores.

---

* This Scale is reproduced in the *HABGT Revised Record Form,* 2nd edition, published by Grune & Stratton, Inc.

† These definitions differ in some important respects from those applicable to the Psychopathology Scale. Use these definitions, only, for this scale.

4. The *Corrected Adience–Abience Score* is obtained by adding +25 to the uncorrected score. The range in Corrected Scores is from +1 to +38; high scores reflect high degrees of adience while low scores reflect high degrees of abience.

5. For Factors 1 and 2, use either the Scoring Template or Table 1 in this volume.

Factors Relating to Space and Size

1. Height and Width

    a.   There are *no* instances in which *either* height or width is *less* than   +1
the limits indicated.

    b.   There are *1 or 2* instances in which *either* height or width is *less*   0
than the limits indicated.

    c.   There are *3 or more* instances in which *either* height or width is   −2
less than the limits indicated.

2. Height, Only

    a.   There are *no* instances in which height is *less* than the limits   +1
indicated.

    b.   There is *only 1* instance in which height is *less* than the limits   −1
indicated.

    c.   There is *more than 1 instance* in which the height is *less* than the   −2
limits indicated.

3. Use of Page (Calculated by imagining a line drawn around all of the drawings and estimating the amount of space utilized in the drawings.)

    a.   Uses *more* than three-fourths of the page, and *no more* than 3   +2
figures are within 1 inch of the left margin of the page.

    b.   Uses *more* than three-fourths of the page, but *more* than 3 figures   +1
are within 1 inch of the left margin of the page.

    c.   Uses *less* than three-fourths of the page, but *no more* than 3 figures   −1
are within 1 inch of the left margin of the page.

    d.   Uses *less* than three-fourths of the page, and *more* than 3 figures   −2
are within 1 inch of the left margin of the page.

Factors Relating to Organization

4. Sequence (Defined as a shift in the direction of successive placements of the figures; i.e., when successive placements have been from left to right, a shift occurs when the next figure is placed above, below, or to the left of the preceding figure, etc. When the edge of the paper has been reached the next placement would normally be at the opposite side of the page—as if the page were a sphere.)

a. Methodical sequence: less than 3 shifts.   +1

b. Irregular or confused sequence: it is *irregular* when 3 or more   −2
shifts occur; it is *confused* when there is an obvious jumble in
placement and no apparent plan is evident.

5. *Placement of First Figure*

a. Normal placement: at least 1 inch from the top and left edges of   +2
the page, and not otherwise an abnormal placement.

b. Normal placement: between ¾ and 1 inch from the top of the page,   +1
and at least 1 inch from the left edge of the page, but not otherwise an abnormal placement.

c. Abnormal placement: less than ¾ inch from the top edge, or less   −1
than 1 inch from the left edge, but not below the upper half of
the page.

d. Abnormal placement: center of figure is within 1 inch of the cen-   −2
ter of the page, or below the upper half of the page.

Factors Related to Change in Form of Gestalt

6. *Closure Difficulty* (Defined as an obvious failure in accurate closure within a
figure or at the joining of contiguous figures. In the case of circles, for example, there is a gap in the closing of the circle, or an overshooting of the
closing; in the case of straight-line figures, the joining at an apex is unclosed or overshot; in contiguous figures, there is a gap or overshooting
at the junction of the figures. *Score only for figures A, 2, 4, 7, and 8.* Note: *no
more than 2 closure difficulties* are counted for a single figure, and on
figure 2, count 2 closure difficulties as a score of 1, and more than 2 difficulties as a score of 2.)

a. Normal closure difficulty: 5 or less closure difficulties.   +1

b. Moderate closure difficulty: between 6 and 8 closure difficulties.   −1

c. Severe closure difficulty: 9 or more closure difficulties.   −2

7. *Crossing Difficulty* (Defined as any obvious difficulty in the crossing on
figures 6 and 7, manifested by redrawing, sketching, erasing, or increased
line pressure where the lines cross. On figure 6, when the two curves do
not cross cleanly—as when there is a merging of the two lines—this is
counted as a crossing difficulty, but when the two curves are drawn as tangential, this is *not* counted as crossing difficulty. Note: there may be two
instances of crossing difficulty on figure 7.)

a. No crossing difficulty.   +1

b. Moderate crossing difficulty: only 1 instance.   −1

c. Marked crossing difficulty: two or more instances.   −2

8. *Change in Angulation* (Defined as a shift of *15 degrees or more* of the
angulation *within* the figure, e.g., when the columns of figure 2 are shifted

toward the upright or toward the horizontal. *Score only on figures 2, 3, 5, 6, and 7*. Use the Scoring Template, using the central axis of each figure as the referent. *Increased* angulation means that the angle within the figure has been made more *acute; decreased* angulation means that the angle within the figure has been made more *rectangular*, e.g., when the secant on figure 5 has been shifted toward the upright position, or when the left-hand figure in design 7 has been shifted toward the horizon.)

 a. No instance of either increased or decreased angulation. +2

 b. Increased angulation: present on only 1 figure, and there is no +1
instance of decreased angulation.

 c. Excessive increased angulation: present on more than 1 figure, 0
but there is no instance of decreased angulation.

 d. Decreased angulation: present on only 1 figure, and there is no −1
instance of increased angulation.

 e. Excessive decreased angulation: present on more than 1 figure, −2
and there is no instance of increased angulation.

Factors Related to Distortion

9. *Rotation* (Defined as a shift in the axis of *the total figure*—not the paper—
from the standard orientation of the card).

 a. Absent or mild: no rotation of more than 14 degrees. +1

 b. Moderate: any rotation of 15–79 degrees. −1

 c. Severe: any rotation of 80 degrees or more. −2

10. *Fragmentation* (Defined as the breaking of the Gestalt into component
parts or the *gross separation* of the 2 parts of the figure as in figures
A, 4, and 7).

 a. No fragmentation present. +1

 b. Fragmentation on only 1 figure. −1

 c. Marked fragmentation: present on 2 or more figures −2

11. *Simplification* (Defined as the use of a "substitute figure" which is simpler
to draw—e.g., the substitution of a rectangle for a hexagon in figure 7—
other than by fragmentation or by making symmetrical figures out of
asymmetrical ones.)

 a. No simplification present. 0

 b. Moderate simplification: present on only 1 figure. −1

 c. Marked simplification: present on 2 or more figures. −2

12. *Elaboration* (Defined as any obvious elaboration or doodling).

 a. No elaboration present. 0

 b. Elaboration present on 1 or more figures. −2

Table 5
Normative Data for the
Adience–Abience Scale, 2nd Revision*

Group	N	Mean	SD
Normals	140	25.8	3.5
Outpatient neurotics	125	23.8	3.6
Inpatient neurotics	55	21.0	3.8
Chronic schizohrenics	155	18.3	5.1
Organic brain damage	98	15.1	6.2

* The population for this table has been described in our discussion of Table 3.

Normative Findings

At present we have fairly well-established norms on adience–abience for adults, based on slightly more than 500 cases, and these are presented in Table 5. Our norms for older children are based on a much more restricted sample and are presented in Table 6 as tentative norms for these groups.

It will be noted that there is a steady decrease in the mean Adience–Abience Scale scores as one proceeds down the table from "normals" to organic brain-damaged cases, while the standard deviations increase through the same progression. The differences between each of the pairs of means reaches a p value of .001 or better. Thus the adience–abience score is able to differentiate quite satisfactorily among these groups. Tests were run to determine the relevance of chronological age and sex in relation to these scores. For all of the subpopulations both age and sex were

Table 6
Tentative Normative Data for the
Adience–Abience Scale: Children

Group	CA Range (years)	N	Mean	SD
Normals*	10–12	102	21.3	3.9
Disturbed*	10–12	109	18.2	4.1
Boys' Club**	10–16	120	17.7	2.6

* These populations are described in connection with Table 4.
** These cases were drawn from Project Gamit, a research project in connection with the Boys' Club of Royal Oak, Mich., which is, as yet, unpublished.

insignificantly related ($p < .01$). The only group for whom we had data on education was a population of outpatients being treated at the Psychology Clinic of the University of Detroit. Utilizing highest grade achieved as a rough indication of "intelligence," it was found that the correlation of Adience–Abience score with educational grade was .052 ($p < .001$; $N = 100$). Thus, we can suggest that for this group, at least, intelligence, as estimated, is unrelated to the Adience–Abience score.

We have lumped the age groups since we have no reason to believe that age, within this range, significantly affects Adience–Abience score. (See later discussion.) The large majority of the Boys' Club children were in the 11–13 age categories; most of these children had been referred to the Club in connection with delinquent acts against persons or property.

The norm for Adience–Abience for "normals" is comparable to that of inpatient neurotic adults reported in Table 5; it is 4.5 points lower than the norm for "normal" adults. Hence different norms are justifiable for children. The differences between the "normal" children and each of the problem populations of children are significant at the .001 level. The difference between the norms for the "disturbed" and "Boys' Club" groups is statistically insignificant ($p < .05$), if we demand a higher order of probability.

Clinical experience has suggested that the higher the Adience–Abience score the more likely, other things being equal, that the child will be able to profit from a large variety of "learning" or "therapeutic" experiences. If the score is above 21 on the revised scale, the chances are good that significant improvement may be expected. The meaning of scores for children below 10 years of age remains to be explored, and great care should be taken in attempting to extrapolate from these findings to younger groups.

Research Findings

Let us consider aspects of the reliability of the Adience–Abience Scale. In one study, a rho of .912 was obtained for scores obtained with two judges, one experienced in scoring and the other relatively inexperienced, for a sample of schizophrenic patients (Hutt & Miller, 1975). Other studies, in progress, reveal comparable results, the lowest interjudge correlation obtained being .90 and the highest .94. We can conclude that objectivity in scoring is fairly high. With regard to test–retest reliability there are more extensive data. In the same study noted above, test–retest correlations, over an interval of two weeks, for each of two different groups were found to be .84. Moreover, the four major components of the scale also proved to be quite reliable, the highest reliability being found for the component of "Organization" and the lowest for" Form of Gestalt.'' In the Gamit project, the findings of which are unpublished, as yet, with 120 cases, test–retest results over longer intervals of time yielded an r of .968 ($N = 120$) for children in the age range 10–16 years. Only four cases showed what would be judged to be a significant shift in adience–abience position on a clinical basis.

The problem of validity is, of course, a much more complicated one and demands difficult criteria for meaningful evaluation. We shall present summaries of a number of studies on this score, treating them in a historical perspective.

Our first study, part of the development of the original scale, was done on a population of deaf–retardates. In this study (Hutt & Feuerefile, 1963), a preliminanry analysis and a cross-validation analysis were performed. In the preliminary study, 30 cases were selected randomly from the total population of approximately 200 patients. The copy phase of the HABGT records of these individuals were then scored in terms of the preliminary form of the Adience–Abience Scale, and these records were then dichotomized into two groups: 15 cases relatively high in adience and 15 cases relatively high in abience. In order to test the construct validity of the adience–abience measure, these two groups were compared on six criteria, presumably related to the general hypothesis that more adient individuals would show more effective intellectual and interpersonal functioning than those who were higher on the abient end of the scale. It must be remembered that we were dealing with a highly selected population at the lower end of the intelligence scale, and that this fact would tend to attenuate possible positive findings. Despite such limitations, all but one of the tests turned out to be quite significant, as the data in Table 7 indicate.

All of the differences are in the expected direction, but one (length of hospitalization) does not reach a frequently accepted level of statistical significance. The data indicate that our measure of adience–abience does discriminate, for this highly restricted group, along the lines of our *a priori* conceptualization. Adience is apparently related to more effective adjustment and one can infer that it is related to capacity for making more effective use of one's experience.

In the cross-validation study, the remainder of the experimental population was utilized. Four of the criterion variables used in the phase of the study were retained, and three were added, but our analysis will be limited to two of these three additional criteria (since one is not directly pertinent to our present discussion). Moreover, separate analyses are presented for males and females, since (1) other data from this research project indicated that females tended to show more psychopathology than males, and (2) there were differences in adience–abience scores between females and males for this population. A revised form of the adience–

Table 7

A Comparison of Individuals Who Differ in
Adience–Abience, Based on Six
Criterion Variables*

Criterion Variable	High Adient Group (N = 15)	High Abient Group (N = 15)	t	p (one-tail)
HABGT score on				
Psychopathology	70.1	130.4	13.33	<.01
Rating on				
Psychopathology	2.0	3.2	3.33	<.01
Goodenough I.Q.	70.6	44.9	4.33	<.01
Rating of intellectual				
impairment	3.1	4.1	2.86	<.01
Age at admission to				
hospital (months)	175.9	120.6	2.24	<.02
Length of hospitalization	112.1	147.8	1.20	>.05

* For all personality variables, higher scores indicate greater degree of psychopathology.

abience scale was used. An additional test was made for the possible relationship between age and adience–abience score. A correlation of .09 was obtained between these variables, which is not statistically significant. In the present analysis we compare the means in corrected adience–abience scores of the groups of males and females who lie within the upper 25% of the distribution on each of the criterion variables, since some of these variables are either noncontinuous or are not normally distributed. Table 8 presents our findings.

As predicted, individuals who are high in ratings on psychopathology tend to be more abient than those who are low in such ratings, the differences being considered significant in view of the limited validity of the psychopathology ratings. As predicted, adience is associated with better intellectual performance, on both the Goodenough and the Wechsler scales, the findings being highly significant. We did not obtain a significant difference for males on the rating of intellectual impairment, but did for females. This discrepancy is consistent with the impressions of the clinical staff of the deaf–retarded project that the male population was far less impaired in intellectual functioning than the female population, and ratings of males had lower reliability. It is apparent that age of admission is highly significant in relation to adience–abience in the expected direction: those who were institutionalized earlier were more abient. Our findings on ratings of hostility are difficult to interpret, not only because they are inconsistent, but also because this criterion variable turned out to have very limited validity, as judged by other data obtained in the research project.

There is apparently some degree of commonality between our measure of adience–abience, on the one hand, and psychopathology and intelligence on the other. A correlation of .69 was obtained for 114 cases between our HABGT score on the psychopathology Scale and on the Adience–Abience Scale. This is not inconsistent with our conceptualization that abient individuals would tend to be more maladjused. However, there is still sufficient noncommonality to make these measures separately meaningful. Various correlations between measures of intelligence, ranging from .28 to .73, were obtained for different samplings of this population. Again, we would expect that individuals who were higher in adience would tend to rate and function as more intelligent, or be less impaired intellectually, other things being equal. There is sufficient noncommonality between such measures, however, to indicate that somewhat different functions are being tapped.

All in all, the findings from both phases of the deaf–retarded study suggest that the Adience–Abience Scale enables us to make at least roughly accurate predictions in terms of our major hypothesis, and that therefore this scale has significant possibilities.

Other tests of the scale's predictive potential were made and will be reported briefly, as suggestive rather than conclusive. The interested

Table 8
Adience–Abience Means and Differences for Extreme
Groups on Six Criterion Variables

Variable	Sex	Mean, High Group	Mean, Low Group	t	p (one-tail)
Rating on	M	14.6 (16)*	17.3 (16)	2.39	$<.02$
Psychopathology	F	12.3 (10)	15.9 (10)	2.04	$<.05$
Goodenough I.Q.	M	21.5 (16)	11.4 (16)	4.41	$<.01$
	F	16.4 (12)	8.6 (12)	3.63	$<.01$
Rating, on intellectual	M	14.7 (18)	14.8 (18)	.14	$>.25$
impairment	F	9.9 (10)	14.4 (10)	3.21	$<.01$
Age at admission	M	16.4 (23)	12.5 (23)	2.68	$<.01$
to hospital	F	17.3 (13)	8.5 (13)	4.90	$<.01$
Wechsler performance	M	20.4 (15)	11.2 (15)	4.47	$<.01$
I.Q.	F	16.6 (11)	9.0 (11)	3.76	$<.01$
Rating on overt	M	22.6 (23)	15.0 (23)	3.45	$<.01$
hostility	F	13.9 (13)	12.0 (13)	.95	$>.05$

* Numbers in parentheses represent the N in each group.

reader will wish to examine the data in research publications which are being prepared.

The first of these concerned the prediction of "movement" in psychotherapy. It was hypothesized that those who were higher in adience, as measured, would tend to make greater improvement from dynamically oriented, uncovering therapy, than those who were higher in abience. From our own population of psychotherapy cases, we selected those individuals, ranging in age from 18 to 35 years at the beginning of therapy, on whom we had ratings of degree of therapeutic change. There were 42 such cases in all. All of these had been given the HABGT during the early stages of the therapeutic program. The rating scale involved global judgments concerning: symptomatic improvement, ego functioning, degree of maturity, and absence of pathological anxiety. Each of these was rated on a 7-point scale and the scores were then averaged. The Adience–Abience Scale scores were obtained independently of any knowledge of these ratings so as to avoid possible contamination. Our test of the efficacy of the adience–abience measure was its capacity to discriminate between the upper third and the lower third ($N = 14$ in each group) in overall psychotherapeutic change, as rated. The findings are presented in Table 9.

This significant finding is limited by many considerations. No attempt was made to control for other factors than those already noted, such as initial degree of psychopathology, motivation for therapeutic change, age, etc. The distribution by sex in the two groups was roughly equal, with 8 females in the high group and 7 females in the low group. What appears to indicate promise for the measure of adience–abience is that it discriminated effectively between these two "extreme" groups. This tends to support the notion that adient persons can better profit from at least this type of learning experience.

Our next presentation of findings deals with adience–abience differences between two groups of hospitalized schizophrenic patients. Of a

Table 9
Means and p Values for Adience–Abience
Scores of Two Extreme Groups
Differing in Therapeutic Change

Group ($N = 14$ each)	Mean Score
High in change	29.7
Low in change	23.9
p (one-tail) for mean difference = .01	

population of 100 such patients, we selected the HABGT records of those who had been hospitalized for less than 6 months and those who had been hospitalized for more than 5 years. We wished to test the Adience–Abience Scale's power in differentiating between these two groups, on the assumption that those who had been hospitalized for a long period of time were more likely to be unable to profit from experience (and change) than those who had been hospitalized for less than 6 months and then discharged. Obviously, the two groups must have differed in severity of psychopathology, among other things. Nevertheless, if differences were found between the two groups in the expected direction (that the discharge group would be higher in adience), we would have reason to believe the measure to have some possible value in line with our general theory.

We were able to find 22 cases with hospitalization above 5 years (13 males and 9 females), and selected 20 of these cases, leaving out 2 males. We also found 12 cases with less than 6 months of hospitalization, including 7 males and 5 females. Again, no attempt was made to control for other possibly significant factors, such as intelligence and socioeconomic status, that might influence results. However, at this stage we were still only interested in the general tendency for the Adience–Abience Scale to predict along the lines of our theoretical view. We found that the high hospitalization group had a mean Adience–Abience score of 18.1, while the low hospitalization group had a mean score of 22.6. The difference between the means turns out to be significant at the .01 level (one-tail test), and in the expected direction.

Two other studies deserve special note. In a rigorous study of the predictive power of the Adience–Abience Scale score, we attempted to determine whether schizophrenics who scored higher on the scale had better "inner resources" than those who scored lower (Hutt, 1969b). Two groups of 40 cases each were matched on the basis of age, sex, and length of hospitalization. The groups differed significantly on Adience–Abience scores. They were compared on two tests of creativity: accuracy in reproduction of the figures, and number and quality of associations on the association phase of the procedure. It was found that the two groups were statistically and significantly different on both measures, strongly suggesting the power of the scores on the Adience–Abience measure to tap differences in patients with comparable clinical diagnoses.

A critical study was performed by Credidio (1975). In an attempt to evaluate the construct validity of our measure of adience–abience, he compared two groups of college students who differed in scores on adience–abience with respect to their performance on the Gottschaldt Figures Test. This test yielded an independent measure of perception of novel stimuli and the accurate reproduction of such stimuli. As predicted, those who were high in adience performed significantly better than those who were low in adience or high in abience.

These studies support the predictive and construct validity aspects of the Adience–Abience Scale. Other studies have attempted to evaluate the relationship of this scale to other aspects of the personality. Two studies (Kachorek, 1969; McConville, 1970) explored the relationship of adience–abience to measures of field dependence–independence. As expected, there was a slight tendency for these measures to be related, but the degree of relationship was not statistically significant. Thus, we have some evidence that different functions are being tapped. Similarly, Meyer (1973) has shown that there may be a very small positive relationship between altruistic behavior, as measured by a special test, and adience–abience. In general we find that, as expected, our measure of adience–abience is essentially independent of these other aspects of the personality.

The interrelationship of our Psychopathology Scale and our Adience–Abience Scale has also been investigated with a population of individuals in outpatient therapy (Hutt & Miller, 1976). It was found that the two measures had some degree of commonality (about 15%–18%) in this population, but were essentially independent. However, in the same study, the two measures showed a much higher degree of commonality (40%–60%) in a population of hospitalized schizophrenics. It appears that these measures have much more in common at the extreme in pschopathology.

Implications for Use of the Adience–Abience Scale

We have already dealt with some of the research uses and problems in connection with this scale. The problem of its validity is, of course, by no means settled despite some important evidence of its construct and predictive validities. One of the most important research areas is that of determining under what kinds of conditions adience–abience can be permanently or temporarily modified, if need be. Cross-cultural and experiential effects need to be understood in relation to the phenomenon. The nature of the relationship of adience–abience to other aspects of the personality needs to be much more fully understood. These are but a few of the research areas requiring investigation. We believe that present evidence concerning this scale justifies the effort required in such studies.

At the clinical level there are many possible areas of application. The scale might be used for screening and selection of candidates who are most likely to be ready for some form of ameliorative or therapeutic management. It is useful in any consideration of the nature of the individual's pathology and ego resources. Comparison of findings on this scale with other aspects of the individual's functioning can make the clinical picture much clearer.

If, as we believe, an adient perceptual style is conducive to effective cognitive functioning and healthy personality development, the scale can have important applications in mental health programs. We have detailed some of these possibilities in a chapter of a book about mental health in children (Hutt, 1976a). The scale may be particularly useful in dealing with problems of mental retardation, both in clarifying the exact nature of the retardation and in coping more effectively with it (Hutt, 1976b).

PART II

Clinical Studies

INTRODUCTION TO CLINICAL STUDIES

The following clinical studies of the HABGT are intended to illustrate the various ways in which this procedure can be utilized. In the first clinical study we shall do a "complete" HABGT analysis, demonstrating the following: inferential analysis; configurational analysis; scoring for Psychopathology and for Adience–Abience; and interpretation of these findings in terms of probable conclusions. Following this the HABGT findings will be integrated with other aspects of the case. The busy clinician may not be able to afford the luxury of this type of detailed analysis of one test procedure; he may wish to lessen his burden by utilizing only one or two of the methods of analysis that are available. Too often, the clinician will substitute a large battery of tests, and treat their findings fairly superficially instead of analyzing a more limited sampling of test behavior much more intensively. The *core* of the clinical process is *not* the accumulation of a large number of objective scores, however, but *the intensive and analytical study of a relatively restricted sample of behaviors* and their *integration into an individual picture* in terms of the particular individual's problems, personal history, physical development, and current situation. Simply *scanning* clinical data by means of quick or limited analyses will often lead to inappropriate findings, insufficient understanding of the precise nature of the individual's problems, or only superficial results.

Later clinical studies will highlight different aspects of the various HABGT procedures. In some cases only a limited sampling of procedures will be presented so as to afford illustration of their salience in terms of the limited presenting problem.

It is hoped that the presentation of these cases will not only illustrate the various methods of HABGT analysis but will also serve to introduce the reader to a variety of clinical conditions. Our sampling of cases includes the study of two children and the records of schizophrenic, organic brain-damaged, neurotic, character problem, and mentally retarded patients. A much more comprehensive view of the great variety of phenomena which this procedure reveals will be found in our companion volume, *An Atlas for the Hutt Adaptation of the Bender-Gestalt Test* (Hutt & Gibby, 1970). That volume presents many adult HABGT protocols together with scoring and illustrations of inferential analysis. There is no substitute, however, for first-hand administration and analysis of a large number of clinical records of the HABGT. Only in this manner can the clinician become sophisticated and sensitive to the implications of the test data and accompanying behavior. For didactic purposes, the reader may wish to examine some of the "blind" analyses of HABGT records which have been published in the professional literature (see Hutt, 1949, 1951, 1953, 1960, 1963).

For purposes of scoring the Psychopathology Scale and the Adience–Abience Scale, a *Revised Record Form, 2nd edition,* and a Scoring Template are available*. The *Revised Record Form* provides space for recording important behavioral data (which often makes the meaning of the test performance clearer) and for recording scores and test findings. The Scoring Template, which is included in each package of *Record Forms* makes scoring objective and much more rapid.

In clinical practice the author prefers, generally, to analyze the HABGT protocol by completing the inferential analysis first—before obtaining the total scores on Psychopathology and Adience–Abience. This preference is based on the assumption that obtaining the objective scores first: (1) tends to prejudice the subsequent observations and clinical analyses which inspection of the "raw" test behavior will reveal; and, (2) restricts the free "hovering" attention of the clinician while he empathically tries to trace the patient's test behavior as he proceeds through the various reproductions of the test figures. The objective scores seem to be so "solid" and "substantial" that they may tend to overwhelm the clinician's judgment in analyzing the great many ways in which these scores may have been achieved. If, on the other hand, the inferential analysis (particularly when elaborations and associations have been obtained) is completed first, it is more likely that the clinician will be alert to many alternative explanations for the test findings. He will then be able to "test out" such alternatives, if need be. Consequently, he will be in a much better position to consider alternative and pertinent remedial or rehabilitative procedures for the individual involved.

* Packages of the *HABGT Revised Record Form, 2nd edition,* including the Scoring Template may be purchased from the publisher, Grune & Stratton, Inc.

8
Clinical Studies: Children's Records

The following two case illustrations exemplify some of the ways in which children's records may be analyzed. As we have noted, the basic methods of analysis and the derived scores applicable to adult records are also applicable to the records of children down to age 10 years, unless the individual is significantly retarded. These methods are also applicable to children between the ages of 7 and 9 years, with the proviso that perceptual–motoric development, as tapped by the HABGT figures, has not yet reached its apogee during these years. Hence, some modification in norms for Psychopathology and for Adience–Abience is necessary, as we have indicated in Chapter 7. Children whose general development is retarded are more likely to deviate from the standards, both in projective phenomena and objective scores. Bright children between 5 and 7 years of age are testable with fairly adequate results, but caution should be exercised in interpreting their protocols because of their relative perceptual–motoric immaturity. In questionable cases, it would be advisable to evaluate their perceptual–motoric developmental status first, by scales such as those provided by Koppitz (1963); if their scores indicate that such development has reached at least 7 years, their records may then be interpreted by inferential analysis and other methods proposed in this book with the caution noted above for all children between 7 and 9 years of age.

CASE A: DONALD

This case is presented first so as to give the reader a comprehensive view of the many aspects of behavior revealed by a HABGT protocol.*

* This HABGT analysis was first done as part of a workshop for school psychologists on the clinical use of this procedure.

175

Our presentation will include: a "blind analysis" of the copy phase of the test, utilizing the principles of inferential analysis; a "blind analysis" of the data obtained during the elaboration and association phases; an evaluation of configuration scores; an analysis of the findings on the Psychopathology and Adience–Abience Scales; a synthesis of all of these findings; and, finally, an integration of the HABGT results with data provided by the referring psychologist.

Inferential Analysis: Copy Phase

The only data presented to the writer at the time of the original "blind analysis" were the following. Donald is 12 years and 4 months of age and is in the fifth grade of elementary school. He is right handed. He has no physical handicaps other than a questionable heart condition. The presenting problem was stated as follows: "He has a severe learning problem and is not capable of or able to do regular classroom work." Additional comments were : "A psychiatrist to whom he was referred called him dyslexic. He has lost confidence in himself and is withdrawn."

On the basis of these data one may wonder, immediately, about the severity of Donald's problem. He is retarded in school by two years and may possibly suffer from some organic brain damage. Possibly he is mentally retarded. His problem was regarded as serious enough to warrant referral to a psychiatrist. His "withdrawn behavior" may reflect his response to failure in school work or may be part of a more general personality problem. In any case, it is clear that we are presumably dealing with a very disturbed boy. We will wish to utilize all of the pertinent sources of data available in order to develop an adequate clinical formulation and to provide appropriate recommendations.

We begin by examining the copy phase of the HABGT (see Plate 6). An examination of figure A for placement and special characteristics tells us something about how Donald "enters" this test situation. (The figures were numbered by the writer for purposes of identification.) Donald places this figure in a "normal" position on the page. (This aspect of test behavior is scored as Factor 2, Psychopathology Scale. The factor numbers that follow also relate to this scale.) However, he reduces the size of the design (see Chapter 6 or the Scoring Template). The design is well executed otherwise, except for some degree of closure difficulty in the circle (Factor 6). Close examination of the horizontal axis of the total design indicates that there is a slight degree of clockwise rotation of the figure (about 10 degrees); this degree of rotation is sufficient to merit a score on the factor of perceptual rotation (Factor 10). There is also some indication of impulsively drawn lines, particularly on the diamond or square. (The examining psychologist did not offer any observational data on Donald's behavior while drawing this figure.)

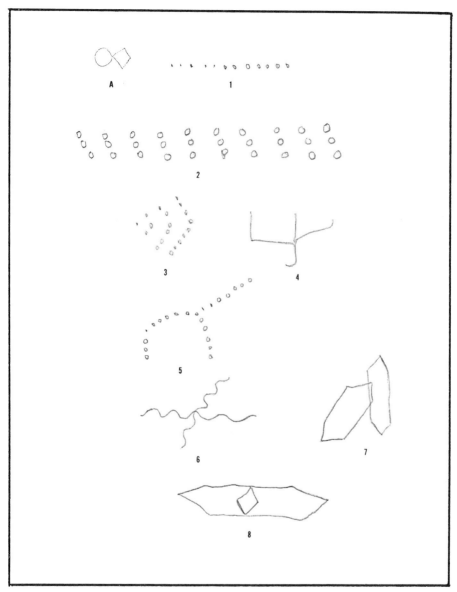

Plate 6.   Case A: Donald—Copy Phase

On the basis of these observations we can offer the following initial and *tentative hypotheses*. Donald appears to approach the test situation with considerable anxiety (small size of the figure), but he is in good contact with reality (normal placement and basically well-executed design). There is a slight tendency to act out impulsively (somewhat poor line quality on the diamond). The small size of the figure together with the slight degree of clockwise rotation mildly suggest a withdrawn style of behavior, and possibly mildly depressive trends. The closure difficulty might be an indication of problems in interpersonal relationships.

All of these hypotheses are offered, of course, quite provisionally and are subject to further evaluation, confirmation, rejection, or modification in the light of other data derived from the test performance. A *second-order inference,* derived from these preliminary hypotheses, is that Donald may tend to defend himself by passive oppositionalism or negative defiance. This type of inference is based on our general evaluation of his apparent pathology. We should also note that, on the positive side, Donald produces a basically good reproduction of the Gestalt; i.e., there is no indication, as yet, of any acute disturbance or any suggestion of the difficulties one might be led to expect on the basis of the referral problem. However, since the maturation level for this design is about 7 years and Donald is 12 years of age, this might be a relatively simple task for him; we shall wish to examine the more difficult figures (such as 6 and 7) to see whether some indication of a severe personality or organic problem is present.

Next, let us examine the sequence employed by Donald in his successive placement of the several figures. This will quickly afford us an overall view of some aspects of his use of spatial relationships and thus some indication of how he relates in this visual–motoric world. From figure A through figure 5 he tends to move in a regular left-to-right orientation, without any deviation in sequence. There is a possible deviation in sequence (Factor 2) in his placement of figure 6 since he has sufficient room on the page to place this design to the right of figure 5 but instead moves down one row. Figures 7 and 8 are then correctly placed in sequence. We should also note that there is a perceptible tendency of a drift in the successive placement of the figures in a southeasterly direction as he moves away from the margin of the page. Our inferences, derived solely from the features of his sequence, are that he is well organized and can plan and anticipate quite well, and thus he shows evidence of some good internal controls. Taking the seriousness of the referral problems into account, one wonders why this boy does not show more overt evidence of his presumed psychopathology on this test. Apparently, some ego functions must be fairly intact!

Next we evaluate Donald's use of space in organizing his drawings (Space I, Factor 3). The space between figures A and 2 is *expansive* according to our criteria (see Chapter 5), whereas the space between figures 2 and 3, and between 5 and 6, is constricted. (Space is within normal limits for the remaining figures.) Therefore, on the basis of admittedly limited data, we infer that his orientation toward the world is ambivalent;

he tends more toward a withdrawn style of adjustment but he also shows some indication of acting out (or possibly of hostility).

Further examination of his use of space in terms of the size of each of the figures reveals that figure A is constricted in both the horizontal and vertical axes, and that figure 1 is constricted in the horizontal axis. However, figure 7 is slightly expansive in the vertical dimension. Again, we note the indication of ambivalence in Donald's use of space. We can now infer more convincingly that he generally tends to reveal a withdrawn style, but he may, on occasion, act out centrifugally. We suspect, therefore, that he is in some inner turmoil, but tends to internalize more than act out (second-order inference). We should emphasize, however, that these trends are offered as hypotheses to be evaluated in terms of additional evidence. Despite his hypothesized inner turmoil, he shows that he generally tends to appear to be in reasonably good control.

Now we shall proceed, in order, to examine the remaining factors of the Psychopathology Scale (along with the other factors noted in Chapter 5) while scrutinizing his performance on each of the several figures. He shows no evidence of collision or collision tendency (Factor 4). On the basis of this finding, we infer that there is no evidence of gross loss of ego controls nor is there any gross evidence of organic brain pathology.

He shows normal use of the margin (Factor 6). Thus, one possible indication of severe, overt anxiety, is absent. We infer that he does not show any indications of much anxiety in his overt behavior.

He does not shift the position of the paper (Factor 5), nor does he shift the position of the test cards (according to the examiner's notes). This possible indication of overt oppositional behavior is not present. If his suspected covert oppositionalism is present, as we have previously inferred, it is apparently not accompanied by any overt oppositionalism.

Our examination for evidence of overall increase or decrease in the size of figures and for progressive increase or decrease in the size of the figures does not reveal such phenomena. Thus, there is no indication of loss of control resulting in tendencies to act out or to withdraw into isolation.

He does show a few isolated changes in the size of some figures. In addition to the constriction of figure A, noted previously, the left-hand portion of figure 7 is changed in size (made "fatter"). The size reduction in figure A may represent his initial anxiety in entering the test situation or it may be an indication of a more general anxiety state. In figure 1, the reduction in size is accompanied by the substitution of circles for dots after the fifth dot. This suggests the presence of *covert anxiety* and regressive efforts at withdrawal. (It is easier to make circles than to focus one's controlled energy in making precise dots.) We should also not dismiss the possibility of impulsive and regressive "break-through" of impulses—an indication of a more serious disturbance in ego functions. The possible meaning of the increase in part of figure 7 is more obscure and will be explored more fully in connection with Donald's performance on this figure during the elaboration and association phases of the test.

We now proceed to an examination for closure difficulty (Factor 6). We note the following instances of closure difficulty as defined by our criteria: figure A, raw score of 1; figure 2, raw score of at least 3; and figure 7, raw score of 1. His total raw score of 5 yields a scaled score of 5.5. This is indicative of a moderate degree of closure difficulty, and suggests that he may have a moderate degree of difficulty in his interpersonal relationships. Taking into account his inferred withdrawal style of behavior, we hypothesize that he tends to act as an "isolate" i.e., his defensive pattern is to avoid rather than to seek personal relationships.

His only evidence of crossing difficulty (Factor 7) is his simplification of the crossing in figure 7. He appears to have difficulty with the right, obtuse angle in the left-hand figure at the point of crossing. We shall score this difficulty as simplification, and give him a scaled score of 1.0 on crossing difficulty. However, this phenomenon may be indicative of a possible difficulty in interpersonal relationships and may indicate some psychological blocking. By now we have considerable cumulative evidence of Donald's interpersonal difficulties. The nature of the evidence suggests that his problems in this area may be more covert and indirectly expressed than overt and directly expressed.

An analysis of his curvature difficulty (Factor 8) reveals that there is obvious "flattening" of the curve in figure 4. He also shows mild distortion and mild "flattening" of the curves in figure 6. His scaled score on this factor is 7.0 and is characterized as moderate. This phenomenon is indicative of flattening of affect. Together with the evidence of his general personality style, one may infer that he is more self-oriented or schizoid than other-oriented or outer-directed.

There is no scorable disturbance on the factor of angulation (Factor 9). Since this factor is usually indicative of disturbance in affective responses, when present, his scaled score of 1.0 tends to lessen the strength of our previous inferences concerning his possible affective disturbance. We shall have to try to understand the significance of these apparently contradictory indications by examining other aspects of his HABGT record.

The very mild degree of rotation on figure A, previously noted, produces a scaled score of 4.0 on this factor (Factor 10). Nevertheless, this is not indicative of any organic brain pathology, and suggests that major aspects of his ego functions are intact.

He shows some mild, scorable evidence on the regression factor (Factor 11). There is a tendency to substitute dashes for circles on Figure 3.

His scaled score on this factor is 4.0. The inference is that, in some situations, he may tend to regress in his behavior.

The apparent crossing difficulty on figure 7 is scored as simplification (Factor 12) because his product shows a somewhat simplified execution of this figure; he thereby avoids the more difficult feature of the crossing or overlapping on this figure. This evaluation is also consistent with our observation that he tends to simplify his test figures, as he does in substituting circles for dots in figure 1 (previously characterized as regressive behavior). His scaled score on simplification is 4.0. This phenomenon may be understood as Donald's attempt to deal with this difficult test situation by expending minimal effort (or trying to avoid the difficult problem). We infer that this may be part of a pattern of passive oppositionalism and withdrawal. Low aspiration level is also suggested. The cumulative evidence in this general area of his defensive style begins to suggest that Donald may be characterized as generally passively hostile, and therefore achieving far less than he is capable of.

We have not scored the record as showing any indication of fragmentation (Factor 13) or of overlapping difficulty (Factor 14). Nor is there any evidence of elaboration (Factor 15). However, there is evidence of perseveration (Factor 16). Perseverative tendencies may be noted in his use of circles instead of dots in figures 3 and 5—type (a) perseveration. It is possible, of course, that this phenomenon may also be explained in terms of regression and simplification tendencies, but the consistency of his persistent use of circles in the latter test figures, after he employed them on figure 1, plus the probable reinforcement of this perseverative tendency by the exposure to the circles in figure 2, suggests that perseveration is a more parsimonious explanation. His scaled score on perseveration is thus 7.0. His perseverative tendencies can be understood as part of his rigid, defensive, passive-oppositional mode. It can be inferred that his loss of adaptive spontaneity reduces his effectiveness in coping realistically with the tasks of his world. This type of rigidity is not suggestive, however, of the possibility of organicity (i.e., organic brain pathology), especially since there is no other test evidence of brain dysfunction on an organic basis.

Donald does not redraw any of his test figures (Factor 17), nor does he show any other pathological indicators on any of the other test factors presented in our discussion of such factors in Chapter 5.

We have now described (and scored) all test factors in the copy phase of Donald's record and have suggested a number of first-order and second-order inferences. There are, however, other features of Donald's drawings in the copy phase which should be noted. First, we should observe that he exercises good "control" in some aspects of ego functions in that he counts the number of dots accurately in the test figures and reproduces the appropriate number (observations by the examiner and analysis of the drawings). We can infer that his compulsive defenses are holding up, and that he has some need to achieve or to please others despite his apparently (inferred) negativistic or defiant orientation. Also, on the whole, he is able to perceive accurately all of the Gestalten although he is inconsistent in his execution of some of the drawings; taken together with his generally good performance on the more difficult items and his chronological age, we can infer that he has about average intelligence, possibly higher. We also note that he has an idiosyncratic style in his arrangement of the figures on the page; to wit, he has arranged the figures symmetrically, with two figures followed by a single "centered" figure. We infer that he is well organized and intelligent, but is possibly excessively self-oriented and/or rigid.

His greatest distortion occurs in figure 4. He shortens the vertical axis of the open square and flattens the curve. If, as is often the case, this figure symbolizes some problems of male–female relationships, we could infer that this area is one of great difficulty for him. We would wonder whether the relationship between his father and mother is disturbed in any aspects and what his relationships have been with each parent. Does he show some oedipal problems?

We also note that on figure 7 he manifests some distortion and simplification, and shows some difficulty with obtuse angles. There is also evidence of poor line quality although he shows good motor coordination on the other figures. He also shows minor evidences of some of these difficulties on figure 8. Are these difficulties primarily perceptual or are they primarily responses to the phallic qualities of these figures? There is evidence that his perceptual abilities are good, in general, and we may infer that his difficulty with these figures stems from his psychological reactions to them.

Before proceeding to analyze the evidence on the elaboration and association phases of the test, let us consider his Psychopathology Scale score, based on the evidence we have already presented in discussing the copy phase. His scores on the several factors of this scale and his total scaled score are presented in Table 10.

Donald's score of 51.5 places him slightly more than 1 SD above the mean for "normal" 12 year olds; it is also almost 1 SD below the mean for "disturbed" 12 year olds (see Table 4, Chapter 7). Even if his scaled score were 6 points higher on the basis of the doubtful scoring on two factors discussed above, giving him a higher score of 54.5, it would still be below the mean of disturbed boys of his age. In any case, judged on the basis of his score, it is apparant that he is not suffering from any profound degree of psychopathology. When one examines the factors that contribute to his Psychopathology score, one notes that his disturbance is most apparent on

Table 10
Donald's Performance on the Psychopathology Scale

	Test Factor	Scale Value		Test Factor	Scale Value
1.	Sequence	1.0	10.	Perc. Rotation	4.0
2.	Position 1st Fig.	1.0	11.	Retrogression	4.0
3.	Space, I	10.0	12.	Simplification	4.0
4.	Collision	1.0	13.	Fragmentation	1.0
5.	Shift of Paper	1.0	14.	Overlapping	1.0
6.	Closure Diff.	5.5	15.	Elaboration	1.0
7.	Crossing Diff.	1.0	16.	Perseveration	7.0
8.	Curvature Diff.	7.0	17.	Redrawing	1.0
9.	Angulation	1.0			

Total scaled score: 51.5

the Factors 3, 6, 8, and 16 (Space I, closure difficulty, curvature difficulty, and perseveration). His perseveration score may be the result of his tendency to do things in the "easiest way" or to be passively oppositional. His problems with the use of space seemed to be related to his ambivalent tendencies to withdraw into himself and to "act out." His difficulty with curves suggested the flatenning of his affective responses. Thus, when analyzed in terms of the components contributing to his score, his pathology suggests a stylistic or characterological inhibition of appropriate and effective grappling with the world of reality.

Inferential Analysis: Elaboration and Association Phases

Now let us turn to the other phases of Donald's test performance. (See Plate 7; the figures have been numbered for purposes of identification.) We shall deal with both the elaborations and the associations at the same time in order to provide more effective integration of the material.

The overall impressions that one gets in examining the elaborations is that they are well executed. There are no marked inconsistencies in the sizes of the several figures. He begins by placing figure A in the center of the page and making it appropriate in size (unlike his small size for this figure in the copy phase), and then places figures 1–3 in correct sequence. Following this, he shifts to the top of the page, placing the remaining figures in good sequence until he runs out of space at the top of the page and finishing the last two figures at the bottom of the page, still in a left-to-right orientation. Line quality is quite good throughout the drawings. Any examiner who has had adequate experience in administering

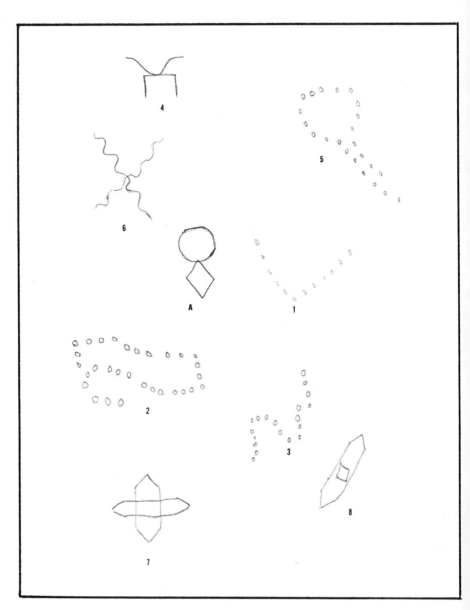

Plate 7.   Case A: Donald—Elaborations

this test to 12-year-old children will recognize at once that this is a superior performance and represents a creative treatment of the test figures. However, one also notes that Donald rotates figures A, 3, 4, 5, 6, and 8, and he rotates part of figure 7. The strong inference is that he adapts by oppositionalism, i.e., by defiance. Moreover, he does not show difficulty with obtuse angles, as he did in the copy phase, so that one gains the impression that his problem is not an organic one, nor is it likely that it is purely maturational–perceptual—it is his psychological difficulties which cause his distortions in the copy phase. Here, then, is a boy whose ego functions are essentially intact, but whose defensive patterns cause him (and others) great difficulty.

His associations add considerable information about the nature of his problems. His association to the figure on card A is: "A tumbling box pushing a ball." In the first place, this response suggests that there is considerable fantasy going on. Beyond this, it suggests considerable inner tension and feelings of great inadequacy, despite the "blandness" of the content. His association to the elaboration he produced (i.e., his projective response, enhanced) is "A head with a big tie on it." This association is indicative of egocentrism, at least, and possibly of narcissism. It is interesting to note that he does not "block" in his ability to associate, so that at least the potential for reaching this boy is there; that is, if he is passively oppositional and obtructionist, as we have inferred, he is still available and willing to respond. There are other things one might say about both the elaboration and the associations to this figure, but we have indicated what seems to us to be most pertinent.

The associations to figure 1 are also original and unique. His association to card 1 is: "A bunch of peeking eyes." The suggestion of paranoidal orientation is clear. Moreover, on the elaboration his associative response is "V," surely an obscurantistic and idiosyncratic response. This response probably involves some effort at denial of what is really troubling him and also may have some symbolic meaning. Does "V" stand for "victory" over his adversaries, or does it have some other special meaning? We can only guess. If the examiner had taken the time to get him to discuss and offer more associative material to this response, we might be in a better position to judge it.

His association to card 2 is: "Football stadium," and to his elaboration it is: "People leaving in cars." The association set off in the response to the card is carried through in his association to the elaboration. The response is highly original and may suggest wishes for attention, desire for power and fame, and an expression of aggressive needs. We can begin to see clearly that whatever other problems this boy has, he does not suffer from lack of imagination, intelligence, or creativity. We also note that he draws circles instead of dots on figures 1, 3, and 5. It now seems more reasonable than before to infer that this type of behavior is more accurately interpreted as parsimonious (i.e., saving of energy or easier to draw) rather than as pathological perseveration.

On figure 3 he associates: "An arrow, a blinking light, a Christmas tree turned sideways," to the card. His association to the elaboration, after a long pause (blocking) is: "Warning signal." The need which may induce the associations of a warning light and signal may indicate apprehension and a need to have more control. Is he constantly alert and on the defensive against imagined danger or threat? The association of the Christmas tree is probably indicative of a normal wish for "supplies, to have happiness, or to be taken care of." These associations tend to reinforce our inference that his orientation toward the world is ambivalent; there is some reaching out and wishing to be nourished but there is also fearfulness and defensive withdrawal.

Both of his associations to figure 4: "A block on the edge of a mountain," to the card, and: "A box underneath a saggy line," to his elaboration (after a long pause), suggest a feeling of precariousness. The fantasy is that of a precarious individual and, perhaps, of one who fears he will be crushed.

On figure 5 he ingeniously completes the original figure in his elaboration, making it more "solid" and "closed." His association to the card is: "Broken magnifying glass," and his association to his elaboration is: "A magnifying glass." Again, these are idiosyncratic responses and suggest that he wishes to see things more clearly or larger; perhaps he is communicating a wish, also, for help.

He shows the same kind of phenomena on figure 6 that he displayed on figure 1, i.e., he lets something "out of the bag" and then covers up. To the card he associates: "A hilly road going up a hill." To his elaboration he responds: "A X". His first association is probably indicative of his view of the world: it is a difficult place and involves struggle. His second response is evasive and, again, suggests helplessness. Is "X" the unknown? It is a literal response to his drawing; perhaps it involves not an "X" but a "cross"; i.e., it may carry symbolic, religious, superego connotations.

His association: "A diamond" to card 7 is unusual. Common responses by children of his age, especially disturbed children, are rockets, bombs, warships or ships, and the like. His association to his elaboration helps us to understand the dynamics of his situation. He says: "A cross." Thus, again, we are faced with data which suggest religious and superego functions. We would infer that he tends to internalize his anger, that he represses his aggressive tendencies, and that he then expresses his problem through oppositionalism or defiance or bland neutrality.

On figure 8 he associates: "A eye," to the card and: "A cat's eye," to his elaboration. These responses are, again, highly idiosyncratic and paranoidal.

Adience–Abience Scale Score and Configurational Data

By now we have a rich source of data about this boy. However, before attempting to integrate the HABGT findings, let us examine two other sources of data: his Adience–Abience Scale score and his configurational data. Table 11 presents his Adience–Abience raw scores and corrected score.

Donald obtains a corrected score of 29. This places him almost 1 *SD* above the norm for "normals" and indicates that Donald is quite high in adience (see Table 5). On this scale, therefore, he shows good promise of being able to profit and develop with suitably constructive experience.

Our only concern with respect to configuration scores is the question of his possible organicity. By consulting the section in Chapter 6 in which the configurational pattern for organic brain-damaged individuals is presented, we find that Donald obtains the following weights: 2 for perseveration; 1 for simplification. Thus his configuration score with respect to possible organicity is 3. This places him well below the marginal score range for this category and does *not* suggest the presence of organic brain damage.

Table 11
Donald's Performance on the Adience–Abience Scale

	Test Factor	Raw Score		Test Factor	Raw Score
1.	Height & Width	−2	7.	Crossing Diff.	−1
2.	Height, Only	−2	8.	Angulation	+2
3.	Use of Page	+2	9.	Rotation	+1
4.	Sequence	+1	10.	Fragmentation	+1
5.	Position 1st Fig.	+2	11.	Simplification	−1
6.	Closure Diff.	+1	12.	Elaboration	0

Raw score: +4
Corrected score: 29

Integration of HABGT Findings

This case presents many intriguing problems. There is little evidence that Donald shows any gross or profound psychopathology. The record does not suggest either the presence of brain damage or the presence of severe psychopathology. However, taking all of the HABGT data into account, we can suggest that there is a *chronic psychological disturbance* in which there is great difficulty to relate easily and nondefensively to others or to function in an appropriately constructive or adaptive manner. Despite the absence of obvious symptomatic difficulties such as one finds in a classical case of neurosis, we infer that the problem is characterologi- cal in structure and that his basic mode of adjustment is maladaptive. There is little evidence of excessive overt anxiety, but there is consider- able evidence of the following: considerable covert anxiety and guilt; an orientation toward the world that is very apprehensive; perception of this world as threatening and hostile; a possibly paranoidal attitude; and a great deal of passive oppositionalism. Nevertheless, many aspects of ego functions are intact; he is bright and creative; and, at some level, he is open to and seeks help and succor. Considering the fact that he is pre- sented as a "severe learning problem" and as dyslexic, we may infer that there is considerable blocking and inhibition. He seems to see himself as impotent and helpless.

On the positive side of the picture, in addition to apparently good intelligence and basically intact ego functions, there is a high potential for growth and recovery and a desire for assistance—even if expressed obliquely.

In a case such as this we would wonder about the causative factors related to the home situation. This boy must have been traumatized quite early in life, and we would suspect that there is profound tension in the home and a highly punitive and guilt-ridden atmosphere. In any event, he has withdrawn into his protective shell and is defensively obdurate. It would seem that this boy can profit greatly from some form of continuous and intensive therapeutic management. We would think that transient or superficial efforts to motivate him or reach out to him would only tend to reinforce his self-image of inadequacy and would cause him to feel re- jected. On the other hand, intensive and continuing therapeutic work with a caring adult, in which his fears could be ventilated and he could be supported in his "reaching out" toward the world, should be very profit- able. Without such assistance, it is likely he would become more self- protective and even more tightly closed off within himself.

Additional Data and Follow-up

To present all of the supplementary data that became available after this analysis was completed and to describe in detail his development after a total therapeutic program was initiated would take us too far afield and is not the focus of this presentation. However, in order to provide some degree of closure, the most salient data will be summarized.

Donald seems to have suffered from severe emotional stress in the family situation, although there were some favorable factors. From his birth on the family suffered financial duress and had difficulty making ends meet. The family atmosphere was one of tension and severity in dealing with the children. Relatives lived with the family for a time; they had lost two of their children in a fire, and Donald was punished severely when, for example, he played with matches. Donald seemed to show good developmental progress until about 3 years of age—a period when stresses in the family situation were most severe. At that time he began to regress in behavior and became enuretic although he had been bladder trained. He began to suck his fingers and became fearful of engaging in any "rough" physical games or activities. He soon became a social isolate. He never liked school and was fearful in school situations. After he learned to read, he regressed to having severe difficulty in reading and made little effort to learn. He displayed grief that was out of all proportion when he learned that people, even those he hardly knew, had died. He had almost no friends, and those he seemed to have begun to make did not continue the relationship.

These few social–developmental facts suggest how severely traumatized and anxious Donald was, and make it evident that his pattern of withdrawal and regression soon led to open or passive defiance and oppositionalism, as our test data seemed to indicate. The home situation also affected his two siblings, both of whom had difficulty in school, showed difficulty in speech, and had problems in social adjustment. The data we have indicate that Donald was never close to either parent and experienced them as nonunderstanding and nonsupportive.

A further indication of the regressive process is suggested by some psychological test data that were obtained. When Donald was almost 9 years of age he was given the WISC test. At that time he obtained a verbal I.Q. score of 88 and a performance I.Q. score of 90. However, his scores on vocabulary, comprehension, picture completion, and block designs were *above* his age level. These scores would indicate that he was above average in complex mental operations, and that his true intellectual level was higher than his I.Q. scores indicated. Three years later, when Donald was retested on the WISC, his verbal I.Q. score was 77 and his performance score was 94. He attained lower scores on this test on comprehension, similarities, and vocabulary than he obtained in the earlier test. His performance scores held up relatively well, improving over the three-year span, except on block designs, on which his score was now lower than it had previously been. Thus, although he "tested" at a full scale I.Q. score of 84, it is apparent that regression had occurred and that his potential was much higher, as suggested by the HABGT findings.

A two-year "corrective" program involving Donald and his mother, as well as a program of planned and supervised recreational and other social activities, produced considerable gain in both cognitive performance and behavioral adjustment. The last report on Donald indicated that he was beginning to make a marginally successful academic adjustment and that his social behavior patterns were fairly adequate.

CASE B: CATHERINE

This case is presented to illustrate the possibilities of rapid inspection and configurational analysis. It is not suggested that the analysis of HABGT records should ever be done in such a limited manner in any individual case, but it is presented in this way so as to highlight the nature of these aspects of the analytic process. Such methods are also useful when a large number of cases have to be screened so that more careful attention can be given to a restricted number of individuals.

Referral Problem

Catherine was referred by her teacher, who indicated that after a few weeks in the persent class (fifth grade) Catherine is still confused about the location of her desk. She also reports that Catherine cannot follow the simplest directions and cannot read. When questioned about her school work or other problems, Catherine begins to weep. She is 10 years of age.

No other data were available at the time of the analysis of the HABGT record. Plate 8 shows her performance on the copy phase of the test. The arrows and numeration were provided by the examiner (not the writer).

Rapid Inspection of HABGT

Our first overall observations reveal that: the page has been rotated; there is obvious distortion in some of the figures, and even destruction of some Gestalten (figures 3, 4, 5, and 7); there is apparent perseveration type (b) on figure 1 and perseveration types (a) and (b) on figure 2; and three figures have been fragmented (figures 3, 4, and 7). Other features of the record are also striking and quite apparent, but we already have enough evidence on this test to suggest that there is a profound disturbance present. Moreover, since she does fairly well on design 8 (roughly at about her own age level), the inference might be that she is impaired in cognitive functioning rather than simply retarded (impaired due to some disturbance which interferes with her capacity for functioning more effectively). In view of the referral problem and these preliminary observa-

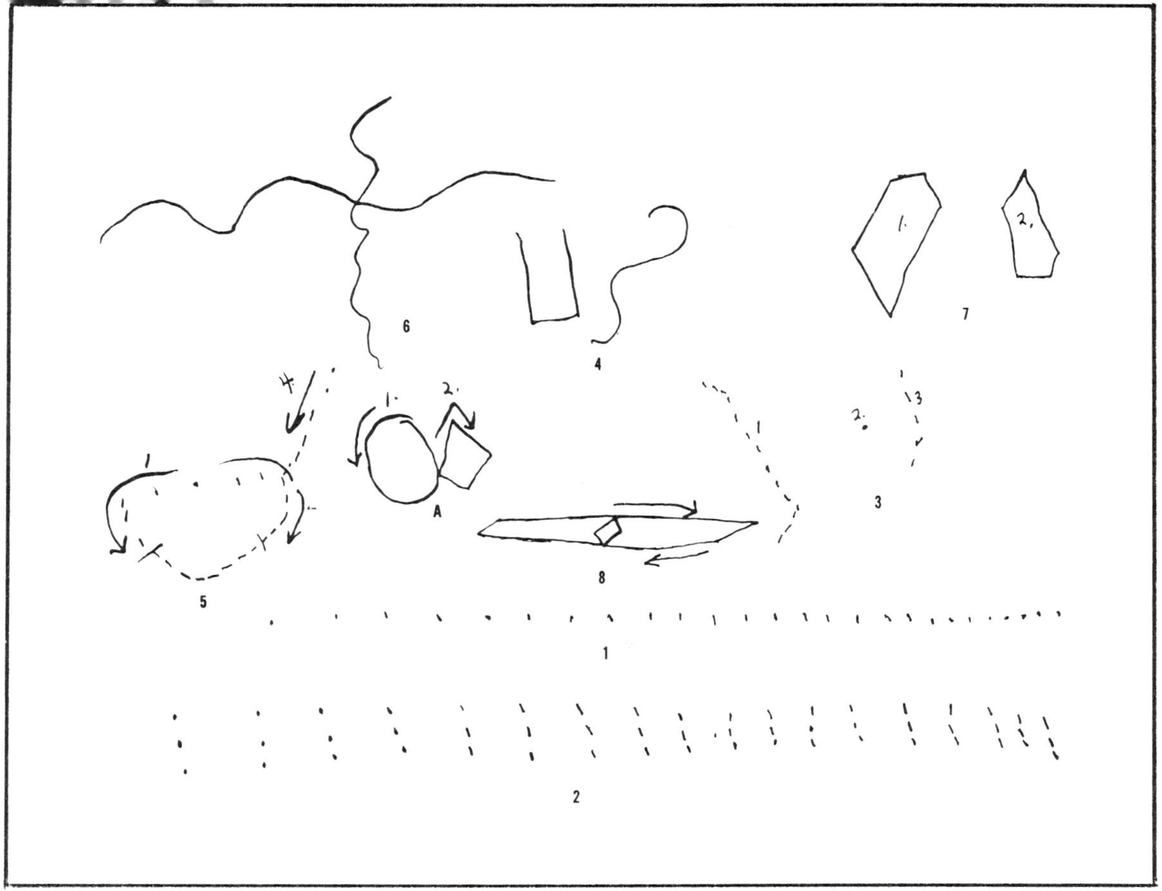

Plate 8. Case B: Catherine

tions of her HABGT performance, it would seem wise to evaluate the record for the possibility of organic brain damage. We shall therefore proceed with a configurational analysis for this factor.

Configurational Analysis

We examine the record for manifestations of the eight critical "signs" listed in the first section, Organic Brain Damage, of Chapter 6. Our findings and weights are presented in Table 12.

Catherine manifests angulation difficulties (of more than 15 degrees) on figures 2 and 6, and possibly on figure 3. There is no perceptual rotation. Collision is absent, but collision tendency is indicated between figures 4 and 6, between 7 and 3; and possibly between A and 5. Severe fragmentation is present on figures A, 3, and 7. We have already commented on the presence of both types of perseveration. There is a doubtful instance of overlapping difficulty on figure 7 (doubtful because the figure is also fragmented). Simplification is obviously present. There is questionable line incoordination on figures A, 4, 7, and 8. Thus there is a weighted score on organicity of at least 9, and possibly 12. A score of 9 is above the marginal score range and clearly falls within the critical score range.

Table 12
Configurational Analysis: Catherine

Factor	Weight
1. Marked difficulty, Angulation	2
2. Severe perceptual rotation	0
3. Collision tendency	2
4. Severe fragmentation	2
5. Perseveration	2
6. Overlapping difficulty	2(?)
7. Simplification	1
8. Line incoordination	1(?)

Weighted score: 9 (possibly 12)

Thus, rapid inspection as well as configurational analysis strongly suggest the presence of some organic brain damage. In examining this girl, in addition to other procedures we might employ to test for organicity, we could conduct an experimental–clinical analysis. We would ask her to attempt to describe what was inaccurate about her figures and try to get her to correct these inaccuracies, as we have discussed in previous chapters. If she were unable to improve her performance significantly, we would have more confirmation of the organic hypothesis.* In any case, we would strongly recommend that this girl have a thorough neurological examination as a primary procedure in any further analysis of her problems and before proceeding with any corrective measures.

Additional Data

A WISC test had been administered to Catherine at the same time that the referring school psychologist administered the HABGT. The findings will help to clarify the clinical picture. Catherine obtained a verbal I.Q. score of 85 and a performance score of 54, with a full scale I.Q. score of 67. Quite obviously, she should not be considered as having a true I.Q. of 67. The great discrepancy between verbal and performance results indicates that something quite basic is amiss. The marked discrepancy in favor of verbal performance suggests the possibility of an organic disturbance—unless there were some other explanation such as severe physical limitations or highly restricted sensory–motor experiences. Moreover, all of the performance scores were severely depressed, the poorest score being obtained on the object assembly test, in which she seemed unable to conceptualize the perceptual problem. She showed fairly even, and higher performance on the verbal subtests, scoring highest on the arithmetic and similarities subtests. These findings, especially her great difficulty with the digits-backward aspect of the digit span subtest (she scored 6 on digits forward and only 2 on digits backward), are further evidence of probable organic brain damage.

It was also learned that Catherine rated at the low second-grade level in reading and at the low third-grade level in arithmetic on standardized tests. Even with a suggested current verbal I.Q. score of 85, such poor achievement suggests that there is severe impairment in her functioning.

* For a discussion of psychological aspects of brain pathology and methods of analysis of the nature of the probable pathology, see Chapter 9.

9
Clinical Studies: Organic Records

Damage to the brain, whether from traumatic or infectious causes, *always* has diverse effects with different individuals. In the first place, as is now well known, the brain tends to act as a whole; the individual organism attempts to compensate for whatever trauma it suffers. The nature of these compensatory attempts depends on residual functions and strengths of the individual as well as on the nature of the organic damage. Further, it is extremely rare that an injury, much less a disease process affecting the brain, is confined to a restricted area or zone of the brain; there are other kinds of brain tissue damage than that resulting from the primary organic insult, such as concussive effects, hemorrhaging and related tissue damage, and other secondary damage. The effects also depend on such other factors as: the personality of the individual; the age at which the damage occurred; and the degree of lateralization of the damage (damage to the dominant hemisphere tends to have more serious effects than those to the nondominant hemisphere). In short, there is always an interactive effect involving the person, the nature of the damage, and the site and extent of the damage.

One should not expect to find highly specific effects of certain types of psychological damage resulting from specified brain damage. The psychological effects, and particularly the perceptual–motoric effects, even though they are quite sensitive to brain dysfunction, are likely to be diverse in different individuals. Hence, the evaluation of brain damage by psychological test—just as by other kinds of tests other then surgical and

194

visual verification—is a complex process. *It involves an evaluation of the nature of the behavioral dysfunction in the light of the individual's pre-damage history.* However, damage to certain zones of the brain tends to produce certain types of effects. In the light of these probabilities, the clinician who wishes to assess carefully for the possibility of brain damage or for the nature of the damage, will *carefully assess the specific parts of the behavioral response which seem to be affected.* Thus, if one attempts to evaluate what kind of brain damage, if any, may be related to aphasia in a given case, one would wish to determine precisely which aspects of the behavioral response in the aphasia are affected, and the correlates with presumed functions of certain areas or zones of the brain. The aphasia may only be expressive, or it may involve difficulty in certain motoric responses, or it may involve difficulty in conceptualization or abstraction, and so on. By determining the exact nature of the deficit, one can evaluate what zones of the brain may be affected.

The HABGT is an extremely sensitive instrument in relation to brain dysfunction, but it, too, taps only certain areas of behavioral response. Thus, despite its efficacy in "screening" for brain dysfunction, as we have reported in previous chapters, it is limited in what it can reveal. In some cases, other psychological procedures are more effective in revealing brain disorders. However, the HABGT does process a great variety of behavioral responses involving fine and gross motor coordination and various kinds of visual perception (space, figure–ground, spatial relationships, angulation, verticality, anticipatory visual planning, etc.), and hence it lends itself to sophisticated clinical interpretation.

In addition to knowing what functions the HABGT taps, it is also important to know how the brain functions. Otherwise, one must rely blindly on test scores and configurational patterns. No matter how valuable these may be, they should be supplemented by intensive clinical analysis and by what we have called experimental–clinical procedures. As an aid to such procedures some generally accepted notions concerning brain functions are summarized below in the hope that they will be of assistance to the clinician.

First, then, let us summarize some general principles concerning brain functions. The brain always tends to act as a whole. Moreover, the action of the brain is either facilitated or inhibited by stimulation, feedback processes, integration of peripheral movements and activities of the body, and the state of health of the body. It is also worth remembering that when one point of excitation occurs it may inhibit the simultaneous excitation by another stimulus. It is also recognized that a pathological condition in any part of the brain tends to change the excitability of the entire cerebral cortex. Finally, complex and higher order functions of the brain, such as conceptualization, abstraction, and symbolization depend on the integrative action of various parts of the brain.

Now let us consider functions and disturbances as they are related to various areas of the brain.

Frontal areas.   Functions of this area, like other areas, are dependent on lower order functions, especially the brain stem and reticular activity. Damage to the frontal area *does not* result in loss in the capacity to recognize known "objects," but it *does* result in loss of recent, associative memory and produces perseverative behavior and *decreases* ability to correct mistakes. Lateral lesions of this area tend to produce loss or impairment in delayed reaction tests or behavior, but such functions are impaired by lesions in other areas of the brain. In general, lesions of the frontal area tend to produce: inertia in behavior, loss in the capacity for scanning, and loss in "searching" for objects. There usually is *passive* looking, which creates difficulty in analysis of pictures or other complex stimuli. Damage to the anterior portion tends to disrupt affective behavior and impairment of judgment. Damage to this area also results in loss of planning behavior and adequate anticipatory behavior. Of course, damage to the frontal area can also produce serious disturbance in motoric behavior.

Parietal-Occiptal Area.   The major disturbance with damage in this area is impairment in visual–spatial organization (and perception). There may also be deficiencies in sensitivity to touch, perception of visual–kinesthetic experience, and spatial planning. Above all, there is a loss in ability to integrate these kinds of experiences.

Damage in the *parietal area* is associated with severe impairment in visual space orientation. Left parietal damage is associated with aphasia, acaluoia, and constructional apraxia.

Damage to the *temporal area,* especially to the left lobe, results in impairment in verbal skills, especially vocabulary, whereas damage to the right lobe causes impairment in such functions as are tapped by the picture arrangement subtest of the WAIS and the WISC.

Damage to the *temporo-occipital area* is related to ability to relate graphic symbols and to auditory perception.

Psychoneural Sensory Area.   Damage results in loss in the ability to perceive and recognize objects and symbols, especially if the damage is in the posterior region of this area. Localization can be assisted by differentiating this loss from loss involving seeing and naming the object or stimulus. If the individual can name or perceive the object but shows a failure of integration or of execution of the desired behavior, the damage results from disturbance in other functions and other areas.

It may also be helpful to list the most common symptoms of minimal brain damage, in general (Clements, 1966). These are: hyperactivity; perceptual–motoric impairment; emotional lability; general coordination deficits; disorders of attention; impulsivity; disorders of memory and thinking; specific learning disabilities; disorders of speech and hearing; and equivocal neurosigns and electroencephalographic irregularities.

Case C was chosen to illustrate the complex interaction between organic and psychological factors as well as to illustrate both inferential and configurational analyses.

Cases D, E, and F are presented primarily to offer some clinical evidence of the nature of reactions to a variety of physical trauma or injuries to the brain. In these cases, so far as is known, the personality of the patient was essentially intact prior to the injury; i.e., the individual was functioning effectively both socially and occupationally. We shall comment only briefly on the outstanding features of the HABGT record.

CASE C: HAROLD

Inferential Analysis

The patient is a 62-year-old black male. His educational history included completion of the tenth grade. His occupational history included work as a cook and unskilled laborer preparing skins for cold storage.

He cooperated fully in the psychological examination. On the HABGT all of the figures were drawn with the right hand. The drawings, shown in Plate 9, were made in a careful manner and were done very slowly.

An initial, overall inspection of the record reveals that the patient utilized one sheet of paper and arranged the figures in an irregular sequence. (The first change in sequence occurs following figure 3, when he shifts from a vertical to a lateral progression in his placement. Figure 6 presents the second shift in sequence, and figures 7 and 8 indicate additional shifts.) The spacing of the figures is unusual: figures A, 1, and 2 are grouped, with a normal amount of space between them; figure 3 is isolated, and separated from figure 2 by an unusually large amount of space; and the remaining five figures are compressed into less than one-quarter of the page. Furthermore, there is a collision between figures 5 and 8, and collision tendencies involving figures 2, 4, and 6.

The sequential arrangement, spacing, and collision and collision tendencies indicate poor planning and inadequate judgment, suggesting the initial hypothesis of impaired ego functioning. Since the drawings were done slowly, we infer that impulsivity was not a factor and that the patient was, in fact, attempting to overcontrol. The failure of these attempts points up the severity of his ego impairment.

A tendency toward use of the margin is evident in the placement of figures A, 1, 2, and 3, suggesting feelings of insecurity or inadequacy and

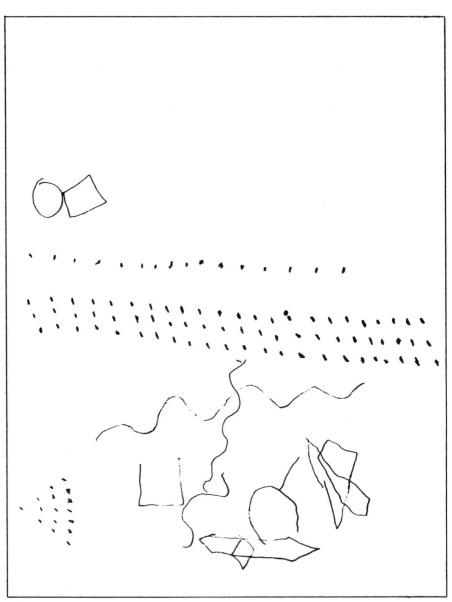

Plate 9. Case C: Harold—An Organic Record

compensatory attempts in dealing with these feelings. The cohesion of the remaining figures also reflects withdrawal tendencies and passivity as an attempt to cope with tension and perceived inadequacies.

The overall line quality of the drawings reveals poor coordination, particularly in the dots, which are quite heavy and irregular. These factors support the impression of compensatory attempts at control on the part of the patient and further suggest that considerable tension and/or neurologic involvement is present.

At this point, the evidence tentatively suggests that we are dealing with an individual whose ego functions are markedly disturbed, who has strong feelings of inadequacy, is anxious, reacts with passivity and withdrawal, and is making strong compensatory attempts at restitution which are relatively unsuccessful.

Turning to the individual designs, figure A is placed in an atypical position and "hugs" the margin. Though the essential Gestalt is preserved, closure difficulty is evident in both the closing of the circle and the joining of circle and square; furthermore, the vertical and horizontal axes of the square are drawn obliquely. The "gaps" in closure suggest difficulty in maintaining interpersonal relationships, characterized by withdrawal; but, in the light of the overall line quality discussed above, it may also reflect motor incoordination, a possibility supported by the lopsided appearance of the square. The atypical placement of figure A supports the hypotheses of an ego disturbance and of fearfulness in interpersonal relations. The relatively larger size of the square in relation to the circle suggests an unconscious need to identify with the masculine role.

The dots of figure 1 are positioned in a wavering line with mild clockwise rotation. Perseveration (a) is indicated by the presence of 16 dots instead of the 12 called for by the stimulus. The dots themselves are overworked and irregular. Depressive features are suggested (clockwise rotation). Attempts at binding tension through the use of internalization and compensatory overcontrol are also supported (dot quality). Loss of ego functioning continues to be indicated (perseveration (b) and wavering quality of the Gestalt).

The same factors observed in figure 1 are present in figure 2 with the addition of perseveration (a). These perseverative factors introduce the hypothesis of rather severe rigidity. In addition, the substitution of dots for circles in this figure is indicative of retrogression on a relatively simple task, mildly suggesting the possibility of diffuse brain damage.

The excessive spacing between figures 2 and 3 with the subsequent placement of figure 3 in the lower left-hand corner of the page would appear to be a result of the patient's attempt to better orient his drawing by using the corner as a guide. However, the increased use of space suggests that hostile impulses are present and tend to find occasional expression. The patient's sequential reaction to this outburst is apparently reflected in the compression of the figure by decreasing its horizontal dimension. This points up his persistent attempts at adjustment through withdrawal. Angulation is decreased, indicating overcontrol and under-reaction to emotional stimuli and/or possible neurologic deficit. Dot quality is consistent in figures 1 and 2 and supports the hypothesis that the patient uses internalization and attempts to overcontrol.

The line quality of figure 4 is tremulous, with evidence of poor coordination and poor control in the "overshooting" at the top of the curved portion of the Gestalt and the top of the right vertical line of the open square. The hostility indicated by the excessive space between figures 2 and 3 now appears to be related to conflict with authority figures (increased length of the right vertical in the open square). The hypothesis is that this patient has strong hostile impulses that are related to basic conflict with authority figures. In general, this patient does not express hostility directly but, rather, suppresses it, as suggested by the persistent tendencies toward withdrawal and by overcontrol and internalization indicated by the data thus far. However, his impaired ego functioning interferes with these defenses to the extent that occasional loss of control occurs, with subsequent expression of hostility. Closure difficulty is also present, as it was in figure A. Difficulty in interpersonal relationships characterized by withdrawal as hypothesized above now seems to be supported. However, since the closure difficulty is accompanied by incoordination, by poor overall line quality in all the figures, and by "overshooting" on the curved portion of the Gestalt, the hypothesis of brain damage is further supported.

Simplification of figure 5 points up the patient's impotence and inadequacy in dealing with a relatively complex stimulus. Here again, tremulous line quality suggests motor incoordination on a neurological basis. The irregular and uneven quality of the curved portion of this figure, the slight counterclockwise rotation, and the severe reduction in size of the figure support not only the hypothesis of diffuse organic damage but also reinforce the impression of a basically passive reaction to unconscious hostile wishes.

Figure 6 is increased in size, particularly in the lateral dimension. There is some irregularity of the curves, with considerable flattening of the vertical curve. The intersecting angle is more nearly square than acute and the entire figure is mildly rotated in a counterclockwise direction. The collision tendencies noted above are present. We can now formulate the hypothesis: loss of control under emotional stimulation is pronounced; with such loss of control, hostile impulses gain expression; conflict with authority figures, as previously suggested, is evident; and a mild tension state with accompanying motor incoordination is indicated.

Overlapping difficulty, simplification, some counterclockwise rotation, and closure difficulty are apparent in figure 7. This Gestalt is drawn as one continuous figure rather than as two overlapping hexagons. The line quality is irregular and changes in pencil pressure, as indicated by dark and light lines, are evident. The patient also spent more time on this figure than any other in the test. For the first time in the test series the essential Gestalt is lost, though it is also evident that the patient tried very hard to preserve it. The patient's performance on this figure points up his inability to deal with a relatively complex stimulus. In spite of this, he persists in his attempt to solve the problem, at the same time revealing his impotence. Compensatory controls are reestablished. The marked evidence of closure difficulty indicates that a frustrating task leads to increased irritability and other difficulties in interpersonal relations. An additional hypothesis is that of sexual impotency.

Figure 8 is slightly reduced in the horizontal dimension. The internal diamond is moved to the left of center and is increased in size so that it extends below the bottom of the lower boundary of the hexagon. In sharp contrast to figure 7, the hexagon form is adequately reproduced, though the patient had difficulty with the left "point." Closure difficulty and incoordination are again manifest. Collision with figure 5 is evident. Impaired ego functioning and inability to plan adequately are indicated. Feelings of impotence (treatment of points) and compensatory attempts at a masculine identification (increased size of diamond) are suggested along with his tendency toward withdrawal (decreased horizontal dimension).

This record is striking in the consistency of factors which suggest rather severe impairment of ego functions. There are several clinical syndromes which could produce such impairment.

Mental deficiency can be ruled out on the basis of the maturity of the patient's reproduction of the Gestalten, particularly figure 8, and his attempt at figure 7 as a continuous line, which suggests his previous functioning at a better than average intellectual level. Furthermore, the mental retardate characteristically simplifies Gestalten by separating the figures into their essential elements.

Such impairment of ego functioning may occur in instances of acute, though transitory, anxiety reactions. Though it is evident that tension is reflected in this record, the anxiety is not severe, and slow, methodical methods of work are not consistent with such a reaction.

Consequently, the problem posed at this point is the differential diagnosis between psychosis, functional or organic, and organic brain damage.

There is little evidence of regression in the protocol, and though deficiency in ego functioning is present, reality testing appears adequate. Only one of the Gestalten is inadequately reproduced, and even in this case the relationship between the elements of the figure is preserved. Rather, the specific ego deficiency appears to be related to poor judgment and planning ability. Furthermore, despite ample evidence of incoordination, the patient appears to be manifesting a perceptual difficulty rather than difficulty in execution. The adequate hexagon drawn in figure 8 suggests that the difficulty with figure 7 resulted from an inability to organize the Gestalt perceptually rather than from an inability to reproduce the hexagonal figures. This marked difficulty in perceptual organization of a relatively complex stimulus is suggestive of diffuse intracranial pathology rather than psychosis.

The evidence of impotence, rigidity, and compensatory attempts at control in this HABGT record are personality factors also associated with organic brain damage.

At this point, it is evident that the patient is a brain-damaged individual who is mildly depressed and anxious, feels impotent, and has apparently reacted with rigidity and with compensatory mechanisms to attempt to maintain his adjustment. What, then, can be said of his premorbid personality?

The primary personality appears to be that of an individual who has difficulty in establishing enduring interpersonal cathexes, utilizes passive mechanisms, and tends to withdraw rather than act in an aggressive manner. Tension is dealt with by internalization. A basic area of conflict appears to be associated with authority figures, and the resulting hostility is repressed. Under the impact of emotionally laden situations, some loss of control occurs, with accompanying tendencies toward impulsivity.

As a result of the brain damage, several major factors appear. There is an intensification of his feelings of impotence and an exaggeration of his previous attempts at adjustment through the use of suppressive techniques. The patient's attempts at compensatory control, so evident in the test data, are a consequence of this. But his defenses, though intensified, are less effective and he also tends to lose control more easily.

Configurational Analysis

Although the evidence concerning the presence of probable organic brain damage is quite strong, and although psychological factors appear to be quite important, it will be useful to check the likelihood of the organic factor by completing a configurational analysis on the basis the factors presented in the first section of Chapter 6. Harold's scores are given in Table 13.

Harold obtains scores on all of the ''organic'' factors except severe perceptual rotation (he showed only mild rotation). His weighted score is 12, which places him well above the critical score of 9 for this syndrome.

Table 13
Configurational Analysis: Harold

Factor	Weight
1. Marked difficulty, Angulation	2
2. Severe perceptual rotation	0
3. Collision	2
4. Severe fragmentation	2
5. Perseveration	2
6. Overlapping difficulty	2
7. Simplification	1
8. Line incoordination	1

Weighted score: 12

This score offers corroborative evidence that there is brain dysfunction with an organic basis.

Additional Data

Approximately 18 months prior to testing, the patient became aware of a sudden weakness of his left arm and leg, causing him to fall to the ground. Initially, there was some slight improvement so that he was able to walk into his home. However, the following morning there was complete paralysis of the left side of his body. Upon hospitalization, the medical findings included bloody spinal fluid. Recovery was good, so that at the time of the psychological evaluation, there was only slight residual weakness of the left extremities. The patient walked with a slight limp and had good use of his left arm and hand.

A recent medical examination disclosed weakness of the left arm and leg, slightly accentuated deep tendon reflexes on the left, positive Hoffman, positive Babinski on the left, a sustained clonus in the left ankle, and a slight loss of tactile sensation on the left side. Ophthalmic examination revealed bilateral arcus senilis, tortuosity of the fundi, silver streaking of the arterioles, and minimal arteriovenous compression. The final impression was cerebral arteriosclerosis and residual left hemiplegia resulting from a mild cerebral vascular accident.

Clinically, the patient appeared neatly dressed and well groomed. He spoke coherently using good vocabulary. His conversation during casual interaction seemed adequate; however, when relatively complex instructions were given he was unable to understand them fully and act accordingly.

The patient arrived for his appointment two hours late, explaining that he was unable to find the building. However, evidence from the nursing home at which he resided indicates that he is forgetful. In this connection he insisted that his stroke took place in 1957 despite hospital records which indicated its occurrence in 1958.

Additional clinical findings include a WAIS I.Q. of 78 with component I.Q.'s of 87 on the verbal scale and 70 on the performance scale. There was evidence of concrete thinking, poor memory, and inability to organize and synthesize. On the block design subtest he confused the yellow with the white colors. The overall impression derived from the patient's performance on the WAIS was that of organic brain damage.

Consequently, both medical evidence as well as the additional psychological evidence supported the impression of this patient derived from his performance on the HABGT—namely, diffuse intracranial damage.

Cases D, E, and F offer some clinical evidence of the nature of reactions to physical trauma or injuries to the brain. So far as is known, the personality of the patient was essentially intact prior to the injury; i.e., the individual was functioning effectively both socially and occupationally. I shall comment only briefly on the outstanding features of the HABGT record.

CASE D: WARREN

This individual was a 31-year-old soldier who suffered a penetrating wound in the left temporal portions of his skull and brain. The test was administered preoperatively, at which time he manifested post-traumatic epilepsy, moderate expressive aphasia, and mild receptive aphasia along with agraphia. His drawings were done with his dominant (right) hand (see Plate 10).

The clinical symptoms suggest that damage was quite diffuse and involved the parietal area (see previous discussion). There are a number of outstanding factors in his drawings. Great anxiety and insecurity are revealed by the placement and size of figure A. Rotation of total and partial figures is evident. Regression and simplification are apparent on several drawings. Figures 5 and 6 show unusual attempts at simplification; he apparently has difficulty both in recognizing and performing these relatively simple figures. The greatest difficulty occurs on figure 7, which involves spatial relationships, obtuse angles, and more difficult figures. Here we note, among other things, simplification, fragmentation, difficulty with overlapping, and closure problems. We note that when he was offered a simpler version of this Gestalt (overlapping elipses drawn in figure 7a), he was much more successful with the problems of overlapping of the figures and in reproducing the total Gestalt. He also shows some difficulty with problems of angulation. However, he does not show any collisions between figures, although a collision tendency (and problems of spacing) is open to question.

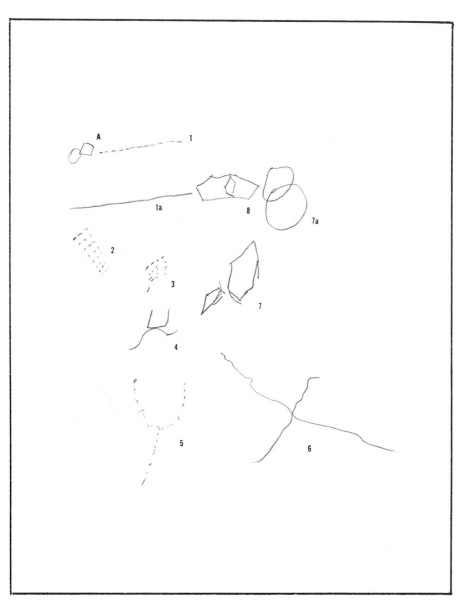

Plate 10.   Case D: Warren

CASE E: RANDOLF

At 19 years of age Randolf suffered a severe and penetrating bullet wound, with explosive effect, to the left posterior temporal and parietal areas of the brain. Surgery was necessary. Preoperatively he showed traumatic epilepsy, but no aphasic signs. He completed his drawings using his dominant (right) hand (see Plate 11).

Sequence is regular through the figure 5; then, due to inadequate space at the bottom of the page, he shifts appropriately in sequence for figures 6 and 7, but does not take into account the space limitations of the page. Figure 8 is "squeezed" in between figures A and 1. In general, spacing between figures is very irregular and inappropriate, and anticipatory planning is poor. He rotates figure A more than 90 degrees and does considerable redrawing of the lines. Although he tries to compensate for some loss in motor control by making his figures large and sweeping, in this and other figures line control is poor. Regressive features can be seen in figures 1, 3, and 5 (the substitution of dashes for dots). He redraws figure 2 in an attempt to get the right angulation. He has difficulty in making even, smooth curves in figures 4 and 6. Severe rotation occurs in figure 7, but he is able to perceive the positional qualities of the overlapping figures (and execute them) when he is given two overlapping elipses as a substitute figure. He shows the classic sign of difficulty with overlapping figures on this Gestalt when he redraws the crossing portions a number of times. Both collision and collision tendencies are present. His great disturbance in affective behavior can be inferred from the nature of his flattened and irregular curves (even though this drawing difficulty may, in part, be accounted for by loss of motor control). Simplification is present as one of his organic signs, but there is not readily apparent fragmentation.

CASE F: EDWARD

This 33-year-old man had a fractured frontal bone of the skull (compound) and a marked depression of the frontal sinuses as a result of his injury. Bone fragments had to be removed surgically. No aphasic symptoms were present. Edward was able to draw the figures with his dominant (right) hand (see Plate 12).

As one first inspects this protocol, there appears to be a great deal of confusion. Some of this is due to the fact that Edward constantly rotated the paper as he struggled with the figures. (The carrots which have been inserted indicate the position of the page for each drawing.) Nevertheless, after successive and regular sequential placement of the figures from A (which was done twice) through 3, Edward continued his placements

Plate 11.   Case E: Randolf

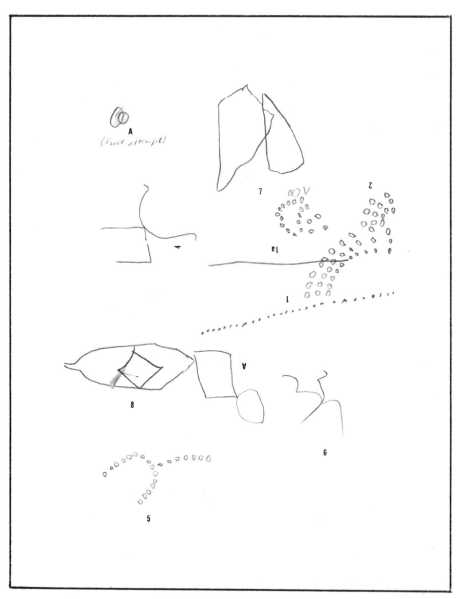

Plate 12.   Case F: Edward

in a spiral fashion, centering figures 4 to 8 around figure A, which was used as a pivot. His great insecurity is revealed in his initial attempt at figure A (which he drew as two elipses); this figure is dramatically reduced in size. His second attempt at Figure A is then placed near the middle of the page, but is rotated some 45 degrees. Figure 1 shows perseveration and is rotated in a counterclockwise direction. The spatial pattern of figure 2 is quite confusing to Edward; he also seems to have great difficulty with the angulation of the columns. His final product represents a destruction of the Gestalt, and the angulation problem causes him to rotate the entire figure in a counterclockwise direction. (Note that he did better with the directional feature of figure 1, when he was asked to copy a straight line.)

Figure 3 shows both perseveration and destruction of the Gestalt. He does remarkably well with figure 4, however, even though he had to rotate the page before doing this figure. Figure 5 shows both perseveration and severe perceptual rotation. Figure 6, with its simplified "waves" and marked irregularities suggests he must have severe problems with affective behavior and emotional control; both the angle of crossing and the crossing are simplified. The Gestalt is destroyed in figure 7; there are great problems with both angulation and overlapping. The difficulties with figure 8 (smudging, extra line drawings, problem with acute angle, closure difficulty) suggest feelings of sexual impotence and inadequacy. This record suggests that there has been damage to many parts of the brain, in addition to the specific area of the penetrating wound. We should also note that the collision of figure 1a with 2, and the collision tendencies suggest that inner controls have been badly damaged.

10
Clinical Studies: Psychotic Records

The diverse phenomena and differing dynamics of psychotic patients are, by now, well known. In this chapter we shall present two cases involving the HABGT records of schizophrenics. Schizophrenia (or, more accurately, the schizophrenias) may differ markedly in the depth and nature of psychopathology. Whether or not there is good compensation, whether the condition is acute or chronic, and whether the defensive system is still intact or not, all influence the nature of the patient's personal and social adjustment. There are many cases of schizophrenia which escape the attention of the clinician since bizarre symptoms are absent and the individual may make at least a marginal adjustment. As a consequence, the maladaptive process may be difficult to see and more difficult to assess. Objective scores and configurational patterns may not reveal the pathology. Only very careful analysis of the myriad inappropriate aspects of behavior or the characteristics of the test record will reveal the nature of the pathology. Case G is an example of this kind. On the other hand, some cases are quite bizarre, if not striking, and these are readily diagnosable. Even in such instances, much can be gained from a careful evaluation of the personality structure and the defensive system. Case H is an example of this kind.

Case G has some historical significance in that it was studied in 1951 as part of a research project. The original analysis, as published, contains a detailed discussion of the process of inferential analysis and shows how such a complicated and obtuse case can be better understood on the basis of an HABGT evaluation. We have included an addendum involving the Psychopathology Scale to show the limitations of this measure in this instance.

Case H presents an example of a rapid inspection and indicates how this assists in understanding other aspects of the "known" clinical history and findings.

CASE G: DAVID—AN APPARENTLY BENIGN RECORD

The HABGT record of this 25-year-old male is presented in Plate 13. The record was obtained as part of a psychological evaluation and was then given to the present author with only the information summarized in the next paragraph. The interpretation is quoted essentially as it was presented and published in the volume by Shneidman, Joel, and Little (Hutt, 1951). Following the summary, we shall comment briefly on the problems which this record presents and on the clinical and therapeutic findings which were later made available and summarized in the volume by Shneidman et al (1951).

It shall not be our purpose to discuss the types of qualifications one must bear in mind in discussing this record, qualifications arising from a situation in which the interpreter is in ignorance of such things as the nature of the setting in which this examination was administered, the sequence of tests, the therapy preceding the test, if any, the nature of the interpersonal relation, and the like. This interpreter had at his disposal the test record (photographic reproductions) and some very brief notes on methods of work (both of which are included with this record of interpretation). The only other information available were these limited identification data: age, 25 years; sex, male; marital status, single; education, high school; handedness, left; no gross physical limitations.

Inferential Analysis

Our first "general" inspection of the test protocol reveals the following: the drawings are arranged in "correct" sequence from A, the introductory design, to 8, the last design, and the patient "lines" his drawings up along the left margin until he has reached the bottom of the sheet, then proceeds by "completing the available space," introducing design 7 to the right of and under design 2, and follows this, again in sequence and in the vertical plane, with the last design. We note further that design A is attempted in a locus slightly to the right of the next six designs which follow it. Our first hunches then are: this individual has strong orderly, i.e., compulsive, needs, tending toward a sort of compulsive ritual, but tries to deny them (the aberrant position of A plus the examiner's comment on this design, " Draws fast, without hesitation"), and he is oppressed with some (probably) generalized feelings of anxiety and (more specifically) personal

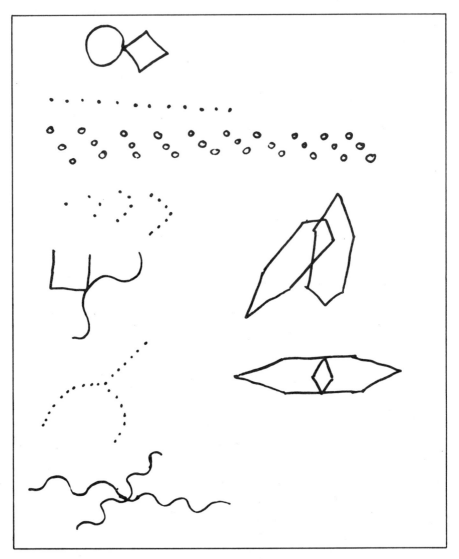

Plate 13.   Case G: David—An Apparently Benign Record

inadequacy (clings to the left margin and is "constrained" to use all of the space available to him on this one sheet). We raise the question for consideration, at once, "How strong and from what source is this anxiety and what is his defense?" We can speculate, from his use of space, that he attempts in some way to "bind" his anxiety, i.e., he cannot tolerate it for long or in large amounts, and that one of the features of this young adult's functioning is the need of control. Taken together, the compulsivity, the "binding" of anxiety, and the need of control offer the first general inference: the superego is very strict.

Permit us to interrupt the formal analysis at this point to review some features of our method of interpretation, since what we have attempted to demonstrate thus far is characteristic of our approach to the analysis of this test. We examined two main features of the test record: spatial arrangement (sequence) and use of the total space area. We correlated extreme orderliness of sequence with compulsivity in functioning (based on the normative findings from our clinical samples from young adults) and the fairly extreme use of the margin with anxiety (again a normative clinical finding). These are considered *tentative* formulations at this point, to be confirmed, modified or rejected in the light of subsequent analysis. We also noted that the "locus" of figure A was slightly deviant from the others (in the use of the margin), considered the examiner's comment regarding subject's haste in drawing, and offered the implication: "but tries to deny them," i.e., his needs for control. Next, utilizing our general knowledge of pathology (or, better, personality dynamics), we tried to speculate concerning the meaning of these clinical manifestations and offered the *inference:* "the superego is very strict." This, in microcosm, is our method of analyzing traits, needs, defenses, symptoms and function. The test is a sample of the nonverbal, perceptual-motor behavior of the individual. As such it has intrinsic validity as a behavioral representation of the patient's adaptation at the moment. We utilize our normative data as cues to interpretation for this particular sample of this particular individual. Some of the cues may appear to be contradictory; others may supplement and confirm each other. The clinical task is to make meaning not only of the cues but their interrelationships and, based on the frame of reference for all humans from a similar population (i.e., the personality dynamics of young, American, ostensibly white, high school graduate adults, in this case), to predict the underlying kind of personality which could be responsible for this total production.

Returning now to the test record, we examine figure A more carefully. The size is slightly smaller than the original. The horizontal axis of the figure is rotated slightly in a clockwise direction. These suggest: fear (self-critical attitude) and depressive reaction, respectively. Both figures are of proportionate size (no specific, exaggerated reaction to either male or female sex symbol), but, perhaps, the moderate rotation of the horizontal axis of the total figure is due to a specific reaction (dread of, hostility toward or lack of identification with, the male parent or surrogate). The latter possibility, or a derivative of it, is supported by the difficulty in "joining" the two figures (exaggerated, redrawn, over-emphasized junction of the figures). This point is the more likely to be significant in view of the patient's speed in drawing and in view of the apparently impulsive, concave sides of the square.

Figure 1, the twelve dots, is also drawn fast, with "no checking back on number of dots," the examiner notes. The number of dots is correct (confirms the patient's need for exactness, i.e., his compulsive trend), but the line of dots is wavy, the dots are filled in, and they are somewhat uneven in size and intensity. Here again, we find the apparent dilemma proposed above: the patient is compulsive but attempts to deny it. For a person who arranges his drawings on the page so methodically this "carelessness" in the alignment and size of the dots is striking. Perhaps he perceives the task of figure 1 as too simple to require careful effort. His tendency toward "haste" on all of the drawings suggests: impulsivity *or* a derogatory attitude toward the test *or* inner tension which is flowing over. The fact that the dots are heavily (and unevenly) filled in suggests that it is the last alternative which fits best. General, tentative inference: high aspiration level in a tense individual unable to accept simple experiences as nonchallenging. It is also worth noting that the dots tend to follow a downward trend: depressive reaction.

Figure 2, the ten diagonal columns of circles, offers further evidence of the marked variability which begins to appear to be characteristic of this patient. The examiner notes, "Checks number of rows (i.e., columns) about two-thirds through." We note that the angles of the columns of dots differ, becoming more obtuse (from the vertical) with a correction toward the end. The whole figure is exaggerated in the lateral plane. Together, these findings suggest a strong need to relate to people, but difficulty in establishing such relationships. The orientation of the first column is correct, so the variation in "angulation" is not a simple perceptual difficulty. The patient gets the number of columns correct, but varies both angulation and spacing. We have evidence, then, for the presence of considerable internal tension with an attempt at denial of its existence. How can we explain the apparent contradiction of the need for order and control with the speed and variability of performance? His compulsive defenses do not function effectively enough. In addition to the postulation of his impulsivity, we must add some mechanism which permits him to react so emotionally, i.e., so violently. This is especially necessary in view of "collision tendency" (figures 1 and 2). We therefore think of "acting-out," a mechanism in which ego controls are cut off (cease to function temporarily) and regressive impulsivity breaks through. If this is indeed the case, we can argue that superego demands can be side-stepped, guilt is temporarily overcome only to return in increasing intensity once the ego is later able to survey the transgression. This would thereby satisfy the patient's masochistic needs (to expiate his guilt) and thus serve a doubly useful purpose. Another possibility, which we should like to consider, is that of psychotic episodes, but the evidence for this in the record is lacking (there is no indication of a full-fledged psychotic process in the record), so we abandon this for the more parsimonious explanation already given.

Figure 3 is elongated laterally, a further indication of the patient's attempt to relate to others. The dissociation of the parts of the "arrowhead" supports the possibility of the "acting-out" mechanism offered above. The downward orientation of the figure again suggests depressive reaction. The correct number of dots and the intensity of the dots indicate: orderliness (i.e., compulsive trend) and inner tension. The Gestalt is accurate, although, again, in the segment consisting of five dots, the "postmark" of impulsivity is revealed. The increase in the horizontal dimension of the figure is accompanied by a decrease in the vertical dimension; is he fearful of authority figures?

In figure 4, the patient has increased the vertical sides of the open square; (there are no notes by the examiner); this is deduced from the "breaks" occurring in both vertical lines. His reaction to authority figures can now be inferred more completely: he is hostile to such figures, unable to express his hostility directly, and reacts either symbolically or impulsively. In line with the "acting-out" hypothesis, the former is more likely. The curved portion of this figure is enlarged, flattened out in the middle, and reveals an impulsive flourish at the upper end. Now we may speculate that his major identification is with a female figure, but she is perceived as more masculine (i.e., dominant, aggressive) than feminine and is reacted to openly with antagonism. It is interesting that the upper portion of the curved figure extends well above its position on the stimulus card, and is at least as high up as the vertical lines. Here we may conjecture that his mother (or surrogate) was stronger psychologically than his father, or at least seemed so to him, and that he would like to use his mother (or women) to defy his father (or men).

The depressive coloring in the patient's attempt at figure 5 is striking (clockwise orientation of the total figure). He has difficulty with the projecting line of dots, attaching it about midway on the circumference of the "semicircle" of dots, although it is off-center on the stimulus. Despite this, other features of the drawing are precisely accurate: the number of dots in the "semicircle," the number of dots in the projection, and the position between the seventh and eighth dot of the circumference for the point of union. Here is, indeed, compulsive attention to detail, despite which, the figure in toto is distorted. If we accept the premise that this figure "stands for" the mother surrogate, we may then infer that his vehemence against this symbol can be, and is, expressed in an open-structured figure, while he cannot so distort it in the simpler, more conventional symbolism of figure A. Again, this would support the premise of a symbolic acting-out of his conflict with his mother (and with women), although conventionally he is deferent, obedient and conformist.

Figure 6, the sinusoidal curves, taxes him to the utmost. Affect is strong (amplitude of curves), but is expressed unevenly (uneven wave lengths). Marked difficulty occurs at the crossing. (E's notes support this.) The excessive loop at the top of the vertical curve plus the fact that this curve was drawn first, from the top down, express the patient's suppressed hostility to male, parental symbols. The Gestalt is accurate, but the difficulty with this figure is apparent in the drawing. One would expect this patient to show some apathy in his typical behavior, but react on occasion with outbursts, probably of a sexual, or, better, sexual-symbolic, character.

On figure 7, the right-hand figure is rotated slightly in a clockwise direction and all of the joinings show "closure difficulty." There is an exaggeration of the lower section of the left-hand figure. The Gestalt is accurate. We infer: depressive reactions; difficulty in maintaining interpersonal relations; feelings of sexual inadequacy (possibly feelings of impotence).

The same closure difficulty is noted on figure 8, on which E says, "Draws small inside diamond first, then encloses." The figure is increased in size laterally and the ends are exaggerated. Inferences: difficulty in interpersonal relations; major identification with female figures; sexual impotency (or fear thereof).

One final observation: the spacing between successive figures is constricted. This fits in with our conception of him as essentially anal in fixation and generally suppressive of conscious hostility feelings.

From all of the above, we may attempt to etch out the personality as it functions on this psychological task, and offer some predictions to be considered in the light of other data.

We would suspect that this individual tries to give the impression of a sophisticated, but conforming, individual. He has unusually high aspirations, but feels limited and inadequate, although ordinarily denying this to others and attempting to deny it to himself. He is subject to marked inner turmoil, but attempts to conceal this, too, from others and himself. His ambition and drive toward achievement, and in general his compulsive controls offer some compensation, but they are not enough. He suffers from melancholy and intense feelings of frustration. He finds it increasingly difficult to work effectively. At the root of his difficulty lies an identification with a dominant, and to him, unrewarding mother-figure, toward whom he reacts with some hostility, but toward whom he is very attracted sexually. For some reason (the record is not indicative) he is also fearful (and unable to express it) toward the father-figure. We may speculate that the father is perceived as strong but ineffectual in relation to the mother (for some reason) and that he has guilt over his attraction to the mother, who is objective, strong, just, but unobtainable. With this nucleus in this type of oedipal conflict as a base, his development was attended by deep guilt reactions stirred by a strict superego development. A relatively strong ego enabled him to move along for a time until late adolescent and young adult situational factors decreased the effectiveness of ego functions, at least for a time. It is suggested that then either Don Juan behavior or symbolic acting-out occurred (possibly both), and guilt increased until the prevalent masochistic pattern was reestablished. One would suspect that depressive reactions, possibly suicidual preoccupation, began as the cycle became tighter and as the vocational-occupational sublimations became less effective with decreased efficiency in total functioning. The Don Juan hypothesis is in line with the speculation that he tried to act out his needs for masculine competence in the face of increasing feelings of sexual inadequacy and guilt. The anchorage of good, intense relationships with peers is lacking, although wished for.

Superficially, this young man may give the impression of control and fair effectiveness. If our speculations concerning the nature of his difficulties are substantially correct, we may suggest that he will be able to make very effective use of analytically oriented therapy, providing this is both intensive and fairly extensive.

Additional Data

The above analysis of a record attempts to present an illustration of inferential analysis. We can evaluate it in terms of effectiveness against the extensive clinical and treatment findings which Shneidman et al (1951) subsequently presented in the same volume.

Insofar as basic dynamics are concerned, the HABGT analysis comes remarkably close to the findings of this man's therapist; not only are the statements of the nature of the conflicts and their attempted resolution the same or very similar, but even the rhetorical phrasing of the problem in the HABGT report and in the report of the therapist is very similar, almost identical.

It might also be pointed out that the report of the psychology staff of the hospital where this man was under study and treatment, based upon a battery of tests and interviews, also arrived at findings essentially similar to those of the analysis based on the HABGT.

Specifically, the psychiatric history indicated that this man, a patient in a neuropsychiatric hospital, was admitted with the following symptoms: insomnia, palpitation, night sweats, trembling when people observed him, and feelings of inadequacy. His difficulties were reported as having begun some six months after he entered the Navy, in which he was assigned to the medical corps. Since his discharge his concentration had become quite poor and his symptoms had increased progressively.

At the hospital his first diagnosis was psychoneurosis, anxiety type, acute and severe. Later, psychiatric consultation suggested that he was most likely an obsessive–compulsive, but the diagnosis was "between obsessive–compulsive neurosis, anxiety–hysteria, and schizophrenia." The discharge diagnosis was that of anxiety reaction.

Following discharge from the hospital, the patient was seen in therapy at a mental hygiene clinic. The patient terminated therapy, which had been conducted by a psychiatric case worker under close psychiatric consultation. The closing note on this case may be of interest. "The material obtained seemed to indicate more and more clearly that his defenses were crumbling and that he was either close to a psychotic break or actually psychotic. . . . Diagnosis: schizophrenic reaction, paranoid type."

We cannot take the space to review the specific dynamic findings of the therapist which confirmed those of the HABGT, but the interested reader may study these for himself in the fairly exhaustive summary which Shneidman presents (Shneidman et al, 1951).

Addendum

This patient's Psychopathology Scale score is presented in Table 14. An examination of these scores indicates that there is little scorable pathology on this scale. This is an excellent example of the limitations of any objective scale, not only this one. There are many instances in which a low Psychopathology score is not suggestive of the severe disturbance that may be present. Casual inspection of such scores might lead to the

Table 14
Psychopathology Scale Findings: Case G, David

Test Factor	Scale Value	Test Factor	Scale Value
1. Sequence	1.0	10. Perc. Rotation	1.0
2. Position 1st Fig.	3.25	11. Retrogression	1.0
3. Space, I	1.0	12. Simplification	1.0
4. Collision	2.5	13. Fragmentation	1.0
5. Shift of Paper	1.0	14. Overlapping	1.0
6. Closure Diff.	5.5	15. Elaboration	1.0
7. Crossing Diff.	4.0	16. Perseveration	1.0
8. Curvature Diff.	4.0	17. Redrawing	1.0
9. Angulation	2.0		
Total scaled score: 32.25			

inaccurate conclusion that there is no pathology. The same conclusion might be reached by a casual inspection of the actual or test behavior. One of the major reasons for such possibilities is that the pathology may be disguised by compensatory processes. Many disturbances involve an insidious process which is not easily detectable. *Low scores on objective scales do not necessarily mean, however, that there is an absence of pathology.* High scores are more likely to be indicative of such pathology. The advantage of a careful, detailed inferential analysis, as this case illustrates, is that the trained clinician is much more apt to pick up subtle signs and, especially, contradictions in the record, which finally leads to a more accurate appraisal.

CASE H: BILL—AN OBVIOUSLY PSYCHOTIC RECORD

This is the case of a white male patient, 38 years of age, who was hospitalized for severe personality disturbance because of inability to maintain himself in society and who had periods of violent acting out. His diagnosis was chronic, undifferentiated schizophrenia, and it was estimated that the outbreak of the psychotic reaction had occurred some 10 years before. Plate 14 presents his responses on the Copy Phase of the HABGT. As we have already indicated, we shall simply note some of the test factors which characterize this record and comment on the nature of his configuration.

Sequence. The sequence is methodical since only two figures indicate a deviation from a regular pattern (a deviation after figure 3 and another after figure 7). Thus, sequence is atypical for schizophrenia.

Position of the first drawing. The placement of figure A is clearly atypical or abnormal.

Use of space I. The record must be characterized as constricted. Moreover, spacing is very uneven.

Use of space II. Again, this is a constricted record. In both aspects of the use of space this record is clearly atypical and is consistent with the configurational findings for schizophrenia.

Collision. An actual, but slight, collision occurs between figures 3 and 6 and between 7 and 8, and collision tendencies occur between other figures: e.g., 3 and 6, 6 and 7, and possibly 4 and 5. These findings are consistent with the configuration for schizophrenia.

Use of margin. This factor is not present. Except in schizophrenics with intense anxiety or in incipient stages of this disorder, this factor is not likely to be present.

Shift in the position of the paper. This does not occur.

Shift in position of the stimulus cards. There is no examiner's notation of this phenomenon.

Plate 14.   Case H: Bill—An Obviously Psychotic Record

Overall change in size. This record does not meet the criteria for this test factor.

Progressive change in size. This is not present.

Isolated change in size. This factor is clearly present. It will be noted that the circle in figure A, for example, is disproportionately small in relation to the square. Similarly, one part of figure 6 is disproportionately small. Although this factor has not been included within the configuration for schizophrenia presented in Chapter 6, it is significant in evaluating the dynamics of the individual case.

Closure difficulty. This is present and very pronounced. This finding is not unique to schizophrenia, by any means, but again, in inferential analysis it would be of importance.

Crossing difficulty. This factor is present for both figures 6 and 7. It is an associated discriminator in schizophrenia.

Curvature difficulty. Flattening occurs in figure 4. Both irregularity and flattening occur in figure 6. These are the most pronounced indications of curvature difficulty in this record. This finding is consistent with schizophrenia as an associated discriminator.

Change in angulation. This is present in figures 2 (the decreased angulation of the columns of circles), 3, 7, and 8. The defenses of this patient against emotional impact of the stimuli represented by these figures may be inferred.

Rotation. Mild rotation occurs in figures 5 and 6. Moderate rotation occurs in figure 8. This factor is of borderline significance in this record with respect to schizophrenia.

Retrogression. This is marked. Note the dashes in figure 3 and the pronounced difficulties in figures 7 and 8. The presence of this factor in two or more figures is consistent with the diagnosis of schizophrenia.

Simplification. This also is marked. It may be noted in figures A, 3, 4, 6, 7, and 8. This is still another essential discriminator for schizophrenia.

Fragmentation. This factor is present in figures A, 4, 6, and 8. Again, this is an essential discriminator for schizophrenia.

Overlapping difficulty. Present on all three criterion figures: 4, 6, and 7.

Elaboration or doodling. Not present.

Perseveration. This may be present in figure A, in which the circle is repeated; it may also be noted in figure 2 (the excessive number of columns), and is present in figure 6. However, these type (b) perseverative tendencies are not pronounced, nor is type (a) perseveration present. Perseverative tendencies, particularly of type (b), are much more marked in organic records, but we can suggest on this and on other bases, that this record is not likely to be that of an organic.

Table 15
Configuration Analysis Bill: Case H

	Factor	Weight
1.	Confused placement	0
2.	Retrogression	2
3.	Abnormal placement of 1st fig.	2
4.	Elaboration	0
5.	Very severe closure difficulty	1
6.	Very severe curvature difficulty	1
7.	Moderate fragmentation	1
8.	Perceptual rotation	1
9.	Simplification	1
10.	Crowding of figures	1?

Configurational score: 9–10

The test record alone is insufficient to judge the test factor of *line movement,* and there is no clear indication of any significant disturbance in the factors of *line quality.*

An evaluation of this record on the basis of the configuarational weights for schizophrenia, presented in Table 15, clearly indicates that this record fits this category.

The score on the schizophrenic configuration is at least 9, possibly 10. This is well above the critical score of 7 presented in the section on configurational analysis of the schizophrenias in Chapter 6, and hence provides confirmatory evidence of the presence of a probable schizophrenic condition. Of course, in actual practice the clinician will wish to consider additional evidence.

11
Clinical Studies: Neurotic Records

The richness of HABGT records is no more evident than in the protocols and associations of neurotic individuals. Each record is unique. We can do no more than offer a glimpse into the diverse patterns of response among these individuals. Three records have been chosen to illustrate the great variety of neurotic manifestations. The first will be presented in some detail, but the other two will only be commented on briefly.

CASE I: JOHN—NEUROSIS AND THERAPEUTIC MANAGEMENT

John, as we shall call him, had been referred by his psychiatrist, who had a number of questions concerning the nature of his problems and this patient's suitability for psychotherapy. John had sought the help of the psychiatrist at the urging of his wife, who felt that her husband was showing increasing difficulties in holding down a job and who wished assistance for John with his problem of alcoholism. She stated that their marital relationship had never been entirely satisfactory but that John had been a good provider and that he was considerate. John was not sure that he needed psychotherapy, admitted to periods when he felt tense and irritable, explained that he was getting bored with his job and that he drank, only on occasion, to relieve his feelings of boredom and tension. The psychiatrist, who had seen John for a short consultation, wondered how "sick" John might be and how well motivated he was for psychotherapy. John was 48 years old at the time of examination. His wife was 35 years of age.

John was quite cooperative during the psychological examination. He appeared obviously tense and a mild expressive aphasia was suspected on the basis of his speech patterns. His mood was slightly depressed, but his judgment and memory appeared to be unimpaired. He gave the impression of being somewhat passive and compliant.

Plate 15 contains the record of the copy phase of the HABGT. It will be noted that only six figures were presented. This was done to save time, since only one visit by this patient was available and sufficient time was needed during this visit to administer a Rorschach test. Clinical experience has indicated that figures A, 2, 4, 6, 7, and 8 furnish a very good sample of all of the basic phenomena in most cases and provide an adequate basis for inferences concerning most aspects of the relevant dynamics.

Inferential Analysis

We note first that all of the drawings tend to be reduced in size, with figures A and 6 showing a marked reduction in size. Moreover, the spacing between some pairs of figures, notably A and 2, 4, and 6, and 6 and 7 is decreased. All of the drawings together occupy slightly less than one-half of the page. The position of figure A is not atypical, but, as we have noted, figure A, and especially the circle in this figure, is markedly reduced in size. The sequence is methodical; there is no collision or collision tendency; and there is no shift in the position of the test paper. These stylistic features tell us that this patient is generally orderly in his approach to new tasks and that he tends to be suppressive in his behavioral modes of expression. The initial reduction in size, the general reduction in use of space, and the reduction in the size of figure 6 indicate, respectively, that he is fearful and anxious, he tends to use repressive mechanisms of defense, and he is especially anxious in emotionally toned situations. These stylistic features suggest that anal modes of adaptation are prominent in this individual's behavior and that, overtly, passivity may be a characteristic personality trait.

In the reproduction of figure A several features may be noted. The marked discrepancy in size between the circle and the square, the reduced size of the square, and the heavy line quality of the square suggest that this patient is attempting to identify unconsciously with a strong male role (as object preference) but that he feels inadequate in his male role. The presence of closure difficulty is indicative of anxiety in interpersonal situations, and this finding, together with the relatively larger size of the square, the elongation of the square in the lateral dimension, the heavy line quality present in the square, and the irregularity in the line quality on the right lower perimeter of the square, suggest that there may be severe conflict in the sexual sphere and that the anxiety may be of the castration

Plate 15.   Case I: John—Copy Phase

variety. More than this, the severity of the conflict as well as the jagged-
ness of the line referred to above may indicate some perverse tendencies,
as well as the inappropriate fusing of sexual and aggressive drives. Finally, the possibility of some mild intracrainial damage should not be
overlooked (the difficulty with the angle of the square at the bottom).

We note, in figure 2, that there is a mild counterclockwise rotation of the entire figure. The columns of circles are so arranged that they form an arc of a circle (with the patient at the pivotal position). The narcissistic, oppositional features of the personality may be inferred from these two factors. Closure difficulty is again present. Another interesting feature is the gradual increase in size of the circles from left to right. This latter phenomenon suggests a tendency to act out, a tendency toward impulsivity in the personality which is otherwise fairly well concealed from overt observation.

The most striking feature of figure 4 is the closure difficulty (between curve and open square) and/or fragmentation of this Gestalt. The blocking in interpersonal situations has already been noted. The possibility that fragmentation is present reinforces the hypothesis of some mild organic damage. The inequalty in the vertical sides of the open square again suggests the difficulty this man is having in maintaining an adequate self-percept in the role of a male, as well as the possibility of difficulty with authority figures. Some poor fine coordination is noted, further indication of the anxiety which is present. The curved portion of the figure is slightly exaggerated but the relative positions of the open square and curve are reproduced accurately. Perhaps the fragmentation enables this patient to handle this situation more easily than he could otherwise have done.

Figure 6 was presented in the same spatial orientation in which the patient reproduces it, i.e., no rotation is present. However, the figure is markedly reduced in size in both dimensions. The curves are drawn (especially the one in the horizontal plane) as a series of connected curves (and not as a smoothly flowing line). The amplitude of the curves is reduced and some "looping" occurs. The abient type of defense which this patient preferentially uses is made quite clear. He is unable to respond spontaneously in an emotional situation. He tries to control by repressive techniques; denial and isolation are suggested as defense mechanisms.

Figure 7 presents severe problems for this patient. The whole figure is rotated in a clockwise manner. Each part of the figure is modified slightly. Crossing difficulty is quite apparent as a consequence of the problem of overlapping. Sketching occurs even when the problem of overlapping is not present. Thus, although we must again suspect the presence of some intracranial damage, the depressive features of the reproduction and the sexually traumatic meaning of this stimulus seem much more prominent. These inferences are supported by the presence of line incoordination and the closure difficulties which can be noted in the response.

The same types of difficulties appear in figure 8, i.e., clockwise rotation, closure difficulty, and difficulty with the "phallic" endings of this Gestalt. Some mild line incoordination is also present. Moreover, the internal diamond is poorly drawn and shows repetitive line movements, suggesting conflict over the presence of this female symbol in an otherwise highly phallic figure. The phenomena which we have noted in common for both figures 7 and 8 suggest that the primary problem is one of psychosexual arrest and conflict. The overall impression, reinforced by the findings on the last two figures, suggest the possibility of some type of sexual perversion as a residual of severe castration anxiety and some attempt at displacement of the locus of the anxiety.

Turning now to the elaborations (Plate 16), we note some striking similarities to the general stylistic features of the copy portion of the test. Methodical sequence is maintained, the drawings are compressed into the upper half of the page, the size of the figures (generally) is reduced, and the position of figure A is about the same. It will be noted that the curved portions of the Gestalt (figures A and 4) are placed *above* the other portions. The patient now has less difficulty with figure A than he had before (closure difficulty is reduced and the relative size of the two components is more appropriate). From these observations we can conclude, in general, that the most prominent inferences we derived from the copy phase are reinforced. Additionally, we can assume that this patient has strong feminine components in his personality, and possibly some exhibitionistic tendencies (the latter to be confirmed as plausible or rejected on the basis of additional evidence, possibly from the associations to the drawings).

We note that figure 2 is again rotated in a counterclockwise fashion, that poor line quality is evident on the open square portion of figure 4, that reduction of the amplitude of the curves again occurs on figure 6 (and this time mild clockwise rotation of the figure appears), that figure 7 is completely separated into two components (in order, presumably, to solve the problem of overlapping), and that the same types of difficulties present in figure 8 in the copy phase are present in the elaboration phase. Thus, again, our previous hypotheses are strengthened. These elaborations are very close to the original in basic Gestalt qualities, i.e., the patient was too fearful or too limited to be able to modify them freely.

And now, we can turn our attention to the associations which were obtained both to the original stimuli and to the elaborations. The patient first gave his association to his elaboration of figure A and then to the stimulus, as follows: "An ornament. A ring with a do-dunny. Could be an ornament for a bracelet or something," and: "Ball and a block." The association to the elaboration suggests exhibitionistic fantasies. The verbal blocking indicates the presence of conflict. The orientation is feminine. The association to the original stimulus is quite concrete and literal. Fantasy is limited and guarded.

Again, on figure 2 the first association is given to the elaboration: "A bracelet or something to me." When asked to associate to the original stimulus, he said: "Both look like bracelets to me." The exhibitionistic

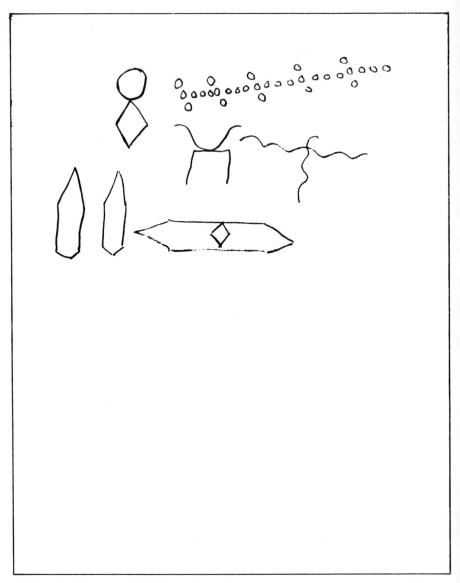

Plate 16.   Case I: John—Elaborations

and repetitive nature of these associations should be noted. It can also be
said that this patient's speech style contains egocentric features.

He associated to the elaboration of figure 4: "A stand and a basin."
He could give no association to the stimulus. The possible superego
characteristics of his association (which may be inferred from the need to

wash oneself) should not be overlooked. The block in associating to the original figure is indicative of the presence of anxiety, which tends to confirm our speculations concerning his difficulties in copying this figure. It should also be noted that his association tends to deny the higher (superior) position of the basin (one wonders why he did not say, "A basin on a stand").

He associated only to the elaboration of figure 6. He said: "A peice of string. Might be a kind of wire—a crooked wire." This association appears to be evasive. The "crooked wire" may be a reference to his self-percept, i.e., distorted or bent.

On figure 7, he responded, again, to the elaboration: "I don't know. Some kind of ornament or something. Something like the top of a picket fence." Again, the exhibitionistic needs of this patient become apparent. The fence may connote the need for protection while the picket-type of fence suggests many possibilities, among which the phallic connotation is the most parsimonious in terms of other evidence already obtained for this figure. He could give no association to the original stimulus.

His only association to figure 8 was to the original stimulus. His association: "Some kind of a sign. They have on fences." The continued association to "fence" suggests a perseverative trend in his thinking as well as the probable need for protection, suggested before. The association "sign" is often related to feelings of guilt and suspiciousness.

Taking into account all of the data from the three phases of the HABGT, we are able to present the following summary of our analysis. This man appears to be a fairly dependent and very anxious individual. He shows considerable concern about maintaining a conventional "facade" and tends to be conforming and compliant in his behavior. There is some rigidity in his behavior. Ego controls are reasonably well maintained except for problems involving specific sexual traumata. Affective behavior is reduced and spontaneity is lacking. He has considerable doubt concerning his adequacy as a person. Superego functions are fairly strict but are insufficient to prevent occasional breakthrough of libidinal impulses.

Although this man is essentially conforming in his behavior, the severity of his conflicts and the possible impairment which intracranial damage has caused, produce some overt types of psychopathology. His strong oral-dependent needs and his internal tension are consistent with his use of alcohol. The narcissistic and oral features of the personality as well as the anal components which are present suggest that he has strong exhibitionistic needs and may engage in some other perverse sexual behavior. In turn, the use of alcohol and the predicted perversions, together with his superego formation, will produce considerable guilt and tension. His feelings of impotence and his sexual–aggressive drives may result in both homosexual needs and practices. Some form of perversion as a displacement of his castration anxiety may also be present.

The basic features of the personality are psychoneurotic in character and the primary features of the defense system are obsessive–compulsive, with denial and isolation, as part of a general repressive orientation, high in the defense hierarchy. The presence of some mild intracranial damage, possibly a small tumor, is suspected and may account for the apparent expressive aphasia and for the reduced effectiveness of ego controls.

It is suggested that this man will be willing to accept psychotherapy if, in fact, his conflicts are as severe as is suspected and he is confronted with them. However, psychotherapy may be expected to be long and difficult. Some reduction in the severity of the superego may be anticipated, some release of anxiety may be accomplished, and more effective ways of sublimating his oedipal problems, and especially his oral and anal needs, may be secured. Careful neurologic examination is also suggested to evaluate the possibility of brain damage.

Additional Data and Follow-up

Subsequent psychiatric and neurologic examination, and subsequent psychotherapeutic intervention revealed the following. Unknown to the wife, this man has been engaging in homosexual practices for almost the entire period of his marriage. So far as could be learned, he had shown no overt homosexuality previously. He described, in his therapeutic sessions, two experiences in which he had exhibited himself before adolescent girls. On one occasion he had sexual relations with a 12-year-old girl, and he had described to the psychiatrist his obsessive concern with smelling and fondling this girl's genitalia. He discussed his strong urges to engage in perverse sexual practices as well as his strong conflicts in this regard. The neurologist reported that this man suffered from a small parieto-temporal tumor for which operative care was not indicated. He did receive concurrent psychotherapeutic and general medical care. The therapist reported that this patient was able to make moderate gains in reducing guilt and anxiety, that he was able to function better on his job, and that there was some improvement, but not complete cessation, in his alcoholism. He had developed a hobby involving sculpturing with clay materials which was very satisfying to him. He left therapy after 72 sessions, spaced over a year and a half, because he felt he was able to get along fairly well and the financial drain was more than he could tolerate.

Configurational Analysis

It is interesting to evaluate this record of the copy phase (Plate 15) in terms of the configurational analysis of psychoneuroses presented in Chapter 6. Although only 6 of the figures were given, this man obtains the following scores for the neurotic configuration: 2 for sequence; 2 for isolated changes in size; 2 for crossing difficulty; 2 for inconsistent line quality; 2 for severe constriction in size; and 1 for mild curvature difficulty. This yields a score of 11 points, which is well above the critical score of 8 for this category. Some of the features that are specific to depressive reactions that have been obtained in research studies (e.g., Johnson, 1973) are also present.

CASE J: HORACE—ALCOHOLISM AND NEUROSIS

Our next case is that of a 37-year-old man, a professional, who had become extremely tense, was finding great difficulty in carrying out his duties, which were formerly quite easy for him, was depressed at times, and finally became alcoholic. This highly intelligent and well educated man (we shall call him Horace) was aware that he had serious psychological problems and sought psychotherapeutic help. The HABGT (all phases) was given to him early in therapy and proved helpful to him and his therapist in evaluating his problems and offering leads for therapeutic working through. Plates 17 and 18 reproduce his copy phase record.

Inferential Analysis

The most striking feature of this record is the use of lines between figures. This, plus the marked increase in the size of the figures and the heavy line quality, suggests that he is using great effort to compensate for feelings of anxiety and insecurity. The increase in the horizontal dimension of figure A, so that the circle becomes an ellipse and the square a diamond, suggest how desperately he is trying to reach out (i.e., the lateral plane being the interpersonal dimension of motoric behavior). Closure difficulty and "overshooting" are also apparent in this drawing, reinforcing the inference of interpersonal problems. On figures 1, 3, and 5 he makes heavily filled in dots, utilizing a great deal of time and energy for such simple tasks. This suggests the high level of his anxiety and the strength of his compensatory efforts. Figure 3 is rotated in a counterclockwise direction; the inference is that he is oppositional. Figure 6, 7, and 8 show markedly increasing size. As he becomes more tense, he makes his figures bigger and bigger.

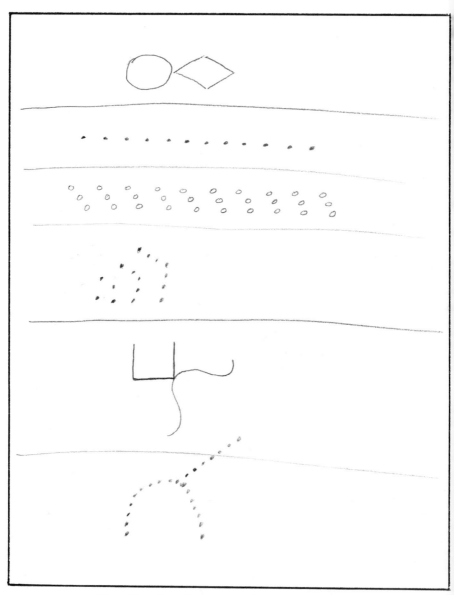

Plate 17.   Case J: Horace—Copy Phase (page 1)

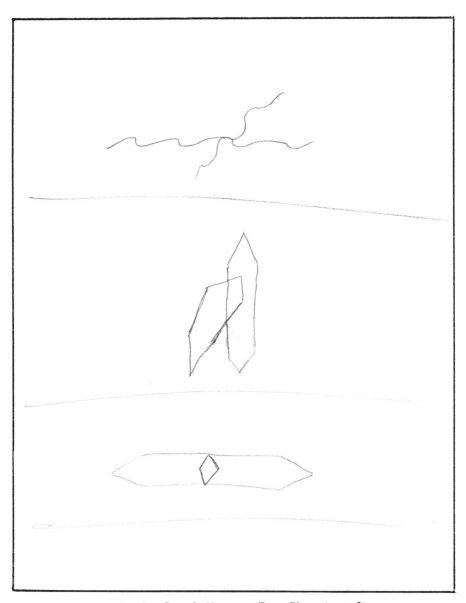

Plate 18.   Case J: Horace—Copy Phase (page 2)

A special problem is his great difficulty with the overlapping hexagons. The simplification and the redrawing in this figure suggests that sexual conflict is severe, and this is "confirmed" by his difficulty with the internal triangle of figure 8.

These are but a few of the outstanding features of this record. He was also given the elaboration phase of this test. He made no effort to change any of the figures, essentially redrawing them once again. This time, however, he drew figure 7 quite accurately, but he had to redraw the lines in this figure a number of times. Figure 8, too, was done much more easily, but some incoordination was shown on the internal triangle.

His associations to both the stimulus cards and the elaborations were extremely limited and literal. Most of his attempts at association ended with a description of the figures. His only nonliteral associations were to figures 4 ("a German helmet") and 6 ("happiness").

Additional Data and Follow-up

Horace was asked to offer his own reactions to his performance on the various phases of the test. He noted how fearful he had been in this simple "test" situation, how constricted he was in fantasy (associations), how angry he felt while drawing the figures, and said: "Quite obviously, you can see that I have serious sexual problems." (Nothing had been said during previous interviews about the existence of such a problem.) The test situation subsequently opened up a flood of associations which he began to deal with in his therapy sessions. He wondered why he had been (and was) so fearful of sexual matters, yet so attracted to them (he was unmarried). He became aware of his repressed rage. He began to see that alcohol was not simply a means of attempting to relieve tension, but also a means of excusing his current incompetence and enabling him to mingle with men at bars and talk about sexual matters in a pseudo-free way.

CASE K: STEPHEN—A CASE OF SEVERE INTERNAL TURMOIL

This is the case of a 26-year-old man who felt that his only problems were those created by his nagging and inconsiderate wife. He did not profess to see any need for psychotherapy for himself, but came for consultation because he felt that his marital problems were serious. He was quite successful in his career as a consulting engineer. However, he recognized that his associates kept at a distance from him and sometimes complained that he was rigid and spiteful. After the HABGT had been administered he was asked to comment on his performance and his reac-

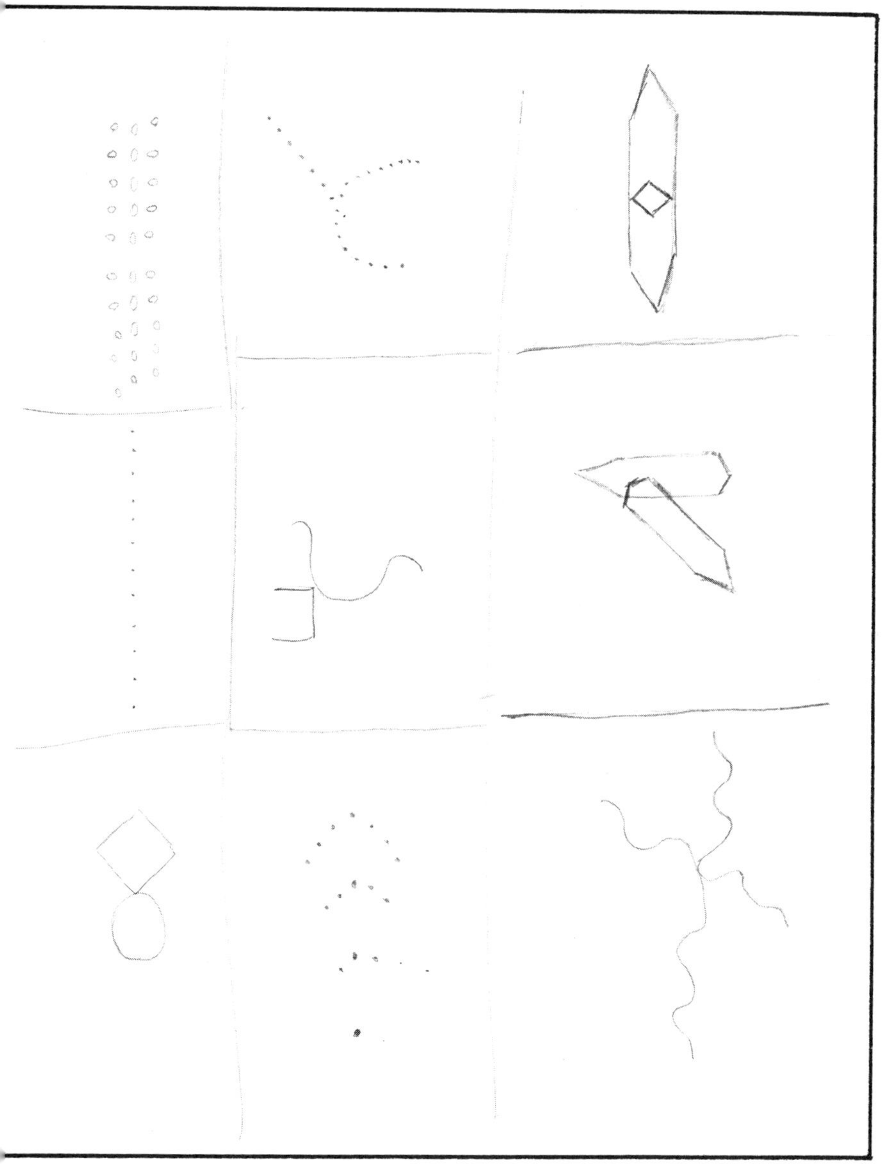

Plate 19. Case K: Stephen—Copy Phase

tions during the test. He felt he had done well, but could not understand why he had "changed" some of the figures. He said he had tried to draw them veridically, yet felt "compelled" to modify them as he did; he was fully aware of the differences between his drawings and those on the test cards. Further discussion of the test and his personal situation convinced him that he had significant intrapersonal problems and he requested therapy for himself.

Inferential Analysis

We shall comment only briefly on the major aspects of his test performance in order to highlight some of the personality characteristics which they suggested.

On the copy phase (Plate 19), one notes his need to compartmentalize completely all of his drawings by enclosing them in "boxes." He boxed in each figure after he had completed it. Figure A is accurate except that he enlarges the diamond; some closure difficulty is noted. Figure 1 is constricted in size. Figure 2 is also constricted (horizontally) and shows some highly unusual and idiosyncratic characteristics. It is composed of two sections, and contains ellipses in the middle row instead of circles. Thus far, we note that this is the performance of a highly compulsive, highly repressed, and overly controlling individual. The unusual features of figure 2, especially the loss of angulation in the columns, with a shift in their orientation toward himself as the focus, suggest that he is very willful, highly egocentric, and possibly paranoidal in orientation. Spacing between the figures throughout the record (space I) tends to be constricted.

Figure 3 is elongated in the horizontal dimension, and the dots are filled in heavily; we would infer that he reacts in the interpersonal sphere by overassertion and aggression. Figure 4 contains a number of distortions. There is a slight "gap" between the figures, the open square is compressed, and the curved portion is exaggerated and off focus. One would suspect that he is a highly tense individual who is overly defensive and has some problems in terms of sexual identity.

Figure 5 is rotated slightly in a clockwise direction. He sketches the curved portion of the figure before filling in the dots. Figure 6 is drawn as two asymptotic curves, rotated slightly in a clockwise direction, and the curves are uneven in amplitude. By now we have indications of depressive features in the personality and indications of poor affective control with a tendency to turn anger inward (which may be a source of his depression). He simplifies figure 7 (perhaps to avoid the difficult overlapping problem) and does obvious sketching and redrawing. Figure 8 is also sketched and shows redrawing. The closure difficulties on figures 7 and 8 plus the "hallmark" on figure 8 of sexual conflict (intensely drawn internal diamond, and difficulties with the "phallic" ends of the hexagon), suggest how impotent this individual feels as "a man" and how much he must overcompensate.

The obsessive and compulsive features of this record are conspicuous. In the light of this, his distortions take on added significance.

Turning now to the elaboration (Plate 20) and association phases, we note first that his compulsive style is quite evident; he still finds it necessary to compartmentalize each figure. (Note: only 6 of the figures were given for the elaboration phase.) With the exception of figures 2 and 4, he simply tries to reproduce, rather than elaborate, the drawings. Figure 2 is "tied together" with straight lines; figure 4 is elaborated into what looks like a "Valentine presentation." Moreover, on figure 4 the open squares are made even smaller and the curved portion even larger.

His associations are quite revealing. He gives two associations to stimulus card A: "A ball that hangs on the end of a chain, knocking down a building;" and, "An error in a computer program. Each symbol represents an action. It should have an arrow." No associations are given to his elaboration. The possible meanings of the associations are quite apparent. They will become even more clear as we examine his other associations. His associations to the stimulus of figure 2 are: "Webbing in a building;" and "Military formation or a disarranged pegboard." His association to his elaboration of this figure is: "Edge of tapestry. Woven material. Woven fabric or frame of a picture." We should comment on the obviously ambivalent characteristics of these associations: militaristic and aggressive, on the one hand, and feminine and soft, on the other.

His association to card 4 is: "A vessel poised on the edge of a table" (note the projection of his self-precarious identity), while his associations to his elaborations are: "My mother; an asymmetrical figure; a design, a nonobject." The possible meanings of these associations were explored in his therapeutic sessions and clearly indicated how tied he was emotionally to his mother, yet how much he "hated" her.

On card 6 he associated: "Looks like uncombed hair; grotesque tree limbs." On figure 7 (to the card only) he responded: "Two geometrical symbols; parts of a plane intersecting, as in teaching parallelograms." On figure 8, he offered his associations to the elaboration: "Kerchief of a Boy Scout's ring; like a totem belt you buy in a souvenir store; pieces of costume jewelry."

We could profitably spend considerable time in dealing with these associations. Suffice it to say that his confused sexual identity, his intense narcissistic attitudes, and his repressed rage seem strongly suggested.

Plate 20. Case K: Stephen—Elaborations

Table 16
Psychopathology Scale Findings: Case K, Stephen

Test Factor	Scale Value	Test Factor	Scale Value
1. Sequence	4.0	10. Perc. Rotation	4.0
2. Position 1st Fig.	1.0	11. Retrogression	1.0
3. Space I	10.0	12. Simplification	1.0
4. Collision	1.0	13. Fragmentation	1.0
5. Shift of Paper	1.0	14. Overlapping	5.5
6. Closure Diff.	10.0	15. Elaboration	1.0
7. Crossing Diff.	1.0	16. Perserveration	1.0
8. Curvature Diff.	4.0	17. Redrawing	1.0
9. Angulation	2.0		

Total scaled score: 51.5

Psychopathology Scale Score

Finally, we should like to present the results of his Psychopathology Scale scoring. This is offered in Table 16.

His score of 51.5 places him close to the mean of outpatient neurotics (see Table 2, Chapter 7) and more than 3 *SD*'s above the mean of "normals." On this basis, he clearly belongs in the category of "neurotics." Our limited inferential analysis presentation suggests that he is a very disturbed individual who has great strengths as well as severe internal stresses. His therapeutic progress was excellent and he was able to "grow" quite markedly in his personality development.

12
Clinical Studies: A Character Problem

This chapter is concerned with the analysis of an HABGT record produced by a patient whose diagnosis is a character disorder. Detailed interpretation of all three phases of the basic method of administration will
be presented, as well as relevant case history material, other psychological
test data, and a summary from psychotherapeutic data.

The patient was a 28-year-old white female. She was a high school
graduate and had had approximately one year of college. She had never
held a full-time job.

The drawings were made with the right hand in a rapid manner. If
counting took place, it was done silently and imperceptibly. The stimulus
cards utilized were the American Orthopsychiatric Association version.*

Inferential Analysis

In the copy phase (Plates 21 and 22) we note that the drawings are
distributed over two pages in an irregular sequence. There are five deviations: figures A to 1, 1 to 2, 2 to 3, 3 to 4, and 4 to 5. In general, the figures
are increased in size; the spacing is irregular, varying from constricted
through adequate to excessive.

The initial impression is that of an outgoing, aggressively oriented
women (size, two sheets of paper) who is markedly conflicted over the
expression of hostility (varied spacing). Impulses are poorly controlled
and ego functions are uneven (irregular sequence). A second-order

---

* The use of these cards limits our interpretations of the reproductions and excludes
the use of our objective scales.

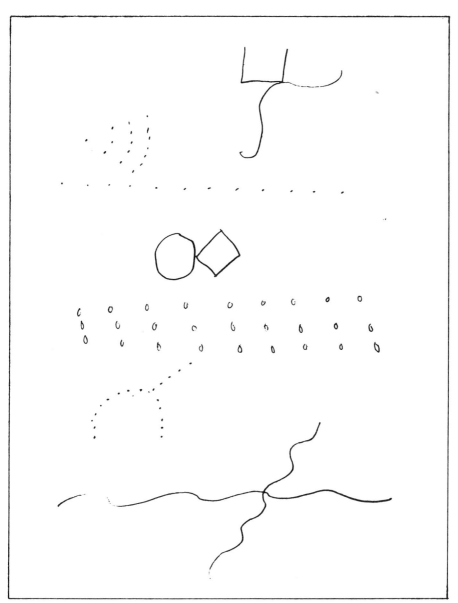

Plate 21.   Case L: Gladys—A Character Problem—Copy Phase (page 1)

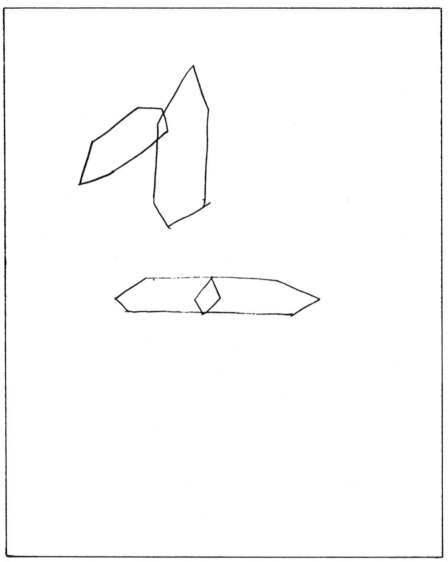

Plate 22.   Case L: Gladys—A Character Problem—Copy Phase (page 2)

hypothesis is that tension is externalized, and as tension becomes pronounced, considerable impulsive acting out can be expected.

The initial progression of the sequence is atypical. After placing figure
A almost in the center of the page, the patient placed figure 1 *above* it,
proceeded downward for figure 2, but then moved from the bottom of the
page toward the top of the page for figures 3 and 4. Only after running

out of space does she regain a more usual sequence by moving downward with figures 5 and 6 and continuing in an orderly fashion with figures 7 and 8 on the second page.

Her initial atypical sequence from figure A to figure 1 suggests oppositional tendencies as well as difficulties with authority figures. The hypothesis advanced is that she reacts to such figures with negativism and resentment. That these feelings are at least preconscious is suggested by her regaining control with figure 2, but the strength of these feelings is again evidenced by her treatment of the next two figures. Conformity is helped by circumstances (the patient "ran out" of space), and with this external aid, she regains control and conforms for the remainder of the copy phase. We infer immaturity and infantile rebellious attitudes at a preconscious level with strong covert dependent needs. Consequently, ambivalence toward strong, authoritarian figures is indicated.

Turning to the individual figures, we note that figure A is placed almost in the center of the page and is reduced in overall size. Closure difficulty is evident in the joining of both parts of the figure as well as in the circle and the square. Both the circle and the square are drawn in an irregular manner with fairly heavy pencil pressure. Compared to the square, the circle is slightly enlarged. Despite anxiety (pencil pressure, reduction in size), the patient reacts in an impulsive, egocentric, and narcissistic manner (placement of figure). An inadequate attempt at identification with the mother is suggested (enlarged circle, irregularity) and fearful and conflicted attitudes toward the father are also indicated (decreased square, irregularity). Oedipal difficulty is likely. Inability to establish enduring relationships with the parents and consequent difficulty in maintaining enduring cathexes with people is an additional finding (closure difficulty).

Figure 1 is reproduced with the correct number of dots. It is mildly rotated in a clockwise direction and is increased in its lateral dimension. Depressive tendencies are suggested, and the increased size indicates difficulty in interpersonal relations, with the additional implication that she feels the need to relate to satisfy covert dependency. (Conversely, decreased lateral size would be related to fearfulness in interpersonal relationships and consequent withdrawal.) The manner in which the dots are executed is interesting. The first four are adequate but they then become dashes (retrogression); this appears to be the result of impulsivity and possible regression under tension. Note that the movement from figure A to figure 1 is upward, as previously described; the underlying conflict with authority apparently produces anxiety and depression as the derivatives of her oppositional tendencies. Her impulsivity and readiness to externalize her own feelings indicates unwillingness to accept responsibility for behavior which, in the extreme, could lead to paranoid-like tendencies.

However, in light of the apparent immaturity of this patient, such paranoid-like behavior is closer to the behavior of the child who, when confronted with an empty cookie jar, rationalizes by blaming his toy bear.

Figure 2 is increased in its lateral dimension. The circles vary to loops and ovals and the number of columns is reduced to none. While the angulation is preserved, the upper line of circles is mildly rotated in a counterclockwise manner and the lower line of dots is mildly rotated in a clockwise direction; thus the Gestalt is gradually and successively increased from left to right in its vertical dimension. Impulsive tendencies are pronounced (treatment of circles, incorrect number of columns). Both oppositional and depressive elements are present (rotation) and difficulty in relating to people is apparent, with confirming evidence that she tends to form dependent relationships which she then is unable to accept (increased lateral size).

Proceeding to figure 3, we note that the dots are impulsively drawn, being transformed into dashes (retrogression). The figure is mildly rotated in a clockwise direction and the figure is reduced in its lateral dimension. Confirmation of this patient's depressive tendencies as well as impulsivity are indicated by the rotation and retrogressions. However, the reduction of the figure's lateral size is inconsistent with the previous figure being increased in this dimension. While this change in lateral size confirms the previous hypothesis of difficulty with interpersonal relationships, tendencies toward withdrawal are now also suggested. Perhaps the symbolically hostile values of figure 3 precipitated the patient's reaction. We would then hypothesize that although she usually aggressively seeks dependent relationships, perceived hostility results in her rapid withdrawal with associated depressive feelings. Analysis of the patient's modifications and associations may provide additional clues.

Closure difficulty is evident in figure 4. The tangential curved portion is displaced under the open square and is also increased in size. The patient's treatment of this portion of the Gestalt is similar to her performance on the circle in figure A and confirms her inadequate feminine identification as well as persistent inability to establish and maintain mature interpersonal relationships. Impulsivity is again indicated by the manner in which the curved portion was drawn, rapidly sweeping from right to left with increasing pencil pressure and ending in an additional loop. Considerable tension is suggested by the very fine tremulousness that appears in the upper right-hand portion of the curve. In examining the open square we also find that while the vertical lines are of approximately equal length, they both slant to the right, and the horizontal line joining them is irregularly drawn. Again, confirmation of the finding on figure A appears: conflicted attitudes toward the father.

Again, in figure 5 we find the circular portion slightly increased in size, with an accompanying reduction in the number of dots in the secant (five instead of seven). Impulsivity and tension are evident in the quality of dots and in the irregularity of the circular portion in its lower left extremity. This gives further support to the hypothesis of this patient's difficulty with feminine identification and her conflicted attitudes toward males.

Figure 6 is markedly increased in size in both its dimensions. The curves are both skewed and reduced in amplitude. Pencil pressure increases as the horizontal line is completed. We infer that expansive, aggressive behavior can be expected under the impact of emotionally laden stimuli. Emotional lability is present and attempts at control to prevent overreaction are only partially successful.

Figure 7 is increased in size, particularly the right hexagon. Closure difficulty is evident in the lower corners of the right hexagon, angulation difficulty also appears, and the point of junction between each element of the figure is displaced to the right. The phallic characteristics of this Gestalt and the patient's adient reaction to them points up her oedipal conflicts and her consequent identification with the father, toward whom her attitudes are markedly conflicted. Emotional lability is further suggested by the angulation changes.

Figure 8 repeats the findings in figure 7; increased size, angulation, and closure difficulties. This lends support to the hypothesis developed above, and the proportionately increased size of the internal diamond further supports the inference of an attempted masculine identification.

Turning our attention to the patient's elaborations (Plate 23) and associations, we note that the drawings are distributed on one page in a methodical sequence. In general, size and use of space are adequate. Furthermore, though the patient does make modifications, each Gestalt is recognizable and she returns all of the original elements to her reproductions. That is, dots remain dots, circles remain circles, and so on. Consequently, she continues the sequence begun on figure 5 in the copy phase discussed above. This suggests that although her initial reaction is characteristically impulsive and labile, she nevertheless has the capacity for control as she becomes more familiar with the demands of the situation. Ego resources are therefore good.

Figure A is modified so that the square encompasses the circle. Her comment is that this ''looks better.'' The patient's treatment of this figure points out her attempt at a masculine identification along with denial of femininity.

Figure 1 is transformed into an angular shape, the number of dots is reduced, and the patient associates a ''hatchet'' to her production. Con-

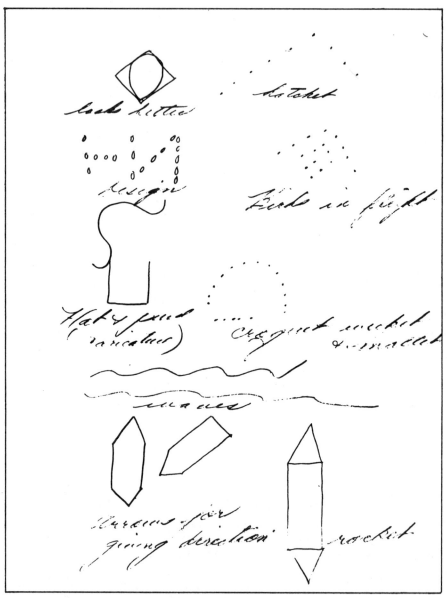

Plate 23. Case L: Gladys—A Character Problem—Elaborations

siderable latent hostility is suggested, as well as emotional lability, by her transformation of a neutral figure into an angular one. Minimal energy is expended in this modification, as was the case in the copy phase, where the patient tended to produce fewer than the required number of elements in all of the Gestalten. We infer that her available energy is limited by repressive defenses as well as depressive tendencies, as suggested above.

Figure 2 offers several leads. It suggests a minimal expenditure of energy, as discussed above, but is also a mirror image of her father's initials, N. H. This provides substantial evidence that her primary identification is with the father and that her attitudes toward him are heavily laden with conflict.

Figure 3 is rotated 90 degrees in a counterclockwise direction and is perceived as a flight of birds. Withdrawal tendencies previously suggested in the analysis of the copy phase of this figure are confirmed. Furthermore, the rotation suggests the oppositional tendencies previously discussed and points up the lability of the patient's potential reactions in her relationships with perceived authority figures.

Moving rapidly through the remaining modifications and associations, confirmation of narcissistic elements is suggested by the ornamental symbolism of a hat and purse (figure 4). The phallic and hostile qualities of the personality are emphasized by the associations to figure 5: "croquet wicket and mallet," a game in which a female symbol (ball) is driven through a series of female sexual symbols (wickets) to make contact (identify?) with a phallic symbol (poles). We might speculate upon the potential oedipal drama of this association in which the patient (ball) conquers the mother (wickets) to possess the father (poles). Further suggestions of phallic and castrating elements in the personality are indicated by the association to figure 8 of "rocket," along with the separation of the pointed ends by horizontal lines. Additional evidence of phallic dependency is also suggested by figure 7, "arrows" for giving directions. With regard to the castrating elements of the patient's personality, note the cut off end of the right "arrow." Finally, figure 6 (association: "waves") suggests orality with its accompanying dependency. This association is also suggestive of possible addictive tendencies.

The test results are, therefore, indicative of a basically narcissistic and egocentric individual who is emotionally labile and can be expected to act out under minimal emotional stress. She is aggressive, and considerable latent hostility is present. She is markedly dependent but is unable to accept this dependency.

The basic conflict appears to be oedipal in nature. The patient has made a paternal identification and at the same time has strongly ambivalent attitudes toward her father. Her identification with the mother is partial and incomplete. Consequently, confusion over her sexual identity is evident and she denies her feminine wishes while attempting to assume a masculine role. Conflict with the father and other perceived strong males results and she reacts with oppositional tendencies and negativism. Overtly she is demanding, infantile, and suspicious, acting out freely and externalizing the basis for her own behavior.

Secondary paranoid reactions are thus likely. She is likely to become anxious easily, react with depression and possible addiction to alcohol and/or drugs, particularly as these would enable her to become more dependent.

Ego functioning, though occasionally uneven, is nevertheless intact. No evidence of psychotic functioning appears in the HABGT record. All Gestalten are adequately perceived and reproduced and no primary psychotic manifestations are present.

The patient's basic modes of adaptation described above appear to be a fundamental and characteristic part of her personality. Her apparent inability to be aware of and modify them suggests that they are ego-syntonic or characterological in nature rather than classically psychoneurotic. The lability, impulsivity, and oedipal nature of her problem further suggest that this is a hysterical character disorder.

Additional Data and Follow-up

As this patient's history is reconstructed, we find that she very early perceived her mother as a weak, ineffectual woman dominated by her husband, and consequently the patient gave her up as a source of identification. On the other hand, she idolized her father, who was perceived as a very intelligent, rigid, moralistic person, and she expressed positive feelings regarding him. He was very affectionate to her when she was a child, but when she was eight years old, her father told her that she was too big to sit on his lap and this made her feel rejected by him. At the same time he also indicated that she was too big to "spank in the regular place" and subsequently punished her by slapping her hands.

After her eighth year, rebellious attitudes toward the father began to develop and she was unable to accept his continual "interference" in her life. Their relationship became so bad that they no longer spoke, but communicated with each other in writing.

She maintained few close interpersonal relationships outside of her home during adolescence and dated very little because of her father's strict demands and interference.

However, away at college, she met a law student and was married, giving up further education to help support him as he continued school. She looked to her marriage as a situation which would bolster her security and unconsciously gratify her dependency wishes. But since her husband was not strong or consistent enough in his own orientation and had marked dependency problems of his own, her conflicts were intensified rather than reduced.

Following the marriage, a series of traumata served to reactivate still further her old conflicts concerning her inadequacy and guilt. She learned to enjoy sexual relations but the birth of her children made her feel trapped, and a congenital heart defect in one of them caused guilt and dependency needs to emerge. Then, separation from her husband due to his military service, her inability to find gratification in an occupation, and her inadequate sublimation in her domestic life reactivated and reinforced old problems. Regression and acting out became means of defending against severe conflicts, and the use of drugs and alcohol offered temporary respite but increased her marital problems.

When initially seen for psychological consultation, the patient appeared clinically to be anxious and mildly depressed. She was consulting several physicians and had obtained copious supplies of amphetamines, barbiturates, and ataraxics. She was also consuming approximately a pint of whiskey each day. Despite heavy medication, she was unable to sleep at night, and though she was taking liberal doses of amphetamine during the day, she was fatigued and unable to do any housework. She insisted on and was able to obtain a full-time maid. Her appearance was poor; she dressed in sweaters and skirts or knit dresses, often wearing the same outfit for days at a time. Little or no makeup was used.

The patient was seen therapeutically for a period of two years. She rapidly formed a positive transference and a highly dependent relationship with the therapist. Her presenting symptoms of anxiety and depression soon remitted, but she externalized and projected the basis of her difficulties upon her husband. She refused to take responsibility for her behavior, acted out impulsively and rationalized her behavior as being the only possible reaction to her impossible situation. Basically unsure of herself and unable to accept the permissive and understanding therapist's interest in her, especially as she became aware of her dependency, she began to test and provoke him, coming 45 minutes late for appointments and then expecting a full session, missing sessions completely, and calling him at 3 or 4 a.m. to dicusss trivial matters which she insisted were emergencies. She made other excessive demands and would react with petulance and negativism when they were not met. When confronted with her inconsistencies, she would respond with anger and bewilderment.

Though she insisted she could not continue in various difficult situations, when she was unable to enlist outside aid she not only functioned but did so in a most adequate manner. As therapy progressed she began to differentiate herself and become aware of and deal more effectively with her reality problems, functioning in a more realistic, independent manner.

Her intake of drugs and alcohol diminished and was finally eliminated. However, before therapy could be completed, circumstances caused her to move out of the area and the therapeutic relationship was terminated.

The characterological nature of this woman's problems is pointed up by the history and therapeutic data. Other psychological test results were supportive of her narcissistic orientation, emotional lability, covert dependency, and overall hysterical orientation indicated by the analysis of the HABGT protocol.

13
Clinical Studies: The Problem of Mental Retardation

The modern approach to mental retardation requires the consideration of physical history, social development and adjustment, and cognitive functioning (Hutt & Gibby, 1976). There are excellent tests for assessment of intellectual functions, but there are few, and hardly adequate ones, for the assessment of social maturity and adjustment. The HABGT can prove to be particularly useful in that it not only provides information about aspects of cognitive functions, as these are evaluated nonverbally on the basis of perceptual–motoric functions, but it simultaneously offers evidence concerning aspects of personality adjustment.

The following case material also demonstrates the possibility of differentiating mental retardation from problems of impaired functioning due to schizophrenic regression or organic brain damage. Such differentiation is highly important in clinical practice since other conditions often masquerade as mental retardation. The crucial question in such cases is: Is the mental impairment due to overall retardation in development or is it a resultant of some regressive process or damage to the organism after "normal" development was present?

Only the copy phase is presented (Plate 24), and only the most pertinent features of the record, in relation to the problem of mental retardation, will be analyzed. The patient is a 25-year-old white female. After failing to complete the second grade, she was placed in special education classes until the school authorities dismissed her as "unable to learn." She has never held a job.

She was fully cooperative during the testing and used her right hand in drawing all the figures. She worked slowly and carefully, taking a longer

251

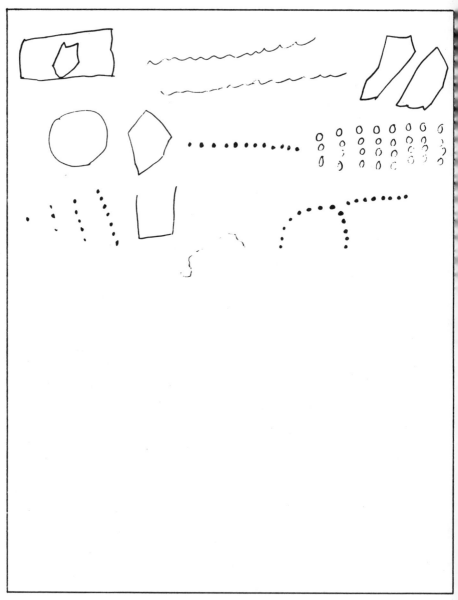

Plate 24.   Case M: Roberta—A Case of Primary Mental Retardation

than average amount of time to complete her drawings. Her comments during the testing were: "I can't do it," "I don't know," and, "It's confusing."

Initial inspection of the record indicates that the patient has arranged her drawings on one sheet of paper in a methodical sequence. (Only two changes in direction occur: between figures 5 and 6, and between 7 and 8.) All the figures are placed in the upper half of the page, and are generally appropriate in size, but overall use of space is constricted. These factors suggest that the patient's ego functions are adequate (sequence and size) but that the general orientation is passive and characterized by withdrawal. Such hostile impulses as may occur are repressed (constricted use of space). Line quality is relatively uniform, with little evidence of incoordination. The lines are drawn firmly with good pressure, suggesting that impulses are usually well controlled.

Figure A is placed in a usual locus. It is drawn as a separate circle and square with considerable space between the two elements of the figure. No effort is apparently made by the patient to bring these elements together. For this reason, closure difficulty is not scored; rather, the drawing manifests fragmentation or simplification, and the question is raised as to whether this has occurred because of inability to execute the figure or because of an inability to perceive the total Gestalt. Such separation is frequently found in young children, mental defectives, schizophrenics, and organics.

In examining figure A in detail, we note that the circle has been drawn by joining two segments in a well-articulated manner. The patient, however, had great difficulty with the obverted square, finally producing it as a five-sided figure. We infer perceptual, coordinational, or maturational difficulty in which an earlier level (circle: 3 year old) is unaffected but a higher level (obverted square: 7 year old) has either not been attained or regression has occurred.

The correct number of dots has been reproduced in figure 1. The dots are heavily filled in, suggesting considerable investment of energy in a relatively simple task. We hypothsize that tension is bound through internalization and compulsive ritual. There is a decrease in the lateral dimension of this figure, and it is mildly rotated in a clockwise direction, suggesting difficulty and withdrawal as an interpersonal technique and possible depressive tendencies.

Figure 2 is also decreased in its lateral dimension and is reproduced with an inadequate number of columns (eight instead of ten), but it is composed of well-articulated circles. The reduction in the number of columns appears to be due to poor planning or anticipatory ability in that the design is ended when it reaches the edge of the paper. The angulation of the columns is changed to the vertical. The first column is correctly composed of a series of three circles but subsequent columns consist of series of four circles, a form of perseveration (b). The patient's adequate reproduction of the circles of this figure suggests capable functioning at a lower maturational level. The angulation difficulty may indicate a defensive reaction to emotional stimuli (decreased acuity of angles) but also suggests maturational or organic involvement. Withdrawal in interpersonal relations is also further supported (decreased lateral dimensions). Rigidity is also indicated by the perseveration type (b).

The patient manifests angulation difficulty in figure 3. The angulated lines of dots are drawn straight, with the angulation approximated by rotating each line of dots in a counterclockwise direction, without, however, rotating the figure itself. Consequently, the patient maintains a semblance of the angulation in this figure, but is unable to angulate each line about its midpoint. The basic Gestalt is lost; however, this can also be considered to be a form of simplification and it suggests difficulty in coping with a relatively complex stimulus as well as maturational and/or organic components. The dots in this figure are heavily worked over, supporting the previous inference that the patient internalizes tension.

Turning to figure 4, we find that the patient has again separated the Gestalt into its two separate elements. The open square is well retained, except that the right vertical is somewhat longer than the left vertical. We hypothesize conflict with authority, suppression of hostility, and a probable passive orientation to authority figures (sequence and organization, overworking of dots). The patient has great difficulty with the curved portion of figure 4. The curve is slightly irregular and flattened and an additional tiny loop appears in the lower left-hand corner. We infer difficulty in rhythmic coordination involving complex curved forms, suggesting a maturational deficit and a tendency to underreact to emotional stimuli. The fragmentation and simplification of figure 4 also support the hypothesis that this is a maturational, organic, or psychotic problem.

Figure 5 is well drawn with the exception of a moderate clockwise rotation of the slanting portion. The dot quality is consistent with that previously described. The hypothesis that this patient deals with tension by internalization and controls impulses adequately is supported. The excellent quality of the curved portion of this Gestalt indicates that the patient can function adequately at the mental age of 3 years, at which level a well-differentiated circle can be drawn (see also figures A and 2). The rotation of the slanted portion of figure 5 may be a manifestation of angulation difficulty similar to that found in figure 3, or an attempt to avoid a collision with figure 2. If the latter is the case, it implies adequate ego functioning, suggested previously by the patient's sequence, and tends to rule out a psychotic process.

Fragmentation and simplification again occur in figure 6. Furthermore, flattening of the curves takes place and they are reproduced as a scribble. This treatment of figure 6 is characteristic of children at the 5-year-old level (Bender, 1938), and adds weight to the inference of mental deficiency. The difficulty with the curves (flattening) also suggests under-reaction to emotional stimuli.

Figure 7 again manifests fragmentation and simplification. Further-more, the patient is unable to reproduce a hexagonal shape. At this point, there is clearly indicated an inability to perform complex perceptual-motoric coordinations, such difficulty probably being of maturational origin.

The hexagonal shape in figure 8 is simplified to an acceptable rec-tangle. The internal diamond is inadequately drawn as an irregular six-sided figure. Difficulty with the diamond shape is consistent with the treatment of the oblique square in figure A. The handling of this Gestalt is typical of the mental retardate (retrogression, simplification, and inability to perceive and complete complex Gestalten).

The distortions apparent in this test record could be the result of one of several clinical syndromes. These entities are: schizophrenia, organic brain damage, primary mental retardation, and mental retardation secon-dary to organic brain damage.

In making a differential diagnosis, it should be noted that we would expect, both in cases of schizophrenia and of organic brain damage, evi-dence in the test record of variable levels of adjustment and maturity. That is to say, in both of these types of disorder, the patient would have reached relatively high levels of maturational development but then, as a result of schizophrenic regressions or organic involvement, would have lost "this maturity" and would make an adjustment at a more primitive level on some but not *all* of the Gestalten. From a theoretical point of view, such retrogression is never complete; it is irregular and evidence of the higher level of adjustment persists in behavior as well as in test data. Turning to the record, we find that the patient quite adequately repro-duces the circular forms at every opportunity. Furthermore, from the adequate open square of figure 4 and the rectangular form produced in figure 8, we infer that the patient is capable of producing the square shape, which indicates functioning at the 5-year-old level. The diamond shape (7-year-old level) failed at every opportunity, as did the hexagonal shape. This patient's "even" functioning is not consistent with either schizo-phrenia or organic brain damage.

The patient's relatively adequate ego functions, manifested in methodical sequence, appropriate size of the Gestalten, and the treatment of figure 5 (in which a possible collision is avoided), also is contraindica-tive of a psychosis.

Organic brain damage can also be ruled out on the additional basis of the patient's fairly good coordination, particularly the regularity of her handling of the dots (see the test protocol of Case C in Chapter 9 for comparison), the even quality of lines, and the overall consistent appearance of the test record.

On the other hand, the patient's adequate functioning at a lower maturational level and total inability to function at higher levels, consistent fragmentations, and simplifications of all figures involving disparate elements are striking evidence of mental retardation. Since we find no evidence of organic brain damage the diagnostic impression is that of primary mental retardation.

The patient's I.Q. can also be estimated from this data. She is capable of maturational behavior at the 5-year-old level (drawing a square) but not at the 7-year-old (drawing a diamond) (Terman & Merrill, 1960). The level of some of her other reproductions, particularly figure 5, suggests a probable mental age of 6. The estimated I.Q. is, therefore, 37.

The patient's inadequately developed maturational level makes inferences derived from many of the test factors highly unreliable. Hypotheses associated with the factors of angulation difficulty and the like must now be evaluated more cautiously. But other factors such as sequence, use of space, size, and line quality are little affected by maturational factors. On the basis of hypotheses developed from these latter factors we can conclude that the patient's ego strength is appropriate for her level of maturation, that she has a generally passive orientation, and that she tends to suppress and internalize tension and inhibits impulses and hostility. She is likely to be compliant and cooperative, with little danger of impulsive acting out. These personality characteristics have considerable implications for educational and/or vocational management.

The patient has always been regarded as being "slow." The mother's pregnancy was uneventful and the birth was an easy one. The medical history is essentially noncontributory and there is no evidence of injury or illness of a nature that might have contributed to her deficiency.

She lives at home and is described by her parents as a well behaved, cooperative, and docile person. She never leaves the house unless she is accompanied by a member of the family.

The patient occupies her time by watching television, doing housework, "sewing," and "reading." She can recognize letters as well as simple, one-syllable words and she spells out words to her mother, who pronounces them for her.

Her clinical appearance was congruent with her parents' description. She was neatly dressed and well groomed. In general, her orientation was passive and she did manifest awareness of her inadequacies, as her comments during the testing indicated, although she also attempted to cover them over by talking about her "reading and studying."

The patient's WAIS summary follows:

Verbal		Performance	
Information	3	Picture arrangement	3
Comprehensive	2	Picture completion	0
Digit span	0	Block design	1
Arithmetic	0	Object assembly	0
Similarities	2	Digit symbol	4

Verbal IQ   53
Performance IQ   46
Full Scale IQ   46

The patient's verbalizations were at an extremely concrete level and she approached tasks that called for reasoning (picture arrangement, block design, object assembly) in a trial-and-error fashion. Her I.Q. scores and the relatively even level of her test performance support the diagnostic impression of primary mental retardation.

References

Aaronson, B. S. The Porteus Mazes and the Bender-Gestalt recall. *Journal of Clinical Psychology*, 1957, **13**, 186–187.

Adams, J., & Canter, A. Performance characteristics of school children on the BIP Bender test. *Journal of Consulting Psychology*, 1969, **33**, 508.

Adams, J., Kenny, T. K., & Canter, A. The efficacy of the Canter Background Interference Procedure in identifying children with cerebral dysfunction. *Journal of Consulting and Clinical Psychology*, 1973, **40**, 486.

Allport, G. W. *Personality: Psychological interpretation*. New York: Holt, Rinehart & Winston, 1937.

Alschuler, R. H., Hattwick, L. B. W. *Painting and personality: A study of young children*. Vols. 1 & 2. Chicago: University of Chicago Press, 1947.

Ames, L. B. Calibration of aging. *Journal of Personality Assessment*, 1974, **38**, 527–529.

Armstrong, R. G. A re-evaluation of copied and recalled Bender-Gestalt reproductions. *Journal of Projective Techniques and Personality Assessment*, 1965, **29**, 134–139.

Armstrong, R. G., & Hauck, P. A. Correlates of Bender-Gestalt scores in children. *Journal of Psychological Studies*, 1960, **11**, 153–158.

Barker, B. J. A note on the development of the Western Reserve Hapto-Kinesthetic Gestalt Test. *Journal of Clinical Psychology*, 1949, **5**, 179–180.

Becker, J. T. & Sabatino, D. A. Reliability of individual tests on perception administered utilizing group techniques. *Journal of Clinical Psychology*, 1971, **27**, 86–88.

Bell, J. E. *Projective techniques: A dynamic approach to the study of personality*. New York: Longmans, Green, 1951.

Bender, L. A. *Visual Motor Gestalt Test and Its Clinical Use*. American Orthopsychiatric Association Research Monograph, No. 3. New York: American Orthopsychiatric Association, 1938.

Bender, L. *Instructions for use of the Visual Motor Gestalt Test*. New York: American Orthopsychiatric Association, 1946.

Bender, L. Psychological principles of the Visual Motor Gestalt Test. *Transactions of the New York Academy of Science*, 1949, **70**, 164–170.

Bender, L. Foreword. *An evaluation of the Bender-Gestalt Test*. In A. Tolor & H. Schulberg (Eds.). Springfield, Ill.: Charles C Thomas, 1963.

Benton, A. Visual motor Gestalt test. In O. K. Buros (Ed.), *The fourth mental measurements yearbook*. Highland Park, N. J.: Gryphon Press, 1953.

Billingslea, F. Y. The Bender-Gestalt: An objective scoring method and validating data. *Journal of Clinical Psychology*, 1948, **4**, 1–27.

Billingslea, F. Y. The Bender-Gestalt: A review and a perspective. *Psychological Bulletin*, 1963, **60**, 233–251.

Bilu, U., & Weiss, A. A. A configurational analysis of the Bender-Gestalt Test. *Israel Annals of Psychiatry and Related Disciplines*, 1974, **12**, 37–52.

Black, F. W. Reversal and rotation errors by normal and retarded readers. *Perceptual and Motor Skills*, 1973, **36**, 895–898.

Blum, R. H., & Nims, J. Two clinical uses of the Bender Visual–Motor Gestalt Test. *United States Armed Forces Medical Journal*, 1953, **4**, 1592–1599.

Brannigan, G. G., & Benowitz, M. L. Bender Gestalt signs and antisocial acting out tendencies in adolescents. *Psychology in the Schools*, 1975, **13**, 15–17.

Bravo, V. L. The conservation, stimulation, and development of superior ability. Paper presented to the California Association of School Psychologists, 1972.

Bravo, L. Psychological tests in the diagnosis of infantile minimal cerebral dysfunction. *Revista Latinoamericana de Pscolgia*, 1973, **5**, 131–141.

Breen, H. The differential diagnostic technique as a measure of hostility. Unpublished doctoral dissertation, University of Western Ontario, 1953.

Brown, F. The Bender Gestalt and acting out. In L. E. Abt (Ed.), *Acting out: Theoretical and clinical aspects*. New York: Grune & Stratton, 1965.

Bruhn, A. R., & Reed, M. R. Simulation of brain damage on the Bender-Gestalt Test by college students. *Journal of Personality Assessment*, 1975, **39**, 244–255.

Butler, O. T., Coursey, R. D., & Gatz, M. Comparison for the Bender Gestalt Test for both black and white brain-damaged patients using two scoring systems. *Journal of Consulting and Clinical Psychology*, 1976, **2**, 280–285.

Byrd, E. The clinical validity of the Bender-Gestalt Test with children. *Journal of Projective Techniques*, 1956, **20**, 127–136.

Canter, A. A background interference procedure to increase sensitivity to the Bender-Gestalt Test to organic disorder. *Journal of Consulting Psychology*, 1966, **30**, 91–97.

Canter, A. BIP Bender test for the detection of organic brain disorder: Modified scoring method and replication. *Journal of Consulting and Clinical Psychology*, 1968, **32**, 522–526.

Carr, A. C. (Ed.) *The prediction of overt behavior through the use of projective techniques*. Springfield, Ill.: Charles C Thomas, 1960.

Chorost, S. B., Spivack, G., & Levine, M. Bender-Gestalt rotations and EEG abnormalities in children. *Journal of Consulting Psychology*, 1959, **23**, 559.

Clawson, A. The Bender Visual Motor Gestalt Test as an index of emotional disturbance in children. *Journal of Projective Techniques*, 1959, **23**, 198–206.

Clements, S. D. *Minimal brain dysfunction in children. NIND Monograph No. 3, United States Department of Health, Education and Welfare, 1966.*

Credidio, S. G. A construct validity study of a measure of perceptual approach–avoidance. Unpublished doctoral dissertation, University of Detroit, 1975.

Crenshaw, D, Bohn, S., Hoffman, M., Matheus, J., & Offenbach, S. The use of projective methods in research. *Journal of Projective Techniques and Personality Assessment*, 1968, **32**, 3–9.

Cronbach, L. J. *Essentials of psychological testing.* New York: Harper & Row, 1960.

Culbertson, F. M., & Gunn, R. C. Comparison of the Bender Gestalt Test and Frostig Test in several clinic groups of children. *Journal of Clinical Psychology*, 1966, **22**, 439.

Davis, D., Cromwell, R. L., & Held, J. M. Size estimation in emotionally disturbed children and schizophrenic adults. *Journal of Abnormal Psychology*, 1967, **5**, 395–401.

Dinmore, D. G. Developmental Bender Gestalt performance as a function of educational setting and sex of young Negro children. Unpublished doctoral dissertation, University of Pennsylvania, 1972.

Donnelly, E. F., & Murphy, D. L. Primary affective disorder: Bender-Gestalt sequence of placement as an indicator of impulse control. *Perceptual and Motor Skills*, 1974, **38**, 1079–1082.

Drever, J. Early learning and the perception of space. *American Journal of Psychology*, 1967, **5**, 395–401.

Elliot, J. A. A validation study of the Koppitz and Pascal and Suttell systems with eleven through fourteen year old children. Unpublished doctoral thesis, University of Michigan, 1968.

Fabian, A. A. Vertical rotation in visual–motor performance: Its relationship to reading reversals. *Journal of Educational Psychology*, 1945, **36**, 129–154.

Fabian, A. A. Clinical and experimental studies of school children who are retarded in reading. *Quarterly Journal of Child Behavior*, 1951, **3**, 129–154.

Fanibanda, D. K. Cultural influence on Hutt's adaptation of Bender-Gestalt: A pilot study. *Journal of Personality Assessment*, 1973, **37**, 531–536.

Fuller, J. B., & Chagnon, G. Factors influencing rotation in the Bender-Gestalt performance of children. *Journal of Projective Techniques*, 1962, **26**, 36–46.

Gardner, R. W., & Long, R. I. Cognitive controls as determinants of learning and remembering. *Psychologia*, 1960, **3**, 165–171.

Garron, D. C., & Cheifetz, D.I. Comment on "Bender-Gestalt discernment of organic pathology." *Psychological Bulletin*, 1965, **63**, 197–200.

Gavales, D., & Millon, T. Comparison of reproduction and recall size deviations in the Bender–Gestalt as a measure of anxiety. *Journal of Clinical Psychology*, 1960, **16**, 278–300.

Gesell, A., Ilg, F. L., & Bullis, G. *Vision: Its development in the child.* New York: Harper, 1949.

Gillmore, G., Chandy, J., & Anderson, T. The Bender-Gestalt and the Mexican–American student: A report. *Psychology in the Schools*, 1975, **12**, 172–175.

Gobetz, W. A quantification, standardization, and validation of the Bender-Gestalt test on normal and neurotic adults. *Psychological Monographs*, 1953, **67** (6, Whole No. 356).

Goldberg, L. R. The effectiveness of clinicians' judgments: The diagnosis of organic brain damage from the Bender-Gestalt Test. *Journal of Consulting Psychology*, 1959, **23**, 25–33.

Goodstein, L. D., Spielberger, C. D., Williams, J. E., & Dahlstrom, W. G. The effects of serial position and design difficulty on recall of the Bender-Gestalt designs. *Journal of Consulting Psychology*, 1959, **23**, 25–33.

Greene, R., & Clark, F. K. Predicting reading readiness with the Bender-Gestalt Test in minority students. Unpublished findings, 1973.

Griffith, R. M., & Taylor, V. H. Incidence of Bender-Gestalt figure rotations. *Journal of Consulting Psychology*, 1960, **24**, 189–190.

Griffith, R. M., & Taylor, V. H. Bender-Gestalt figure rotations: A stimulus factor. *Journal of Consulting Psychology*, 1961, **25**, 89–90.

Grinker, R. R., & Spiegel, J. P. *Men under stress*. Philadelphia: Blakiston, 1945.

Guertin, W. H. A factor analysis of the Bender-Gestalt Test of patients. *Journal of Clinical Psychology*, 1952, **8**, 362–367.

Guertin, W. H. A factor analysis of curvilinear distortions on the Bender-Gestalt. *Journal of Clinical Psychology*, 1954, **10**, 12–17. (a)

Guertin, W. H. A transposed factor analysis of schizophrenic performance on the Bender-Gestalt. *Journal of Clinical Psychology*, 1954, **10**, 225–228. (b)

Guertin, W. H. A transposed analysis of the Bender-Gestalts of brain disease cases. *Journal of Clinical Psychology*, 1954, **10**, 366–369. (c)

Guertin, W. H. A transposed analysis of the Bender-Gestalts of paranoid schizophrenics. *Journal of Clinical Psychology*, 1955, **11**, 73–76.

Guilford, J. P. *Personality*. New York: McGraw Hill, 1959.

Hain, J. D. The Bender Gestalt Test: A scoring method for identifying brain damage. *Journal of Consulting Psychology*, 1964, **28**, 34–40.

Halpern, F. The Bender Visual Motor Gestalt Test. In H. H. Anderson & G. L. Anderson (Eds.), *An introduction to projective techniques*. New York: Prentice Hall, 1951.

Hammer, E. F. An experimental study of symbolism on the Bender-Gestalt. *Journal of Projective Techniques*, 1955, **18**, 335–345.

Handler, L., & McIntosh, J. Predicting aggression and withdrawal in children with the Draw-a-Person and Bender Gestalt. *Journal of Personality Assessment*, 1971, **35**, 331–337.

Hannah, L. D. Causative factors in the production of rotations on the Bender-Gestalt designs. *Journal of Consulting Psychology*, 1958, **22**, 398–399.

Hanvik, L. J., & Andersen, A. L. The effect of focal brain lesions on recall and on the production of rotations in the Bender-Gestalt Test. *Journal of Consulting Psychology*, 1950, **14**, 197–198.

Harris, J. G. Size estimation of pictures of thematic content for schizophrenic and normal subjects. *Journal of Personality*, 1957, **257**, 651–657.

Haworth, M. R. *The primary visual motor test*. New York: Grune & Stratton, 1970.

Hebb, D. O. *The Organization of behavior*. New York: Wiley, 1949.

Helson, H. Perception and personality—A critique of recent experimental literature. USAF School of Aviation Medicine, Project 21, July 1953.

Hoch, P., & Rachlin, H. L. An evaluation of manic–depressive psychosis in the light of follow-up studies. *American Journal of Psychiatry*, 1941, **97**, 831–843.

Horine, L. C., & Fulkerson, S. C. Utility of the Canter Background Interference

Procedure for differentiating among the schizophrenias. *Journal of Personality Assessment*, 1973, **37**, 48–52.

Hunt, J. McV. *Intelligence and experience*. New York: Macmillan, 1961.

Hutt, M. L. *A tentative guide for the administration and interpretation of the Bender-Gestalt Test*. U.S. Army, Adjutant General's School (Restricted), 1945. (a)

Hutt, M. L. The use of projective methods of personality measurement in army medical installations. *Journal of Clinical Psychology,* 1945, **1**, 134–140. (b)

Hutt, M. L. The Bender Gestalt Test: The case of Gregor. Interpretation of test data. *Rorschach Research Exchange and Journal of Projective Techniques*, 1949, **13**, 443–446

Hutt, M. L. The Bender Gestalt drawings. In E. S. Shneidman, W. Joel, & K. B. Little (Eds.), *Thematic test analysis*. New York: Grune & Stratton, 1951.

Hutt, M. L. Revised Bender Visual-Motor Gestalt Test. In A. Weider (Ed.), *Contributions toward medical psychology*. Vol. II. New York: Ronald Press, 1953.

Hutt, M. L. The Revised Bender Gestalt Test. In A. C. Carr (Ed.), *The prediction of overt behavior through the use of projective techniques*. Springfield, Ill.: Charles C Thomas, 1960.

Hutt, M. L. The Bender-Gestalt Test. In D. Rosenthal (Ed.), *The Genain quadruplets: A study of heredity and enivronment in schizophrenia*. New York: Basic Books, 1963.

Hutt, M. L. The projective use of the Bender-Gestalt Test. In A. I. Rabin (Ed.), *Projective techniques in personality assessment*. New York: Springer, 1968.

Hutt, M. L. *The Hutt Adaptation of the Bender-Gestalt Test*. (2nd ed.) New York: Grune & Stratton, 1969. (a)

Hutt, M. L. The potentiality of a measure of perceptual adience–abience in predicting inner psychological adaptability. Paper presented at American Psychological Association, Annual Meeting, Washington, D. C., September, 1969. (b)

Hutt, M. L. The significance of perceptual adience–abience in child development. In D. V. S. Sankar (Ed.), *Mental health in children*. Vol. II. Westbury, N. Y.: PJD Publications, 1976. (a)

Hutt, M. L. Perceptual adience–abience and cognitive functioning. Paper presented at the Gatlinburg Conference on Research in Mental Retardation, Gatlinburg, Tenn., March 1976. (b)

Hutt, M. L., & Briskin, G. J. *The Hutt Adaptation of the Bender-Gestalt Test*. New York: Grune & Stratton, 1960.

Hutt, M. L., & Feuerefile, D. The clinical meanings and predictions of a measure of perceptual adience–abience. Paper presented at American Psychological Association, Annual Meeting. Philadelphia, 1963.

Hutt, M. L., & Gibby, R. G. *Patterns of abnormal behavior*. Boston: Allyn & Bacon, 1957.

Hutt, M. L., & Gibby, R. G. *An atlas for the Hutt Adaptation of the Bender-Gestalt Test*. New York: Grune & Stratton, 1970.

Hutt, M. L., & Gibby, R. G. *The mentally retarded child: Development, education, and treatment*, 3rd ed. Boston: Allyn & Bacon, 1976.

Hutt, M. L., Isaacson, R. L. & Blum, M. L. *Psychology: The science of interpersonal behavior.* New York: Harper & Row, 1966.

Hutt, M. L., & Miller, L. J. Further studies of a measure of adience–abience. *Jouranl of Personality Assessment,* 1975, **39,** 123–128.

Hutt, M. L., & Miller, L. J. Interrelationships of psychopathology and adience–abience. *Jouranl of Personality Assessment,* 1976, **40,** 135–139.

Hutt, M. L., & Shor, J. Rationale for routine Rorschach "testing-the-limits." *Rorschach Research Exchange,* 1946, **10,** 70–76.

Johnson, J. H. Bender-Gestalt constriction as an indicator of depression in psychiatric patients. *Journal of Personality Assessment,* 1973, **37,** 53–55.

Jung, C. G. *The integration of the personality.* New York: Holt, Rinehart & Winston, 1939.

Kachorek, J. Relationships between measures of adience–abience and field independence–dependence. Unpublished master's thesis, University of Detroit, 1969.

Kai, T. An examination of the Koppitz Bender Gestalt Test (II); The correlation between each item of emotional indicators (EI) and the emotional problems in younger children. *Memoirs of the Faculty of Education, Kumamoto University,* **20,** section 2, 1972.

Keller, J. E. The use of the Bender-Gestalt maturation level scoring system with mentally handicapped children. *American Journal of Orthopsychiatry,* 1955, **25,** 563–573.

Keogh, B. K., & Smith, C. E. Group techniques and proposed scoring system for the Bender-Gestalt Test with children. *Journal of Clinical Psychology,* 1961, **17,** 172–175.

Kitay, J. I. The Bender-Gestalt as a projective technique. *Journal of Clinical Psychology,* 1950, **6,** 170–174.

Klopfer, B., *The Rorschach technique.* Yonkers, N. Y.: World Book, 1942.

Klopfer, B., Ainsworth, M. D., Klopfer, W. G., & Holt, R. R. *Developments in the Rorschach technique.* Yonkers, N. Y.: World Book, 1954.

Klopfer, B., & Kelley, D. Mc G. *The Rorschach Technique.* New York: World Book, 1942.

Koffka, K. *The growth of the mind.* New York: Harcourt, Brace, 1931.

Koppitz, E. M. The Bender-Gestalt Test and learning difficulties in young children. *Journal of Clinical Psychology,* 1958, **14,** 292–295.

Koppitz, E. M. The Bender-Gestalt Test for children: A normative study. *Journal of Clinical Psychology,* 1960, **16,** 432–435.

Koppitz, E. M. *The Bender Gestalt Test for young children.* New York: Grune & Stratton, 1963.

Koppitz, E. M. Use of the Bender Gestalt Test in elementary school. *Skolepskyologi,* 1965, **2,** 193–200.

Koppitz, E. M. *The Bender Gestalt Test for young children.* Vol. II. *Research and application, 1963–1973.* New York: Grune & Stratton, 1975. (a)

Koppitz, E. M. The Bender Gestalt Test and Visual Aural Digit Span Test and reading achievement. *Journal of Learning Disabilities,* 1975, **8,** 154–157. (b)

Korchin, S. J., & Basowitz, H. The tachistoscopic Bender-Gestalt Test. *American Psychologist,* 1954, **9,** 408, (Abstract).

Korim, H. Comparison of psychometric measures in psychiatric patients using heroin and other drugs. *Journal of Abnormal Psychology,* 1974, **83,** 208–213.

Kramer, E., & Fenwick, J. Differential diagnosis with the Bender Gestalt Test. *Journal of Projective Techniques and Personality Assessment,* 1966, **30,** 59–61.

Krop, H. D., & Smith, C. R. Effect of special education on the Bender-Gestalt performance of the mentally retarded. *American Journal of Mental Deficiency,* 1969, **73,** 693–699.

Lachman, F. M. Perceptual–motor development in children retarded in reading ability. *Journal of Consulting Psychology,* 1960, **24,** 427–431.

Landis, B., Baxter, J., Patterson, R. H., & Tauber, C. Bender-Gestalt evaluation of brain dysfunction following open heart surgery. *Journal of Personality Assessment,* 1974, **38,** 556–562.

Landmark, M., & Grinde, T. *Children's Bender drawings from 1938 to 1962.* Copenhagen, Denmark: Nord Psykology, 1964 (Monograph).

Lerner, E. A. *The projective use of the Bender Gestalt.* Springfield, Ill.: Charles C Thomas, 1972.

Lieberman, L. P. Drawing norms for the Bender-Gestalt figures. *Journal of Clinical Psychology,* 1968, **24,** 458–463.

Lindsay, J. The Bender-Gestalt Test and psychoneurotics. *Journal of Mental Science,* 1954, **100,** 980–982.

Lubin, B., Wallis, R. R., & Paine, C. Patterns of psychological test usage in the United States: 1935–1969. *Professional Psychology,* 1971, **2,** 70–74.

Lyle, O., & Quast, W. The Bender Gestalt: Use of clinical judgment versus recall scores in prediction of Huntington's disease. *Journal of Consulting and Clinical Psychology,* 1976, **2,** 229–232.

Mark, J. C., & Morrow, R. S. The use of the Bender-Gestalt Test in the study of brain damage. *American Psychologist,* 1955, **10,** 323.

Marsh, G. G. Impaired visual–motor ability of children with Duchanne muscular dystrophy. *Perceptual and Motor Skills,* 1972, **35,** 504–506.

McConnell, O. L. Koppitz' Bender-Gestalt scores in relation to organic and emotional problems in children. *Journal of Clinical Psychology,* 1867, **23,** 370–374.

McConville, M. G. Perceptual adience–abience and social field-dependence: An attempt at construct validation. Unpublished master's thesis, University of Windsor, 1970.

McPherson, M. W. & Pepin, L. A. Consitency of reproductions of Bender-Gestalt designs. *Journal of Clinical Psychology,* 1955, **11,** 163–166.

Meyer, R. Altruism among male juvenile delinquents related to offense committed and parents' cultural status. Unpublished doctoral sissertation, University of Detroit, 1973.

Miller, L. J. & Hutt, M. L. Psychopathology Scale of the Hutt Adaptation of the Bender-Gestalt Test: Reliability. *Journal of Personality Assessment,* 1975, **2,** 129–131.

Mills, H. D. The research use of projective techniques: A seventeen year survey. *Journal of Personality Techniques and Personality Assessment,* 1965, **29,** 513–515.

Mira, E. Myokinetic psychodiagnosis: A new technique in exploring the conative trends of personality. *Proceedings of the Royal Society of Medicine*, 1939–1940.

Mira, E. *Psychiatry in war*. New York: Norton, 1943.

Mlodnosky, L. B. The Bender Gestalt and the Frostig as predictors of first-grade reading achievement among economically deprived children. *Psychology in the Schools*, 1972, **9**, 25–30.

Money, J., & Newcombe, P. Ability test and cultural heritage: The Draw-a-Person and Bender Tests in aboriginal Australia. *Journal of Learning Disabilities*, 1974, **7**, 197–303.

Mosher, D. L., & Smith, J. P. The usefulness of two scoring systems for the Bender Gestalt Test for identifying brain damage. *Journal of Consulting Psychology*, 1965, **29**, 530–536.

Naches, A. M. The Bender Gestalt Test and acting out behavior in children. Unpublished doctoral dissertation, Colorado State College, 1967.

Newcomer, P., & Hammill, D. Visual perception of motor impaired children: Implications for assessment. *Exceptional Children*, 1973, **39**, 335–337.

Niebuhr, H. Jr., & Cohen, D. The effect of psychopathology on visual discrimination. *Journal of Abnormal and Social Psychology*, 1956, **53**, 173–176.

North, S. The diagnostic efficiency of a drawing technique. Unpublished doctoral dissertation, University of Western Ontario, 1953.

Olin, T. D., & Reznikoff, M. Quantification of the Bender-Gestalt recall: A pilot study. *Journal of Projective Techniques*, 1957, **21**, 265–277.

Olin, T. D., & Reznikoff, M. A comparison of copied and recalled reproductions of the Bender-Gestalt designs. *Journal of Projective Techniques*, 1958, **22**, 320–327.

Pardue, A. M. Bender-Gestalt Test and background interference procedure in discernment of organic brain damage. *Perceptual and Motor Skills*, 1975, **40**, 103–109.

Parker, J. W. Tactual-kinesthetic perception as a technique for diagnosing brain damage. *Journal of Consulting Psychology*, 1954, **30**, 91–97.

Pascal, G. R. Quantification of the Bender-Gestalt: A preliminary report. *American Journal of Orthopsychiatry*, 1950, **20**, 418–423.

Pascal. G. R., & Suttell, B. J. *The Bender-Gestalt Test: Its quantification and validity for adults*. New York: Grune & Stratton, 1951.

Peek, R. M. Directionality of lines in the Bender-Gestalt Test. *Journal of Consulting Psychology*, 1953, **17**, 213–216.

Peek, R. M., & Olson, G. W. The Bender-Gestalt recall as an index of intellectual functioning. *Journal of Clinical Psychology*, 1955, **11**, 185–188.

Peek, R. M., & Quast, W. *A scoring system for the Bender-Gestalt Test*. Hastings, Minn.: Roland M. Peek, 1951.

Petrie, A. *Individuality in pain and suffering*. Chicago: University of Chicago Press, 1967.

Piaget, J. *The psychology of intelligence*. London: Routledge, Kegan Paul, 1950.

Postman, L. On the problem of perceptual defense. *Psychological Review*, 1953, **6**, 198–206.

Rapaport, D. *Organization and pathology of though*. New York: Columbia University Press, 1951.

Research Report No. 43. *Identification and vocational training of the in-*

stitutionalized deaf-retarded patient. The diagnostic study. Lansing, Mich.: Department of Mental Health, 1964.

Reznikoff, M., & Olin, T. D. Recall of the Bender-Gestalt designs by organic and schizophrenic patients: A comparative study. *Journal of Clinical Psychology,* 1957, **13**, 183–186.

Rock, I. The perception of disoriented figures. *Scientific American,* 1974, **230**, 78–85.

Rogers, D. L., & Swenson, W. M. Bender-Gestalt recall as a measure of memory versus distractibility. *Perceptual and Motor Skills,* 1975, **40**, 919–922.

Ross, N., & Schilder, P. Tachistoscopic experiments on the perception of the human figure. *Journal of Genetic Psychology,* 1934, **10**, 152.

Ruckhaber, C. J., A technique for group administration of the Bender Gestalt Test. *Psychology in the Schools,* 1964, **1**, 53–56.

Sabatino, D. A., & Ysseldyke, J. E. Effect of extraneous "background" on visual–perceptual performance of readers and non-readers. *Perceptual and Motor Skills,* 1972, **35**, 323–328.

Schachtel, E. G. *Metamorphosis: On the development of affect, perception, attention, and memory.* New York: Basic Books, 1959.

Schilder, P. Preface, In L. Bender, *A visual motor Gestalt test and its clinical use.* American Orthopsychiatry Association Research Monograph, Number 3. New York: American Orthopsychiatric Association, 1938.

Schneirla, T. C. An evolutionary and developmental theory of biphasic processes underlying approach and withdrawal. In M. R. Jones (Ed.), *Nebraska symposium on motivation, 1959.* Lincoln, Nebraska: Univseristy of Nebraska Press, 1959.

Schulberg, H. C., & Tolor, A. The use of the Bender-Gestalt Test in clinical practice. *Journal of Projective Techniques,* 1961, **25**, 347–351.

Schwartz, M. L., & Dennerll, R. D. Immediate visual memory as a function of epileptic seizures. *Cortex,* 1969, **5**, 69–74.

Segall, M. H., Campbell, D. T., & Herskovitz, M. J. *The influence of culture on visual perception.* Indianapolis: Bobbs Merrill, 1966.

Sěpic, J. *Detection of simulators with Bender-Gestalt Test.* Psiholŏske razprave: IV Kongres psihologov Serj. Ljubljana, Yugoslavia: University of Ljubljana Press, 1972, 502.

Shapiro, D. *Neurotic styles.* New York: Basic Books, 1965.

Shapiro, M. B., Post, F., Löfving, B., & Inglis, J. Memory function in psychiatric patients over sixty: Some methodological and diagnostic implications. *Journal of Mental Science,* 1965, **102**, 233–246.

Shneidman, E. S., Joel, W. & Little, K. B. (Eds.) *Thematic test analysis.* New York: Grune & Stratton, 1951.

Smith, D. C., & Martin R. A. Use of learning cues with the Bender Visual Motor Gestalt Test in screening children for neurological impairment. *Journal of Consulting Psychology,* 1967, **31**, 205–209.

Snortum, J. R. Performance of different diagnostic groups on the tachistoscopic and copy phases of the Bender-Gestalt. *Journal of Consulting Psychology,* 1965, **4**, 345–351.

Solley, C. M., & Murphy, G. *Development of the perceptual world.* New York: Basic Books, 1960.

Song, A. Y., & Song, R. H. The Bender-Gestalt Test with Background Interference Procedure on mental retardates. *Journal of Clinical Psychology,* 1969, **25,** 69–71.

Sonoda, T. The Bender Gestalt Test for young children: A review of verification studies made on the Koppitz scoring system. *Kumamoto Shodai Ronshu,* 1968, **27,** 1–24.

Sonoda, T. A study of the development of visual–motor perception. *Kumamoto Shodai Ronshu,* 1973, **37,** 1–9.

Sternberg, D., & Levine, A. An indicator of suicidal ideation on the Bender Visual Motor Gestalt Test. *Journal of Projective Techniques and Personality Assessment,* 1965, **29,** 377–379.

Stewart, H. F., Jr. A note on recall patterns using the Bender-Gestalt with psychotic and non-psychotic patients. *Journal of Clinical Psychology,* 1957, **13,** 95–97.

Stewart, H. F., Jr., & Cunningham, S. A note on scoring recalled figures of the Bender-Gestalt Test using psychotics, non-psychotics, and controls. *Journal of Clinical Psychology,* 1958, **14,** 207–208.

Stoer, L., Corotto, L. V., & Curnutt, R. H. The role of visual perception in reproduction of Bender-Gestalt designs. *Journal of Projective Techniques and Personality Assessment,* 1965, **29,** 473–478.

Story, R. I. The revised Bender-Gestalt test and male alcoholics. *Journal of Projective Techniques,* 1960, **24,** 186–193.

Suczek, R. F., & Klopfer, W. G. Interpretation of the Bender-Gestalt Test: The associative value of the figures. *American Journal of Orthopsychiatry,* 1952, **22,** 62–75.

Sullivan, H. S. *The interpersonal theory of psychiatry.* New York: Norton, 1953.

Sullivan, J. J., & Welsh, G. S. Results with the Bender Visual Motor Test. In E. L. Phillips et al. (Eds.), *Intelligence and personality factors associated with poliomyelitis among school age children.* Monographs of the Society for Research in Child Development, 1947, **12,** No. 2.

Sundberg, N. D. The practice of psychological testing in clinical services in the United States. *American Psychologist,* 1961, **16,** 79–83.

Suttell, B. J. & Pascal, G. R. "Regression" in schizophrenia as determined by performance on the Bender-Gestalt Test. *Journal of Abnormal and Social Psychology,* 1952, **47,** 653–657.

Taylor, H. D., & Thweatt, R. C. Cross-cultural developmental performance of Navajo children on the Bender-Gestalt Test. *Perceptual and Motor Skills,* 1972, **35,** 307–309.

Taylor, J. R., & Schenke, L. W. The Bender-Gestalt Test as a measure of aggression in children. *Proceedings of the Iowa Academy of Sciences,* 1955, **62,** 426–432.

Terman, L. M. & Merrill, M. A. *The Stanford-Binet Intelligence Scale: Manual for the third revision.* Boston: Haughton Mifflin, 1960.

Tiedman, R. A comparison of seven-year-olds around the world. Lecture, San Jose State College, June 1971.

Tolor, A. A comparison of the Bender-Gestalt Test and the digit-symbol span as a measure of recall. *Journal of Consulting Psychology,* 1956, **20,** 305–309.

Tolor, A. Further studies on the Bender-Gestalt Test and the digit-span test as a measure of recall. *Journal of Clinical Psychology,* 1958, **14,** 14–18.

Tolor, A. The "meaning" of the Bender-Gestalt Test designs: A study in the use of the semantic differential. *Journal of Projective Techniques,* 1960, **24,** 433–438.

Tolor, A. The graphomotor techniques. *Journal of Projective Techniques and Personality Assessment,* 1968, **32,** 222–228.

Tolor, A., & Schulberg, H. *An evaluation of the Bender-Gestalt Test.* Springfield, Ill.: Charles C Thomas, 1963.

VandenBos, G. An investigation of several methods of teaching experiential focusing. Unpublished doctoral dissertation, University of Detroit, 1973.

Verms, S. K. Some perceptuo-motor disturbances on the Bender Gestalt test as effected by changes in orientation of the paper. *Journal of Clinical Psychology,* 1974, **1,** 61–63.

VonBékésy, G. *Sensory inhibition.* Princeton N. J.: Princeton University Press, 1967.

Weiss, A. A. Incidence of rotation of Bender-Gestalt figures in three age groups of normal Israeli school children. *Perceptual and Motor Skills,* 1971, **32,** 691–694.

Werner, H. *Comparative psychology of development.* New York: International Universities Press, 1957.

Wertheimer, M. Studies in the theory of Gestalt psychology. *Psychologische Forschung* 1923, **4,** 301–350.

Wiener, G. The Bender Gestalt Test as a predictor of minimal neurological deficit in children eight to ten years of age. *Journal of Nervous and Mental Diseases,* 1966, **43,** 175–180.

Witkin, H. A., Dyk, R. B., Faterson, H. F., Goodenough, D. R., & Karp, S. A. *Psychological differentiation.* Princeton, N. J.: Princeton University Press, 1967.

Wolff, W. *The expression of personality: Experimental depth psychology.* New York: Harper & Row, 1943.

Wurst, E. Factors in visual perception. *Zeitschrift für Experimentelle und Angewandte Psychologie,* 1974, **21,** 491–498.

Author Index

Aaronson B. S., 79, 258
Adams, J., 41, 82, 258
Ainsworth, M. D., 125, 263
Allport, G. W., 107, 258
Alschuler, R. H., 29, 258
Ames, L. B., 116, 258
Andersen, A. L., 78, 261
Anderson, T., 112, 260
Armstrong, R. G., 35, 40, 79, 258

Barker, B. J., 82, 258
Basowitz, H., 77, 263
Baxter, J., 41, 264
Becker, J. T., 81, 258
Bell, J. E., 23, 258
Bender, L., 7, 19, 22, 23, 49, 258, 259, 266
Bennowitz, M. L., 27, 103, 108, 259
Benton, A. L., 23, 36, 259
Billingslea, F. Y., 19, 22, 34, 128, 259
Bilu, Y., 144, 259
Black, F. W., 112, 259
Blum, M. L., 46, 263
Blum, R. H., 81, 259
Bohn, S., 22, 260
Brannigan, G. G., 27, 103, 108, 259
Bravo, V. L., 41, 113, 259
Breen, H., 103, 259
Briskin, G. J., 22, 34, 63, 75, 95, 111, 126, 150, 158, 262
Brown, F., 116, 127, 259
Bruhn, A. R., 144, 259

Bullis, G., 10, 260
Butler, O. T., 84, 259
Byrd, E., 24, 25, 88, 90, 92, 95, 97, 100, 105, 107, 109, 113, 119, 121, 123, 259

Campbell, D. T., 84, 266
Canter, A. A., 41, 82, 258, 259
Carr, A. C., 46, 54, 259
Chagnon, G., 111, 260
Chandy, J., 84, 260
Cheifetz, D. I., 39, 260
Chorost, S. B., 112, 259
Clark, F. K., 84, 261
Clawson, A., 25–26, 50, 88, 92, 96, 97, 101, 102, 103, 105, 106, 107, 109, 113, 116, 125, 126, 128, 259
Clements, S. D., 196, 260
Cohen, D., 38, 82, 265
Corotto, L. V., 33, 38, 267
Coursey, R. D., 259
Credidio, S. G., 169, 260
Crenshaw, D., 22, 260
Cromwell, R. L., 92, 99, 260
Cronbach, L. J., 23, 260
Culbertson, F. M., 92, 260
Cunningham, S., 79, 267
Curnutt, R. H., 38, 267

Dahlstrom, W. G., 79, 261
Davis, D., 92, 99, 260
Dennerll, R. D., 80, 266
Dinmore, D. G., 81, 260

269

Donnelly, E. F., 88, 145, 260
Drever, J., 10, 260
Dyk, R. B., 158, 268

Elliot, J. A., 27, 101, 260

Fabian, A. A., 37, 260
Fanibanda, D. K., 128, 260
Faterson, H. F., 158, 268
Fenwick, J., 40, 264
Feuerfile, D., 31, 158, 165, 262
Fulkerson, S. C., 41, 261
Fuller, J. B., 111, 260

Gardner, R. W., 158, 260
Garron, D. C., 39, 260
Gatz, M., 259
Gavales, D., 79, 101, 260
Gesell, A., 10, 260
Gibby, R. G., 14, 44, 45, 100, 174, 262
Gillmore, G., 84, 260
Gobetz, W. A., 23, 33–34, 49, 260
Goldberg, L. R., 143, 261
Goodenough, D. R., 158, 268
Goodstein, L. D., 79, 261
Greene, R., 84, 261
Griffith, R. M., 65, 74, 98, 111, 261
Grinde, T., 19, 264
Grinker, R. H., 44, 261
Guertin, W. H., 35, 105, 116, 118, 128, 261
Guilford, J. P., 158, 261
Gunn, R. C., 92, 260

Hain, J. D., 36, 37, 40, 96, 105, 109, 112, 118, 119, 121, 122, 127, 261
Halpern, F., 23, 261
Hammer, E. F., 24, 261
Hammill, D., 39, 265
Handler, L., 127, 261
Hannah, L. D., 65, 74, 98, 261
Hanvik, L. J., 78, 112, 261
Harris, J. G., 92, 261
Hattwick, L. B. W., 29, 258
Hauck, P. A., 35, 258
Haworth, 24, 261
Hebb, D. O., 10, 261

Held, J. M., 92, 99, 260
Helson, H., 10, 261
Herskovitz, M. J., 84, 266
Hoch, P., 44, 261
Hoffman, M., 22, 260
Holt, R. R., 125, 263
Horine, L. C., 41, 261
Hunt, J. McV., 14, 262
Hutt, M. L., 7, 14, 21, 22, 23, 31, 34, 44, 45, 46, 47, 51, 63, 75, 80, 95, 100, 111, 115, 126, 128, 143, 150, 156, 158, 159, 164, 165, 169, 170, 171, 174, 262, 264

Ilg, F. L., 10, 260
Inglis, J., 78, 266
Irion, A. L., 22
Isaacson, R. L., 46, 263

Johnson, J. H., 145, 263
Joel, W., 211, 217
Jung, C. G., 158, 263

Kachorek, J., 170, 263
Kai, T., 27, 101, 108, 116, 263
Karp, S. A., 158, 268
Keller, J. E., 34, 263
Kelley, D. McG., 71, 263
Kenny, T. K., 41, 258
Keogh, B. K., 34, 81, 263
Kitay, J. I., 22, 128, 263
Klopfer, B., 71, 125, 263
Klopfer, W. G., 24, 71, 74, 80, 263, 267
Koffka, K., 10, 263
Koppitz, E. M., 19, 24, 31, 34, 35, 121, 124, 128, 175, 263
Korchin, S. J., 77, 263
Korim, H., 112, 123, 263
Kramer, E., 19, 264
Krop, H. D., 264

Lachman, F. M., 37, 264
Landis, B., 41, 264
Landmark, M., 19, 264
Lerner, E. A., 32, 264
Levine, A., 103, 267
Levine, M., 112, 259
Lieberman, L. P., 125, 264

Lindsay, J., 77, 264
Little, K. B., 211, 217, 266
Löfving, B., 78, 266
Long, R. I., 158, 260
Lubin, B., 19, 22, 264
Lyle, C., 144, 264

Mark, J. C., 112, 264
Marsh, G. G., 264
Martin, R. A., 71, 114, 266
Maltheus, J., 22, 260
McConnell, O. L., 40, 264
McConville, M. G., 170, 264
McIntosh, J., 127, 261
McPherson, M. W., 38, 82, 264
Merrill, M. A., 256, 267
Meyer, R., 170, 264
Miller, L. J., 143, 156, 164, 170, 263, 264
Millon, T., 101, 264
Mills, H. D., 22, 264
Mira, E., 21, 50, 51, 103, 125, 264, 265
Mlodnosky, L. B., 92, 265
Money, J., 128, 265
Morrow, R. S., 112, 264
Mosher, D. L., 36, 40, 88, 96, 109, 119, 122, 126, 265
Murphy, D. L., 88, 145, 260
Murphy, G., 9, 10, 266

Naches, A. M., 27, 101, 265
Newcombe, P., 128, 265
Newcomer, P., 39, 265
Niebuhr, H., Jr., 38, 82, 265
Nims, J., 81, 259
North, S., 103, 265

Offenbach, S., 22, 260
Olin, T. D., 78, 79, 265, 266
Olson, G. W., 79, 265

Paine, C., 19
Pardue, A. M., 37, 41, 82, 264, 265
Parker, J. W., 82, 265
Pascal, G., 22, 33, 34, 49, 77, 79, 81, 83, 115, 118, 121, 122, 124, 127, 128, 265, 267
Patterson, R. H., 41, 264

Peek, R. M., 23, 29–30, 79, 101, 109, 118, 125, 126, 265
Pepin, L. A., 38, 82, 264
Petrie, A., 158, 265
Piaget, J., 92, 99, 265
Post, F., 79, 266
Postman, L. 158, 265

Quast, W., 23, 101, 109, 118, 126, 144, 264, 265

Rapaport, D., 11, 265
Rachlin, H. L., 44, 261
Reed, M. R., 144, 259
Reznikoff, M., 78, 79, 265, 266
Rock., I., 113, 266
Rogers, D. L., 80, 266
Ross, N., 76, 266
Ruckhaber, C. J., 81, 266

Sabatino, D. A., 41, 81, 258, 266
Schachtel, E. G., 158, 266
Schenke, L. W., 26, 101, 127, 267
Schilder, P., 7, 20, 76, 266
Schneirla, T. C., 266
Schulberg, H. C., 7, 19, 23, 39, 63, 78, 111, 259, 266, 268
Schwartz, M. L., 80, 266
Segall, M. H., 84, 266
Šepic, J., 266
Shapiro, D., 51, 88, 266
Shapiro, M. B., 88, 266
Shneidman, E. S., 211, 217, 266
Shor, J., 51, 71, 263
Smith, C. E., 34, 81, 263
Smith, C. R., 264
Smith, D. C., 71, 114, 266
Smith, J. P., 36, 40, 88, 96, 109, 119, 122, 126, 265
Snortum, J. R., 76, 266
Solley, C. M., 9, 10, 266
Song, A. Y., 82, 267
Song, R. H., 82, 267
Sonoda, T., 19, 84, 266, 267
Spielberger, C. D., 79, 261
Spivack, G., 112, 259
Sternberg, D., 30, 103, 267

Stewart, H. F., Jr., 79, 267
Stoer, L., 33, 38, 267
Story, R. I., 27–29, 50, 70, 103, 105, 106, 107, 109, 113, 267
Suczek, R. F., 24, 74, 80, 103, 267
Sullivan, H. S., 158, 267
Sullivan, J. J., 103, 140, 267
Sundberg, N. D., 21, 267
Suttell, B. J., 22, 33, 34, 49, 77, 79, 81, 83, 115, 118, 121, 122, 124, 127, 128, 265, 267
Swenson, W. M., 80, 266

Tauber, C., 41, 264
Taylor, H. D., 84, 267
Taylor, J. R., 26, 101, 127, 267
Taylor, V. H., 63, 74, 98, 111, 261
Terman, L. M., 256, 267
Thweatt, R. C., 84, 267
Tiedeman, R., 81, 267

Tolor, A., 7, 19, 21, 23, 39, 63, 74, 78, 103, 111, 259, 266, 267, 268

VandenBos, G., 157, 268
Verms, S. K., 74, 112, 268
vonBékésy, G., 159, 268

Wallis, R. R., 19, 264
Weiss, A. A., 112, 144, 259, 268
Wells, F. L., 21
Welsh, G. S., 103, 140, 267
Werner, H., 10, 29, 268
Wertheimer, M., 7, 18, 19, 49, 268
Wiener, G., 37, 40, 110, 268
Williams, J. E., 79, 261
Witkin, H. A., 11, 158, 268
Wolff, W., 107, 125, 268
Wurst, E., 36, 123, 268

Ysseldyke, J. E., 41, 266

Subject Index

Abience, 31, 158, *see also*
  Adience–Abience Scale
Abstraction, 118
Acting out, 59, 92, 100, 101, 102, 103,
  107, 126, 179, 183, 214–215, 217,
  219, 242, 248, 249
Adaptive factors, 92
Adience, 31, 91, 245, *see also*
  Adience–Abience Scale
Adience–Abience Scale, 90, 92, 158–171,
  187
  and age, 164
  and altruism, 170
  and brain damage, 163
  derivation of, 31, 159
  and field dependence, 158, 170
  and intelligence, 164, 166, 167
  meaning of, 158–159
  normative data, 163–164
  and psychoneurosis, 163
  and psychopathology, 166–167, 170
  and psychotherapy, 164, 168
  rationale for, 158–159
  and reliability, 164–165
  and schizophrenia, 163, 168–169
  and sex, 163–164
  test factors, 159–162
  validity, 164–170
Adolescence, 27, 101, 103, 108
Affect, 180, 183, 206, 209, 216, 236
Affective stimuli, 108–109, 136, 139, 254,

  see also Emotional adjustment
Aggression, 26–27, 101, 116, 127, 134,
  137, 158, 185, 236, 244, *see also*
  Antisocial behavior; Hostility
Agraphia, 204
Alcoholism, 27–29, 105, 107–108, 109,
  113, 231, 234
Altruism, 170
Ambivalence, 94, 178–179, 183, 186, 243,
  247
Anality, 137, 141, 216, 229–230
Anticipatory controls, 132, *see also*
  Planning
Antisocial behavior, 27, 103
Anxiety, 30, 50, 59–60, 77, 89, 99–100,
  101, 123, 126, 127, 132, 135, 139,
  140, 177, 201–202, 204, 211–213,
  231, 243, 248
  covert, 97, 100, 179, 188
  latent, 54, 58
  overt, 54, 120, 179, 188
Aphasia, 195, 204
Approach-avoidance, 30–31, 91, 94, *see*
  also Abience; Adience
Arteriosclerosis, cerebral, 203
Aspiration level, 181, 216
Assertiveness, *see* Hostility
Assessment methods, 3–5
Association Phase, 69–71, 89, 103,
  185–188, 234, 237
Attitudinal orientation, 93, 123

273

Augmentation-reduction, 158
Authority figure, 103, 125, 138, 200, 202, 215, 243, 254
Autistic perception, 10–11
Autocentrism, 158
Axiomatic propositions, 8

Background interference procedure, 37, 41, 82
Behavior, ix-x, see also Process Phenomena
  complex, 8, 10
  configurations and psychodiagnosis, 44–45
  covert, 133
  nonverbal, 11
  overt, 133
  simplex, 8
  traits, 45–46, 60
    source, 60
    surface, 46
  withdrawn, 101
Bender cards, 7
Bender-Gestalt Test
  and brain damage, 33–34, 36–37, 39–41
  for children, 34–36
  and copy method, 19
  and ego functions, 33
  and emotional factors, 35
  factor analysis, 36
  manual, 22
  and passivity, 26–27
  and reading ability, 35, 41
  and Rorschach, 26
  and schizophrenia, 36, 37, 38
  and school achievement, 35, 41
  scoring methods, 32–34
  signs, 34, 36–37
  as a "test," 18
Benton Visual Retention Test, 36
Brain damage, x, 51, 69, 71, 75–77, 78–79, 82, 83, 84, 88, 95, 96, 97, 110, 111–112, 114, 117, 119, 122, 124, 126, 132, 135, 137, 139, 142–143, 144, 145, 153, 154, 179, 180, 181, 187, 188, 192–193, 194–209, see

also Bender-Gestalt Test and brain damage
Brain dysfunction, general, 194–197

Case studies
  alcoholism and neurosis, 231–234
  apparently benign record, 211–219
  behavior revealed by HABGT, 175–190
  character problem, 240–250
  experimental–clinical method, illustration of, 51–54
  mental retardation, 251–257
  neurosis and therapeutic management, 223–231
  projective analysis, using, 54–61
  psychotic record, 219–222
  rapid inspection and configurational analysis, 190–193
  reactions to trauma of the brain, 204, 206, 209
  relationship of organic and psychological records, 197–204
  severe internal turmoil, 234–239
Castration anxiety, 224–225, 230, 247
Centralization, 92
Character disorder, 111, 188, 240–250
Children, 100–101, 105, 107, 108, 109–110, 111–112, 113, 115–116, 121, 124, 125
  gifted, 112–113
  norms for Adience–Abience Scale, 163, 164
  norms for Psychopathology Scale, 155
Clinician
  definition of, 43–44
  role of, 9, 47–48, 84–86, 143–144, 173–174
Cognitive style, 88, 171, 190
College students, 89, 96, 97, 101, 105, 117, 122, 125, 144
Compulsivity, 182, 211–219, 236, 237, 253
Concretism, 127, 145
Configurational analysis, 142–148, 187, 192–193, 202, 222
  critical and marginal scores, 143, 145–147

normative groups, 143
validity, 143–145
Configurational scores, 145–146
Conflict, 9, 11, 244–245
Conscious factors, 8–9, 12
Copy Phase, 11, 50, 176–83, 190–193,
    197–202, 204–209, 211–217,
    219–222, 223–237, 240–245,
    251–255
Criminal behavior, *ix*
Cultural influences, *ix-x,* 84, 89, 128

Deaf-retarded study, 31, 165–167
Defenses, 138, 216–218
    and adience–abience, 158–159
    compensation, 219, 231
    compulsivity, 211–213
    denial, 185, 211, 213, 216, 230
    intellectualization, 12
    internalization, 254, 256
    isolation, 226, 230
    reaction formation, 158–159
    repression, 224, 236, 247, 253
    retrogression, 50, 255
    vigilance, 158
Delinquency, 51
Dependency, 137, 138, 243, 244
Depression, 79, 88, 107, 113, 125, 135,
    137, 139, 145, 153, 154, 178, 199,
    202, 213, 214, 215, 216, 231, 236,
    243, 244, 247, 248, 253
Diagnosis
    differential, 82, 201, 251, 255
    inferential, 4
    process, 4–5
Don Juan hypothesis, 217
Doodling, 141
Draw-a-Person, *see* Goodenough Test
Dream material, 9
Drives, 8–9
Dyslexia, 176, 188

Egocentrism, 29–30, 57–60, 89–90, 91,
    98, 135, 136, 185, 236, 243, 247
Ego control, 95–96, 100, 102, 111, 115,
    117, 122, 132, 136, 137, 138, 141,
    179–180, 181, 185, 188, 197,

199–202, 242, 245, 248, 253, 254
Ego strength, 33, 77, 88, 256
Elaboration Phase, 11, 28–29, 50, 67–69,
    86, 89, 114, 140–142, 234, 237,
    245–247
    doodling, 141
    interpretation of, 183–187
Electroencephalogram, 112
Emotional adjustment, 24–26, 105, 107,
    109, 121, 137–138, 209, 245
Emotional disturbance, 25–26, 71, 101,
    105, 107, 111, 245, *see also*
    Emotional adjustment; Emotional
    indicators
Emotional indicators, 35, 99, 121, 124
Empathy with patient's performance, 131
Epilepsy, 80, 84, 204, 206
Exhibitionism, 227, 229–230
Experimental–clinical method, *ix–x,* 5,
    51–54, 155–157, *see also*
    Testing-the-Limits
    and card sorting, 74
    and interview analysis, 72–73
    and malingering, 74–75
    modification of, as a feature of process
        diagnosis, 51–54
    and performance analysis, 73–74
Extraneous background, 41

Factor analytic studies, 36, 105, 107,
    122–123
Field dependence, 158
Field independence, 11
Fixation, 137
Focusing, 157
Frostig tests, 36
Frustration tolerance, 102

Gestalt theory, 7
Goodenough Intelligence Test, 166, 167,
    see also Draw-a-Person
Guilt, 139, 188, 217

HABGT, general considerations, 62–63
    administration, 62, 64–70, *see also* Test
        administration
    applications, 11–15, 49

HABGT, general considerations (*cont.*)
  Atlas, 174
  basic method, 50
  characteristics, 7–8, 10
  and children, 23–24, 80–82, 92, 95, 175
  group administration, 80–82
  history, 18–42
  and motor behavior, 79–80
  and objective scores, 32
  with older adults, 116
  Revised Record Form, 67
  scoring template, 174
  as a "test," 18
  test figures, 7, 21
HABGT, use of, 3, 11–17, 19, 21–22, *see
    also* Adience–Abience Scale;
    Configurational analysis;
    Psychopathology Scale
  and adolescence, 27, *see also*
    Adolescence
  and aggression, 27
  and alcoholism, 27–29, *see also*
    Alcoholism
  and anxiety, 30
  and brain damage, 194–197, *see also*
    Brain damage
  as a buffer test, 15, 63
  with children, 24–25, 175, *see also*
    Children
  and communication difficulties, 14
  and conflict, 27
  and cultural influences, 14–15, 16, 84
  and egocentrism, 29–30, *see also*
    Egocentrism
  and ego strength, 33, *see also* Ego
    strength
  and emotional disturbance, 25–26
  and illiteracy, 14, 15–16
  and intellectual impairment, 16, *see also*
    Brain damage; Intellectual
    functioning
  and malingering, 16, 74–75
  and mental retardation, 13–14, 16, 41,
    see also Mental retardation
  norms for, 154, 163, 164
    children, 155, 163, 164
  and passivity, 26–27

primary factors, *see* Test factors
projective analysis, example of, 54–61
and projective features, 18–19, 20,
    22–23, 24–32, 62–71
in research, 17
and the Rorschach, 26
and school achievement, 16
and symbolism, 24, 30
and verbal communication, 13, 14–15,
    16
Hain's scoring methods, 36–37, 40, 110,
    112, 121
Hemiplegia, 203
Heroin, 112, 123
Homosexuality, 59–60, 139, 140
Horizontal plane, 103
Hostility, 92, 93, 94, 127, 138, 181, 200,
    202, 215, 216, 240, 247, 253, 254,
    256, *see also* Aggression
  latent, 59
Huntington's disease, 144
Hutt's designs, 6, 22
Hutt's signs, 36–37
Hutt's Tentative Guide, 21, 24
Hypotheses, formulation from test
    findings, 26, 28–29, 85, 130, 177,
    213
Hysterical behavior, 77

Identification, 60, 213, 215, 216, 243, 245,
    247, 248
Impotence, 97, 100, 126, 136, 145,
    200–202, 209, 216, 229, 237
Imprinting, 10
Impulsivity, 54, 57–59, 88, 95, 107, 120,
    138, 139, 214, 215, 240, 243, 244,
    245, 256
Inferential analysis, 46–47, 49, 89,
    129–142, 176–187, 197–202,
    211–219
Inhibition, 183, 256
Inspection method, 190–192, 204–209,
    219–222
Intellectual functioning, 182, 185, 201, 256
Intelligence
  and recall method, 78
  and perceptual-motoric behavior, 85

and perceptual rotation, 112–113
Interpersonal relations, 103, 104–105, 125, 136, 139, 140, 178, 180, 199, 202, 214, 215, 231, 236, 243, 244
Interview analysis, 72–73
Intracranial pathology, see Brain damage
Introversion, 158

Leveling–sharpening, 158
Line movement, direction of, 125, see also Test factors
centrifugal and centripetal, 179

Malingering, 5, 12, 16, 74–75, 91, 117, see also HABGT, use of
Manic-depressive psychosis, 41, 88, 89, 90
Masochism, 137, 214, 217
Memory in relation to performance, 79–80
Mental retardation, 13–14, 16, 41, 51, 109, 111–112, 120, 147–148, 159, 165–167, 251–257
Micropsia, 100
Mira's study, see Horizontal plane; Vertical plane
Motor control, 95, 182, see also Test factors and line quality
Motor Free Test of Visual Perception, 39
Motoric behavior, 50, 80, 141

Narcissism, 57, 91, 135, 136, 185, 243, 247
Negativism, 89, 182
Neuroticism, 79, 90–91, 101, 105, 108, 110, 115–116, 117, 118, 122, 124, 147, 153, 154, 223–239
Nomothetic approach, 4, 14, 149
Normals, 153, 155, 163
Nosology, 44–45, 69, 142, 143

Objective norms, 3, 32, 149–162
assumptions, 3–4
limitations, 3, 218–219
values, 149
Obsessive-compulsive behavior, 135, 138, 237, see also Neurosis
Oedipal problem, 60, 141, 182, 217, 243, 245, 247–248

Open heart surgery, 41
Oppositionalism, 98, 113, 178, 179, 181, 185, 186, 231, 243
Orality, 141
Organic brain damage, see Brain damage

Paranoidal behavior, 135, 138, 139, 185, 187, 188, 236, 243–244, 248, see also Schizophrenia
Pascal-Suttell scoring method, 22, 33, 40
Passivity, 26–27, 45–46, 100, 101, 134, 137, 138, 253–254, 256
Pedantry, 98
Perception
autistic, 10–11
development of, 7, 85
distortions of, 49–50
Gestalt principles, 7
maturation of, 59, 185, 254, 255, 256
Perceptual–motoric behavior, 10–11, 37–38
and developmental lag, 37, 175
and motor impairment, 38, 39
nonprojective use of, 32–42
and organic brain damage, 39
and reading ability, 37
Perceptual rotation, 51, 111–114, see also Test factors
rotation of test materials, 65–66, 73–74, 112–113
Perceptual style, 130–133, 141, 157, 182
Phallic characteristics, 138, 139, 140, 141, 182, 236–237, 245, 247
Planning, 88, 95, 123, 132, 197, 202, 253
Prediction, x, 45–46, 61, see also Nosology
Process phenomena, x, 4–5, 45–46, 47, 48, 49, see also Assessment methods
Project Gamit, 163, 164
Projective tests, values of, ix, 47–48
Psychodiagnosis, 43–61
relation to behavioral configurations, 44–45, see also Process phenomena
Psychological blocking, 180, 188
Psychometrician, 43
Psychoneurosis, see Neuroticism
Psychopathology, general, 33, 110

Psychopathology, general (*cont.*)
   psychopathic behavior, 90, 91, *see also*
      Delinquency
Psychopathology Scale, 92, 150–157,
      182–183, 218–219, 239
   and adience–abience, 169, 170
   and age, 155, 156
   derivation of, 34
   history of, 150
   and intelligence, 156
   normative data, 153–155
   normative population, 154–155
   rationale for, 150
   reliability of, 155–156
   and research studies, 155–157
   and sex, 163
   test factors, 150–153
   validity of, 154, 157
Psychosexuality, 215–216, 234
Psychosis, 110, 114, 118, 145, 210–222,
      see also Schizophrenia
   prediction of, 45–46
Psychosurgery, 41
Psychotherapy, *ix-x,* 168, 188, 217,
      223–230, 249–250

Rapport, establishment of, 63
Regression, 59, 179, 189–190, *see also*
      Defenses and retrogression
Research Report # 43, 156
Rigidity, 88–89, 122, 181, 182, 199, 202,
      254
Rorschach, indices, 22, 26, 96, 101, 105,
      116
Rotation, 51, *see also* Perceptual rotation
   of test materials, 65–66, 73–74, 112–113

Schizoid, 180
Schizophrenia, 36, 37, 44, 78, 79, 89, 90,
      92, 96, 97, 111, 115–116, 117–118,
      122, 124, 135, 146, 154, 210–222
Second-order inference, 178–179, 181, 242
Selective attention, 158
Self-percept, 131, 134
Set, 122
Sexuality, *see* Psychosexuality

Sexual identity, 60, 103, 134, 137, 140,
      236–237, 244–245
Sexual perversion, 139
Size estimation, 92, 99–103
   slips of the tongue, 103
Sketching, 138, 139, 140
Style, 130–133, 135
Suicide ideation, 30, 217
Superego, 139, 186, 213, 217
Symbolism, 30, 74, 126, 134, 137, 139,
      182, 185, 215, 247
Synthesis, 118

Tachistoscopic method, 75–77
Taylor Manifest Anxiety Scale, 101
Test administration, 62–83
   association phase, 69–70
   copy phase, 11, 64–67
   elaboration phase, 11, 67–69
   group method, 80–82
   multiple choice, 82
   position of cards, 112
   recall method, 77–80
   tachistoscopic method, 75–77
   variations in, 82
Test factors, 84–128, *see also individual
      case studies for examples of the
      usage of test factors.*
   angulation, change in, 108–110, 136
   closure difficulty, 51, 104–105, 138,
      140, 151
   collision, 94–96, 103, 142, 197, 203,
      204, 206, 209, 218, 219
   compartmentalization, 231, 236, 237
   crossing difficulty, 106
   and cultural influences, 84–85
   curvature difficulty, 106–108
   elaboration, 120–121
   factors considered by other researchers,
      127–128
   fragmentation, 118–119
   isolated change in size, 102–103
   limitations of, 105, 107
   line movement, 29–30, 107, 135
   line quality, 126–127, 137, *see also*
      Sketching
   major groupings of the factors, 86

margin, use of, 96–97, 133
movement, direction of
  deviation in, 124–125
  inconsistency in, 125–127
overall change in size, 100–101, 179
overlapping difficulty, 51, 119–120
perceptual rotation, 37–38, 110–114,
  137, 138
perseveration, 121–123, 136
position of first drawing, 90–91, 132
position of paper, shift in, 97–98, 133
position on stimulus card, shift in,
  98–99, 133
redrawing, 123–124
retrogression, 114–116
sequence, 86–90, 131–132
simplification, 116–118, 138
size of figures, 27, 99–100
  overall change in size, 100–101
  progressive change in size, 102
space, use of in relation to test stimuli (I),
  91–93, 131
space, use of in relation to adjacent
  figures (II), 93–94
Test figures, individual, 134–140
Testing-the-Limits, 51–53, 71–75, 114,
  143, see also Experimental–clinical

method
  levels of response, 71
Test materials, 64
Test observations, 64–70, see also Test
  figures
Test performance, 85
  analysis of, 73–74
  and motivation, 12, 85
Test signs, 25, 26, see also Test factors
  and abuse of, 27, 45
Twins, 54–61

Unconscious factors, 8–9, 12, 74, 200

Vertical plane, 103
Visual–motor behavior, 10–11
  and projection, 31–32

Wechsler Intelligence Scale for Children,
  189, 193
Wechsler Intelligence Test (WAIS), 166,
  204, 257
Wechsler Memory Scale, 80
Wertheimer figures, 19, 24
Withdrawal behavior, 102, 103, 179, 180,
  199–200, 244, 253